DAVID SAWYER is not a guru. He's just ░░░░░░░░░░
Glasgow PR guy who woke up one day v ░░░░░░░░░░░░░░ ___ years later,
the result is *RESET* – the unconvention... ░░░░ for midlife professionals that will
wipe the windscreen of life so you can see again. Find out more at toreset.me/800.

Praise for RESET

"Reading this book will guide you in the pursuit of change but it will not make change occur. You have to do that."
CHARLIE SPEDDING, LA Olympics medallist, London Marathon winner and author of *From Last to First*

"Hidden in plain sight within the 300 or so pages of *RESET* is an elegant synthesis of the latest thinking in financial independence, lifestyle design, and age-old philosophical wisdom – cunningly disguised as a breezy pep talk from your witty mate down the pub. In a world that's forever racing past us on a screen, it's a reminder of the potentially life-changing power of a book."
MONEVATOR, www.monevator.com

"If you feel normal in today's world – that is – less than joyful, bored, unfulfilled, overworked yet not-meeting-your-potential, trapped, or simply apathetic about your current state of affairs, David Sawyer's *RESET* is the refreshing splash of water you need to put yourself right. A terrific book."
CYRUS SHEPARD, founder, Zyppy

"Tempted to throw in the towel and run away? Tempted by the greener grass on the other side? Well...be tempted no more...this book will actually let you 'reset'. It's a fun, compelling and, dare I say, tempting prescription to a different approach to life, work and play. *What Matters To You* is a global movement in healthcare aimed at improving experience of patients and families; this book makes you ask this question of yourself and then encourages you to do something about it. Tempted? I am..."
PROFESSOR JASON LEITCH, national clinical director, healthcare quality & improvement, Scottish Government

"A comprehensive introduction to things you didn't learn in school but should have. *RESET* is a complete program with enough motivation and details to make it easy to begin without being too complicated. You'll feel like doing something right now."
JACOB LUND FISKER, PhD, author, *Early Retirement Extreme*

"Sawyer's *RESET* shows us how to achieve material wealth. It emphasizes discipline, sacrifice, and hard work. No argument here. However, we must also reflect on the wisdom from Benjamin Franklin's 1758 essay on *The Way To Wealth*: 'Do not depend too much upon your own industry, and frugality, and prudence, though excellent things, for they may all be blasted without the blessing of heaven.' But even with this admonition, Franklin truly understood human nature, concluding that the people heard it, approved the doctrine, and immediately practiced the contrary. My advice: approve of Sawyer's doctrine. It makes good sense."
WILLIAM D. DANKO, PhD, co-author of *The Millionaire Next Door* and *Richer Than A Millionaire ~ A Pathway To True Prosperity*

"*RESET* is an incredibly detailed and comprehensive guide to planning and achieving the life you desire. But that's only true if what you desire is to work on your own terms, to achieve goals that are meaningful to you, and to move rapidly towards *your* financial independence."
JOHN KINGHAM, managing editor, *UK Value Investor* and author of *The Defensive Value Investor*

"This might just turn out to be one of the most influential books many people ever read – and most likely *the* most influential one any of them read over 40!"
STUART MACDONALD, entrepreneur and CEO, Seric Systems

"*RESET* is a guidebook for life. Whatever age or stage you're at you'll find it a helping hand towards well-being, positive mental health and financial independence. It's both personal philosophy and autobiography, in which David Sawyer describes his own 'reset'. We're all finding our way, with varying capabilities, experiences and skill. Add *RESET* to your toolbox and invite David Sawyer to become your mentor."
STEPHEN WADDINGTON, partner and chief engagement officer, Ketchum

"Most of us dream about changing things up, walking away from where we are now, and pushing a giant reset button. But most of us don't know what do next. David Sawyer's life, and new book, is a testimony to the power of restarting and pursuing the work and life that will make you happy. More than a testimony, it's also an instruction manual."
DAVID BURKUS, author of *Friend of a Friend* and *Under New Management*

"Dave was like me; dashing around, time-poor and feeling a bit unfulfilled. Actually, he's probably still time-poor but only because he's taken life in hand and, in the manner of Frank Sinatra, now does things 'his' way. Even better, he's knocked his pan in to write a book that shares accessible logic, real-life stories and the inspiration to freewheel out of whatever rut you may be in. Sometimes you just need a bit of a push and *RESET* is positively nudging. Or maybe you just want to stay doing what you are doing, the way you've always done it. Your choice."
MARJORIE CALDER, director, OceanBlue Consulting

"There is no PR spin here! A frank and honest appraisal of the challenges facing the PR industry and also the immediate future of a generation that is supposedly at its peak earning potential yet woefully unprepared for what comes next."
JIM HAWKER, co-founder, Threepipe

"*RESET* is an eye-opener. It's a very well-written book about the meaning of life, about angst and the search for purpose. Whether you work in public relations or not, view this book as a guide to creating a strategic plan for the rest of your life. It's impressive. It's exhausting. Sawyer suggests he's everyman. I think he's Superman."
RICHARD BAILEY FCIPR, editor, *PR Place*

"As a 25-year-old GB endurance athlete who's had his fair share of injuries, I think, like Dave, that setbacks in any field should be used to propel you forward not hold you back. I found inspiring and relatable advice everywhere in *RESET* and recommend it to anyone with dreams who believes their best years are yet to come."
LUKE TRAYNOR, (as-yet-unsponsored) GB runner: 61:55 HM, 13:39 5K (2018 PBs)

RESET

How to Restart Your Life and Get F.U. Money

The Unconventional Early Retirement Plan for Midlife Careerists Who Want to be Happy

David Sawyer FCIPR

First (paperback) edition published in Great Britain by Zude PR Ltd in August 2018.

A CIP catalogue record of this book is available from the British Library.

ISBN: 978-1-9164124-1-5
eISBN: 978-1-9164124-2-2

DEDICATION

I'M WRITING THIS BOOK for me six years ago. I've been working on it since November 1972. I dedicate *RESET* to:

- My wonderful kids and beautiful wife, who have supported me in every madcap adventure I've embarked on since mid-2012, believing in me, believing that it will always come right.
- My mum and dad, who gave me my education, morals, appreciation of culture, Churchillian curiosity and primal urge to be the best I can.
- Everyone who's lost hope and, worse still, has accepted this is the way of life until they retire, whenever that is.
- You. There is no other book, blog or programme that synthesises such a range of topics. If you *RESET*, it will change your life.
- All the lovely, inspiring, encouraging, clever, thoughtful, adventurous, affectionate, empathetic, exuberant, generous, passionate, sincere, reliable, different and, most of all, funny individuals I've had the pleasure of knowing.

I don't dedicate this book to the unscrupulous, boring, scared-and-scheming, blowhards, dullards and cowardly arseholes I've met in my life. It may be, as Niccolò Machiavelli said, far safer to be feared than loved, but it can't be good for your insides.

Out of the night that covers me,
Black as the pit from pole to pole,
I thank whatever gods may be
For my unconquerable soul.

In the fell clutch of circumstance
I have not winced nor cried aloud.
Under the bludgeonings of chance
My head is bloody, but unbowed.

Beyond this place of wrath and tears
Looms but the Horror of the shade,
And yet the menace of the years
Finds and shall find me unafraid.

It matters not how strait the gate,
How charged with punishments the scroll,
I am the master of my fate,
I am the captain of my soul[1]
William Ernest Henley, *Invictus*

DISCLAIMER

THE IDEAS AND ACTIONABLE advice in *RESET* are potentially life-changing for hundreds of millions of middle-aged midlifers[2] across the globe. However, they represent one person's worldview. They've worked and continue to work for many others and me, but they may not work for you.

As well as a reset button, my advice comes with an override button: there is no such thing as a set of rules that will make you happy and fulfilled. Everyone is different – I don't know what's happening in your life any more than you know what's happening in mine.

If you want *tailored* digital, career, business, tax, budgeting, or investing advice, seek professional help. And be prepared to pay handsomely for it. If you want certainties, do nothing, live for the moment. Suck. It. Up. And give this book to someone else.

But if, like me, you believe that when pointed in the right direction, there's not much you can't do yourself, read on. After these three caveats:

1. Any name changes or composite characters have been introduced to protect the innocent (or guilty, as the case may be). Otherwise, every single sentence in *RESET* is true.
2. Although this book makes all attempts to provide authoritative and accurate information, I'm not taking any responsibility for what you do with it. None.

3. I'm also taking zilch responsibility for anything that dates, albeit the advice in this book is timeless and 99% will be as relevant in 2028 as 2018.

That's not to say I don't care. I do. Deeply. Otherwise, what would I be doing writing a book like this? However, as *RESET* stresses, you are responsible for what you do with your only life. When your kids and partner have gone to bed or you're driving to the office, it's just you, baby. You, your thoughts and dreams. At these times, take heart and remember: *you* are the master of your fate; *you* are the captain of your soul.

CONTENTS

FOREWORD

WHEN I JOINED A running club at the age of 16, I followed the advice of the day. I used a method of training that was generally accepted as the best way to develop a middle- and long-distance runner. For the next twelve years, I ran well without doing anything exceptional. I won the occasional race and gained an occasional international vest. A lot of runners would have been delighted to have my career. However, I was frustrated because I felt that I was capable of more but it was not forthcoming. At the age of 28, I realised that time was running out, and I had to do something to bring about the change I craved. I convinced myself that if I was going to make changes in the pursuit of improvement, I may as well make big ones.

I resigned from my job, sold my car, rented out my house and moved to America. When I was there, I rejected the conventional wisdom that I had followed in my training for so many years and developed a new approach that I believed would work for me. I didn't just change my physical training; I altered my entire mental approach. I began with the vocabulary I used because I reckoned that by changing my vocabulary I would change my thoughts. If I changed my thoughts, I would change my actions and if I changed my actions, I would get different results. In the words of David Sawyer, I pressed the reset button.

The next four years were the most successful of my entire career. I ran for Great Britain at 10,000 metres in the European Championships and Commonwealth Games. This success boosted my confidence to aim even higher and when I moved up to my best event, I won the London Marathon and an Olympic Bronze medal in the marathon at the Los Angeles Games. The year after that, I set an English marathon record that stood for 29 years. None of these achievements could have been predicted by my first 12 years in the sport.

After more than a decade of comparative mediocrity, I could have given up or I could have plodded on doing the same things in the hope that some miraculous change would occur. I did neither of these; I decided to alter my life for the better by creating a new sense of purpose. It transformed my running career and transformed my life.

This book covers a much wider scope than becoming a better runner but my experience convinces me that change comes from within and the principle can be applied to all aspects of our lives.

Reading this book will guide you in the pursuit of change but it will not make change occur. You have to do that.

Charlie Spedding
LA Olympics medallist, London Marathon winner and author of
From Last to First

INTRODUCTION

Will *RESET* help you?

I'm going to ask 13 questions.

1. Have you forgotten what makes you happy?
2. Did you once have dreams of what you wanted to achieve and who you wanted to be?
3. Do you want to change your life, but figure it's impossible because of your responsibilities?
4. Do you believe in karma, but wonder why it doesn't apply to you?
5. Do you hanker for your childhood, for school, when it was less to do with who you knew and all to do with what?
6. Do you worry about money, but have little idea what you spend it on?
7. Do you know your before-tax salary, but haven't a clue about your net worth?
8. Do you define yourself by the work you do not who you are?
9. Is your job in a constant state of flux, with pressure to do more for less?
10. Is one of your favourite phrases "first world problems", thereby dismissing your angst as trivial and something you have to live with?
11. When someone asks you how you're doing, do you say "not bad"?

12. Lately, have you begun to think there must be more to life? This can't be it, can it?
13. Despite your best efforts, does it feel like, most of the time, you live to work (not the other way round)?

If you answered yes to any of these, *RESET*'s for you.

Problem

Globally, almost one in four of us hate our jobs while a further six in ten are "not engaged" at work[3].

When it comes to people in middle management, their biggest challenge in this hyper-connected world is learning new information, particularly "digital", which is revolutionising their professions. But there's no time to learn, to become the future not the past, to "fit the profile" of the organisation they work for. They have staff to manage, targets to hit, reports to write.

Atrophying skills and decreasing motivation are eating away at their pride. They're trapped, highly paid, with commitments coming out of their earholes. And what's more, there's no way out.

* * *

This causes discord. A lost generation of professionals – sandwiched between the devil-may-care attitude of the millennials and the final salary scheme security of the baby boomers – is stumbling through life unhappy, unhealthy and overwrought.

With little time for their partners and kids, and no time for their dreams. No time for meaningful work but lots of time for their smartphones and the swipe of doom that is social media. They spend so much of their week earning – often with both partners working full-time – that they've little energy left to plan for the future. What remains is spent medicating their dissatisfaction with life through wants that have become needs, and the sweet embrace of Netflix. And so, hundreds of millions of people across the world exist in a state of uncomfortably numb distractedness, reaching for a retirement that is unplanned, uncosted and receding into the middle distance.

Like a frostbitten climber benighted in K2's death zone, they've lost hope.

Solution

What if someone showed you a secret "life" garden? One where the roses smelled good? One you could play in, be yourself, and as long as you pruned the brambles, plants sprang up, vegetables fed your family, and, over the years, mighty oaks grew providing greenery and character.

What if there was another way? Moreover, what if that way didn't involve jacking in your job (like Charlie Spedding did), leaving your partner, having a midlife crisis, uprooting your existence? What if that way just involved small actions, taken every day, compounded over time? With no more effort than you now spend tending your social media flock, superglued to a screen.

Best of all, what if that way cost you little? In fact, what if that way saved you a tonne of money and let you retire a few years earlier than your "finger in the air", "wouldn't it be great to stop working before we're 60? But that'll never happen to us, they'll have pushed the retirement age back to 70 by then", pipedream?

What if someone said that by following this way you would get:

- An idea of what you really really want.
- A practical programme to future-proof your career.
- A plan to declutter your life, so you're able to see and think clearly again.
- A fully costed route to financial independence (you can call it early retirement if you like).
- A system to manage your finances.
- Eleven core principles to guide you.
- Increased happiness, contentment, fulfilment, purpose and meaning.

If you want to reset your life halfway through, as I have, you can. The solution is in this book.

Why listen to me?

I'm you

Well, no, I'm neither the same age nor the same background. But there are similarities:

1. I'm 45. I want to reach at least 90.
2. I live and always have lived a comfortable middle-class life in suburbia: married with two children, a four-bed terraced house, good schools...you get the picture.
3. I've spent most of my working days (20 years) as a middle manager.
4. I'm neither rich nor poor.
5. I have no God-given talents. Anything I've achieved has come through hard work.
6. I've failed at hundreds of things. Most notably A/S maths, skiing, oh and that university talk that went so memorably pear-shaped.
7. I do my best, but I'm no goody-two-shoes. I shout at the kids, sometimes I'm mean to my wife, friends and family. I even buy the odd latte.

In short, I'm a human, with all the concomitant failings. And I know what it's like to have lost my way.

I don't mind working hard

But I do mind over-complicated systems and thoughts that I find hard to remember and follow. Life is busy enough. With the plan in this book, you can set, routine and forget.

I have achieved success in several fields

These are:

- **Traditional public relations (PR):** for five years, I was head of a big city office at one of the world's largest public relations companies. I, backed by my talented colleagues, won 11 awards including one from the United Nations. In 2015, I became David Sawyer FCIPR after receiving a fellowship (the F) from the Chartered Institute of Public Relations (the CIPR) for my "outstanding contribution" to the PR industry.
- **Digital public relations:** over the past six years, I've retrained as a digital PR. I write for *Social Media Examiner*, *SEMRush*, *MuckRack*, *Business 2 Community*, *PRWeek*, *Be Yourself* and others.
- **Business:** I run a company called Zude PR. Making clients happy is my priority.
- **Mountaineering:** two traverses of the Cuillin Ridge and an ascent of Mont Blanc.
- **Marathoning:** since 2012, I have run marathons. After two years out through injury, I came back in September 2017, posting a 2 hours 40 minutes performance at Berlin.

A willingness to leave no boulder unturned in the pursuit of knowledge is the common thread that binds these achievements, an approach I have applied to researching and writing *RESET*.

I've lived the advice in this book for the past 2,000 days

My six-year quest for happiness and meaning began in mid-2012, but unless you're a runner, it warms up one-and-a-half years in. So we'll start with the interesting bit. In January 2014, after 17 years in corporate life, I walked through my office door for the last time. This was a wrench, to put it mildly. Overnight I went from 250 emails and 50 questions a day to nowt. I was lost.

In April 2014, I founded my own business and times were tough. So I did what any rational human would do having invested a load of money and personal capital but with few clients – I threw myself into a crash course in digital, reading blog posts and experimenting for eight hours a day. I'd show 'em.

Despite my counterintuitive approach to finding new business, the money started trickling in as my tinkering began to pay off. Along the way, I'd discovered a few physical and virtual mentors, people I'd never heard of. Their thoughts and advice reassured me that the actions I was taking, that no one else in my country was taking, might work.

Flushed with success, having become over a period of two years, expert in digital PR, I went off at a tangent and first tried to find the keys to productivity, then the essence of success in our modern world and, eventually, the meaning of life. And still, despite the tangents, money kept coming in.

Now devouring a book a week, with blog-reading reduced to a mere two hours a day, I decided to test the resolve of my nearest and dearest further by spending six months decluttering our lives and practising the teachings of the largely US financial independence community I'd pored over for the past two years. A true (unpaid) life reset, having discovered what I – and my young family – wanted out of life. I doubled down on this huge risk by, except from a few confidants, isolating myself from professional networks. This would make it easier to follow a true pure path, impervious as I am not to being swayed by the unsought advice of others.

* * *

The result is this book. Sure, you'll take wrong turns of your own after reading *RESET*, but it's my sincere hope that the systematic plan in these pages will help *you* find *your* own way. Just as it has me these past six years, the happiest, best – occasionally worst – times of my life. I've done all the procrastination, driven down all the cul-de-sacs, made all the mistakes...*so you don't have to.* I have something new to say that is helpful and universal. *Listen* because you won't find this plan anywhere else. And trust me, it works.

Can't is spelt W-O-N-T

If you're anything like me, I can sense your brain finding all sorts of reasons why *not* to visit the lush garden of self-discovery contained within the covers of *RESET*. So, just to help out your Chimp[4], and save it the bother of scratching its head and raising these objections, I'll oblige.

I'm too old

Life may be passing you by right now, but you are never too old to do anything. Peter Roget invented the thesaurus at 73. Paul Cézanne held his first art exhibition at 56[5]. Charles Darwin was an obscure naturalist before he published *On the Origin of Species* in 1859, aged fifty[6].

In the late 1950s, Harlan (Colonel) Sanders lost his successful business and was on the dole. In his sixties, he and his wife got in their car (packed with a couple of pressure cookers, flour and spice blends[7]), to demonstrate, sell and franchise his secret recipe. He was turned down 1,009 times[8] before someone said yes.

Or how about British sprinter Charles Eugster[9], who, in 2015, took two seconds off the world record for the 200 metres in his age category? He was 95. He took up bodybuilding when he was 87 – to improve his appearance.

Napoleon Hill wrote *Think and Grow Rich!*, rated one of the best personal finance books. "I discovered, from the analysis of over 25,000 people," he wrote, "that men who succeed in an outstanding way, seldom do so before the age of forty, and more often they do not strike their real pace until they are well beyond the age of fifty[10]."

I'm not asking you to muster a scientific breakthrough, found a billion pound company, or summit Everest. All *RESET* is suggesting is you spend time sorting your shit out so you're happier. That, for the rest of your days, *you* engineer *your* life. You have generations left in you. Too old?

I can't do it: I don't have the willpower

When I was growing up, my mum used to say: "Can't is spelt W-O-N-T." She left the apostrophe out for dramatic effect.

Willpower has nothing to do with your current state of mind. And others who leave their beds and go to the gym aren't super-human people whose grit and determination will conquer all.

Can I let you in on a secret? There is no such thing as willpower, or superheroes. Just action and inaction.

If you rely on summoning your reserves of strength to do X or Y, your success rate will not be high.

You may not have this mythical willpower: no one does. But you are capable of taking small actions, which, over time, become routines and get stuff done.

I'm too busy

Don't misunderstand me, modern life is tough. Yet sometimes it's not that we're busy with family commitments and work. It's that we're busy meddling in unproductive activities, brought on by our need to de-stress from a life we've unwittingly designed.

How many times a day do you check your smartphone?

How many boxed sets have you watched recently?

In 1994, J.K. Rowling was "as poor as it's possible to be in this country[11]", and could scarcely afford to feed her baby. Nevertheless, she still found time to type copies of a 90,000-word manuscript to send to publisher after publisher because her social security money wouldn't stretch to the cost of photocopying[12].

And tennis stars Venus and Serena Williams[13] were out every morning at 6am hitting tennis balls aged seven and eight before going to school.

There's always time to be carved from every day – it's what you choose to do with it that counts.

I don't believe in self-improvement: it's too touchy-feely

"I don't have time to meditate. Tracking stuff is boring. I don't get five minutes a day to help my 'self'. Who wants to be perfect? All this self-help malarkey isn't me: it's too touchy-feely, too American."

I have a theory. In this millennium, the most advanced thinking, systems and processes originate in America. Even now, in our internet age, they take a couple of years to navigate the Atlantic and go mainstream in London, and a further two to reach Glasgow, where I live. I can't wait for that four-year time lag. In 2012, the sole self-improvement book I'd read was Stephen Covey's *The 7 Habits of Highly Effective People*[14], a quarter of a century ago. And I only got a quarter of the way through.

Over the past six years, I've read hundreds of (mainly US) self-help, business, biography, specific-skill-learning books. And that's not to mention the tens of thousands of blog posts, podcasts and videos I've absorbed. Why? Because I want to be able to take what I've learned and apply it to my life, for the benefit of me, my family, my friends and the community I've created around Zude PR.

It's not that the pre-2012 me was deficient. Far from it. But I wasn't happy. It's not that this self-help book offers a quick fix, or you're going to whizz around every corner of your life and make it perfect. And it's not about transforming your personality. That's yours and no one's going to – or wants to – change it. It's just some ideas, a plan, to make your life a little better. That is all.

I'm a cynic by nature, but embracing lifelong learning has worked for me, as it has for millions of others across the world. Think of it this way, learning is the best way of improving your wealth in the long-term. If you practise the principles in *RESET* for no other reason, do it for that.

I don't have 10,000 hours to master new skills

If this is your first foray into self-improvement books, welcome, you've picked a good place to start.

If not, you may be familiar with the idea, popularised by Malcolm Gladwell's *Outliers*[15] and expanded on by Matthew Syed in *Bounce*[16], that it takes ten thousand hours – or ten years – of practice to achieve mastery in a field.

Two points here. One, it's not just about putting the hours in. It's how you direct that time that counts[17]. For two people, mastery of anything can take 5,000 or 20,000 hours. For the 5,000 variation, you need to head in the right direction: you need to know the way. You need a good coach.

Second, this book isn't about making you an expert. It's about sharing vital principles you can apply to any field, and practical, simple-to-do, tactics. So you can amass enough money to live the life you want to lead.

It's easy for you to say

Well no, it's not actually. I'm not sitting on a million pounds. I'm not wildly successful, super-handsome, or immune to criticism.

I'm right here, fighting the good fight, raising a young family. Living and breathing the advice I give in this book. Barring luck of our own making, my wife and I won't be retiring any time soon.

Life's still a struggle, just the way I like it. As Baron Pierre de Coubertin, founder of the modern Olympics, said: "The most important thing in the Olympic Games is not to win but to take part, just as the most important thing in life is not the triumph, but the struggle. The essential thing is not to have conquered, but to have fought well[18]."

* * *

This book is *my creed*, the truth as I believe it to be. A unique plan for midlife professionals to reset and restart their lives. I promise that after you read *RESET* – and carry out its recommendations – you'll be **happier at work and home**, **better/proud at your job** and have a **practical financial independence/early retirement/escape**

<u>**plan**</u>. It won't happen overnight, but without taking drastic action such as quitting gainful employment, <u>**within a year, you will have transformed your future.**</u>

And finally...

Every year from age 30, I made eight New Year resolutions and gave up by June. One of them was always to sort the money pots my wife and I had filed away in a cupboard. It took me until my forties to tackle those boxes. In the intervening years, we lost tens of thousands of pounds in fund management charges and poor invest-ment performance – adding years on to our full-time working lives. Another resolution was to read a book a month (I hadn't discovered blogs or podcasts back then). I managed a handful a year. I was approaching 40 when I decided to start learning again. I figured I'd done enough reading for the first 22 years of my life: my biggest mistake in lost opportunities, experiences and earning potential. And it was only in 2012 I rediscovered the joys of exercise after ten years spent two stone overweight.

Your point, caller?

Everything can wait. But I warn you, the longer you leave it, the more you'll regret. You picked up this book for a reason. Carpe diem, I say. *RESET* will show you how.

STATUS QUO

Status quo, you know, is Latin for 'the mess we're in[19]'.
Ronald Reagan

WE'RE NOW INTO THE meat of *RESET*. The six main parts comprise a step-by-step transformation programme, with a handy recap in the form of an "index card" at the end of each one. I hope you read it in a glorious oner for full impact; then dip into parts in future when you come to perform your own *RESET*.

This book has 511 Notes (you'll have noticed them by now). So if you find yourself stroking your chin thinking *what does he mean by that*, it's likely explained and referenced there. Also at the back, there's a Glossary of Terms to save you googling the 20 or so words and phrases repeated in this book, which may be unfamiliar to you.

The six parts are bookended by Status Quo and Nirvana, which sketch the beginning and end of the *RESET* journey. Where we are today, and what it will be like when we defeat the troll, cross the humpback bridge and reach the green fields on the other side.

In Status Quo, you'll meet my good friends Brendan and Mary Fazackerley, before taking a quick look at the world we midlife professionals find ourselves in today.

I'll hand you over to Bren now. Let's look at *his* status quo.

One year in the life of Brendan Fazackerley

Bren, they call him Bren, he hates that *they* call him Bren, that's what his friends call him. But he doesn't let on; it pays to allow people in. He doesn't see his friends anymore, anyway. They've even stopped ringing. He's just too busy.

Bren Fazackerley is director of communications for a middling-size local authority in northern England. He sits on the council's management team alongside the directors of housing and HR, and that special adviser type whose sole purpose is to undermine him.

Bren reports to the chief executive who is, well, not to put too fine a point on it, exacting. It's like being married but without the reward of regular sex.

His day job involves doing more for less, motivating a staff team who haven't had a pay rise in eight years and humouring stakeholders (internal and external) who feel the fact they can post on Facebook entitles them to "reframe" *his* digital strategy.

It's January 1st, New Year's Day, Bren's birthday. He's 48. Bren's been on Facebook for seven years, Twitter for four. Why? Because he has to. In his organisation, part of the management team's implicit job description is to like and retweet his boss's latest proclamation to her 657 followers. Every time he does this a speck of his soul decays. When he was a kid, he was going to be an astronaut, an inventor, write the next *War and Peace.* How on earth has it come to this?

Bren makes one resolution this year – he read somewhere that any more than one is unachievable in this modern world of ours. He's going to spend less time on his smartphone and more time *present* with his family. This will be the year things change.

It's February now. Bren, his wife Mary, and kids Henry and Sarah, are away for a weekend break at Center Parcs – the posh holiday camp he loves to hate. They're paying a small fortune, but it's the only place they feel relaxed, so they don't mind splashing the extra cash for quality "family time".

While Mary takes their children to the pool, Bren snatches his chance to do the family *admin* that's been lying around for weeks.

He doesn't have time to look for the best electricity and gas provider, so signs up for another year. He rings his local car dealer and arranges a meeting to talk about a three-year contract hire on that new Audi he's had his eye on. It's got great boot space, and he's had his current car five years. He deserves it.

Months go by and suddenly Bren's the apple of his young chief executive's eye. (She's ten years younger with five more letters after her name and a star that's on the rise. And if he swallows enough shit, his will be, too.)

May brings a pay rise. Ten thousand pounds (with strings attached). Bren's having to take on more responsibility. As well as his own department, he'll now head the internal transformational change team, looking at "cross-cutting new ways of working" across the local authority. It's been explained to Bren that although his deputy can still handle on-call media enquiries, he's expected to be available 24/7 – even on holidays – should his chief executive need him. Bren is not sure this is legal; it's certainly not desirable. Still, Bren and Mary have had their eyes on a new pad for months. It's a four-bed townhouse on a modern estate with a great catchment area. The kids are six and eight and although their primary school is good, the high school it feeds to is not. After a few visits, they sign on the dotted line and their once-25-year mortgage, which they'd been paying down for 20 years, gets £220,000 and 17 years added to it.

August comes. The Fazackerleys are taking their annual two weeks in mainland Europe. It's pricey, but they live for their holidays, and it's worth it to have proper time as a family. But Mary's noticed a change in Bren. Ever since he got the promotion, he's been distracted around the kids and they've argued more.

And that bloody nightmare ("the commandant", Bren calls her). Since they left Manchester airport, she's never off email, sends Bren personal messages through Facebook Messenger and calls him night and day. When he's not dealing with perceived crises – everything's urgent – that somebody else could handle, he's de-stressing by watching the telly or losing his temper with the children.

Time passes. It's cold in the huge hangar that passes for a regional football centre. *What did I expect*, thinks Bren, *it's early November.* Bren's sitting on a plastic seat, watching Henry play fives. It's a 90-minute session on a Friday evening; *who calls a training session between eight and half past nine on a Friday?* he muses. But Bren's not watching Henry. He's hunched over his laptop sifting through the 256 emails – he's counted them – that have amassed since he checked his work email on the toilet at 05:15 that morning.

Bren casts his envious eye around the stand at the pockets of dads laughing and joking, leaning on the barriers, watching their children play football. He thinks back to his own childhood, his dad running the local kids' football team, doing the garden, holding down a good job. He remembers playing soccer, bike rides, adventures, trips to the mountains, dreaming of being the next Clive Sinclair. He snaps back to the present. Lately, he's become prone to melancholic ruminations about how his life might have turned out. But none of this is getting the work done. Brendan plops £2 into the slot of the fanciest coffee dispenser he's ever seen, steels himself and opens the final six emails, those he's left until last. The ones from his chief executive who, as usual, will have tracked if he's opened them or not. She doesn't like to be kept waiting, so he knows that as soon as he clicks the emails he'll have to move heaven and earth to "provide solutions".

The festivities are over. It's December 28th and Bren's back at *work* ("the gulag", Bren calls it) for the best two days of the year. Those between Christmas and new year when "the commandant" is on holiday and, for once, otherwise engaged. There are a skeleton staff in his department – both of whom he likes – and, Brendan decides, *transformational change can, frankly, go fuck itself.*

Bren should be happy. But with time on his hands for once, he's able to take stock. And when he looks down on his life, he doesn't much like what he sees. He's almost 49. He's been working 25 years and can't see an end in sight.

He joined the local authority in 2015, after they closed the final salary scheme, and he's never been in a job more than five years, so God only knows what private pensions he's got.

He's on a good whack and they have Mary's wage as a reporter at the local paper (she returned to work four days a week once the kids were old enough). Their children aren't at private school and they've never been big spenders. But they always seem to be skint. There's the mortgage, two car leases, health club, the kids' sports lessons, a weekly Sainsbury's delivery, holidays, facials and the cleaner to pay for. They're so busy working that they need before-and-after-school childcare as well as expensive school holiday clubs – the bills are astronomical.

Bren retires to the work toilet; there's sanctuary in a bog. He rises to wash his hands and spies his reflection in the mirror: the weird stretched-skin indentations by his earlobes, the crow's feet and darkness ringing his eyes. When Bren takes a good look at himself, when he thinks about it, he knows he's unhappy. He's so stressed he's forgotten who he is, albeit he's certain of one thing: what's looking back at him ain't it.

Outwardly successful, inwardly seething and beaten down, Brendan Fazackerley (aged 48 and 99 hundredths) needs to reset.

He resolves to read some self-help books in the new year. In secret, he won't even tell Mary. He doesn't want her to worry.

* * *

Let's say Bren and Mary are on a combined annual salary of £90k (70 Brendan, 20 Mary). This places them well in the top quintile[20] of median annual household salaries in the UK. Bren's £48,616[21] net (after-tax) salary puts him among the top 0.17% of income earners in the world[22]. Rich? Yes, undoubtedly. Yet not happy, not fulfilled, with, in Brendan's case, a cluttered mind.

There are hundreds of millions of people in the world like Bren.

Good people. Bright people. People with huge potential, trapped in lives *they* have engineered to make them unhappy. Or at least, they could be a lot happier.

I know loads of them. I was one of them. And if you're reading this book, you're one of them, too.

The world we live in

In 1957, a decade before Bren was born in Leeds General Infirmary, the then British prime minister, Harold MacMillan, told us: "Most of our people have never had it so good[23]." Life has got a whole lot better since. There's less famine and poverty, fewer deaths from war and greater democracy[24].

Psychologist Abraham Maslow was on to this in 1943 when he published his hierarchy of needs theory[25], outlining what motivates human behaviour. For midlife professionals living in the 21st century, the basic physiological, safety and social belonging needs are all met.

Which, according to Maslow and his famous pyramid, just leaves esteem, self-actualisation (and, at its apex, self-transcendence) to work on.

Now we have food, shelter, money, a bed to sleep on, a flushing toilet, and no one trying to kill us, we can do anything we want, if our aim is to exist. Hell, we needn't bother with the top of the pyramid at all.

But what if we *want* to be happy, too? Fulfilled maybe? Or find a purpose?

What if existing is not enough?

A brief history of work

Earth is 4.54 billion years old. Life began on this planet 3.8 billion years ago, whereas our species, *Homo sapiens*, has only been around since 200,000BC, 0.004% of Earth's history[26]. The first cities and states appeared somewhere between 4000 and 2000BC[27], while the Industrial Revolution and the onset of modern life started in Great Britain, a mere 250 years ago. If we were to look at man's time on this planet as a day, modern life as we know it began around six minutes before midnight. The post-second world war era has brought immense benefits. We can travel from one side of the globe to the other in 24 hours. We live longer, can treat once incurable diseases and music and art are now a mass pursuit.

Yet one of the drawbacks is we've become conditioned not only to compartmentalise our lives but also to spend a great deal of them either working or thinking about work.

This is a modern phenomenon.

As Dr Frithjof Bergmann explains: "For most of human history, people only worked for two or three hours per day. As we moved from agriculture to industrialization, work hours increased, creating standards that label a person lazy if he or she doesn't work a forty-hour week."

He added: "The very notion that everyone should have a job only began with the Industrial Revolution[28]."

There was a brief attempt to turn the tide in the early years of the 20th century with working hours coming down from an average 60 in 1900 to 35, as workers successfully argued for the fruits of the spoils of the many gains from huge advances in trade and commerce.

But the Depression put paid to that.

And the post-war boom in consumerism and a world run by advertising has sealed the pact, creating a society where we define ourselves by the job we do, not who we are.

Our aim? Instant, easy gratification by earning more money to use more resources.

Although by no means as bad as the 1900s, long working days are not unusual with managers and knowledge workers worst affected.

A recent survey found that 80% of white-collar employees work more than 40 hours a week with a third clocking more than 50[29].

All this toil leads to what British writer Oliver James calls: "The Affluenza Virus...a set of values which increase our vulnerability to emotional distress."

He adds: "It entails placing a high value on acquiring money and possessions, looking good in the eyes of others and wanting to be famous... [increasing] your susceptibility to the commonest emotional distresses: depression, anxiety, substance abuse and personality disorder (like 'me, me, me' narcissism, febrile moods or confused identity[30])."

Technology and the pace of change

First published in 1984, one of the best books written on understanding human behaviour is *Influence* by Dr Robert Cialdini. His international best-seller, which identifies the techniques people can use to persuade others to take actions, is celebrated, but its most important message is often overlooked – we are making unconscious animalistic, emotion-led decisions on autopilot and it's not good for our minds and souls. We have "created our own deficiency by constructing a radically more complex world[31]."

"Because technology can evolve much faster than we can," he wrote, "our natural capacity to process information is likely to be increasingly inadequate to handle the surfeit of change, choice, and challenge that is characteristic of modern life." Cialdini added: "When making a decision we will less frequently enjoy the luxury of a fully considered analysis of the total situation but will revert increasingly to a focus on a single, usually reliable feature of it[32]."

The internet

He wasn't wrong. Since I graduated from university in 1995, technological change has revolutionised our daily lives. The only thing limiting us now is our imagination: all sorts of communities, ideas and influences have become available to us, at the click of a button. Today, 4.3 billion of the world's 7.6 billion people are on the internet; by 2030, everyone will be[33].

The Canadian prime minister, Justin Trudeau (addressing delegates at the World Economic Forum in Davos in 2018), said: "The pace of change has never been this fast, yet it will never be this slow again[34]."

It took 75 years for the telephone to reach 50 million users[35], 13 for the television, four years for the internet, while Angry Birds did it in 35 days. And don't get me started on Fortnite[36].

This new hyper-connected world has had profound effects on the world of work, too. There's an online tool for everything. Systems, services and software that once were the domain of large companies and organisations are now available to the one-man band (strumming their song in a coffee shop) for nothing.

There's Skype, the cloud, everywhere-wifi and 4G. There is no need for us to be chained to our desks, yet the way we work is still catching up. Flexible working is trumpeted but not implemented. All this change is hard to process; it takes generations.

Change will come and you better be ready

Change will transform what employers look for in their recruits. Although it is commonplace to hire locally now, by the end of the twenties it will be different. According to a 2018 report by management consulting firm McKinsey[37], artificial intelligence, automation and robotics[38] will have made many unskilled jobs redundant, and there'll be a bigger pool of knowledge workers for employers to choose from.

Whether you're a PR consultant, accountant, or lawyer it won't matter if you're in Glasgow, Gothenburg or Ganzhou. All that *will* matter, in the words of *Deep Work* author Cal Newport, is:

"Your ability to quickly master hard things."

"The ability to produce at an elite level, in terms of both quality and speed[39]."

You think your job's in danger now. Try ten years down the line. And it ain't going to get any better unless you do something about it.

They're not real

Before we go any farther in this book, you need to understand something. No matter how much you thrive on your job (and if you're one of those lucky 13%[40] that like to work, that's great), the only intrinsic point of working for money is to be paid. No job gives you anything you couldn't experience somewhere else free.

There may be outliers: brain surgeon and astronaut come to mind. Even then, depending on your motivation, I would wager my last pound you could derive similar satisfaction elsewhere.

And see your colleagues, those people you spend all that time with, whose moods, peccadilloes, hopes and fears you know more about than your own family's? They're not real. They don't care about you. They wouldn't be there if they didn't have to. And neither would you. Once you realise this, it's liberating.

It doesn't have to be this way

Alternatives to 9–5 exist. I am not suggesting you take one. But knowing there are other options once you have your early retirement plan in place – you can call it an escape plan if you want – can only a good thing be. The world *is* changing. We should all be working four-day weeks[41] by now.

As Jacob Lund Fisker writes in *Early Retirement Extreme*: "Many people, particularly young people, are starting to realize that the pursuit of happiness isn't found through the pursuit of accumulating things. They don't drop out, they opt out and forge their own path, starting up Internet companies, traveling the world, and retiring early from the rat race so they can spend their lives living rather than just buying stuff. Which do you prefer[42]?"

It's flexible working, the gig economy, going freelance, contracting, becoming an entrepreneur: the portfolio lifestyle. Whatever you want to call it, it's over here, right now. Another way of living always exists. You – only you – just have to find and design it.

And finally…

What is it you want? What were you deposited on this earth to do? Then do it or don't do it. Easy (when you know how). If I, an ordinary midlifer, can reject the *Status Quo*[43] – I never liked them anyway, even their early stuff – so can you. I can't promise you'll be rockin' all over the world, but *RESET* will give you hope and a plan for your future. So let's stop headbanging for a few hours, gather our hair in a ponytail and turn the volume down on that Marshall amplifier. Are you sitting quietly? If you promise to stay still for ten seconds and concentrate, we'll begin.

PART I

What Matters to You?

IT'S 1983, CUDDINGTON: A large double-village in the never-ending suburban sprawl – punctuated by bucolic, flat, hedgerow-bounded countryside – that stretches south of Manchester. My mum and I are sitting in a light blue Vauxhall Chevette in the tarmacked driveway of our modern, detached home. The car won't start. Mum leaves it for a minute. It's just Mum and me; no Ian, no Dad. I don't know why; maybe Mum's had to pick me up from school because of my latest sports-related injury, which typically involved heading a cricket ball or dropping a five-a-side steel crossbar on my foot. I'd just finished *The Hitchhiker's Guide to the Galaxy* and was fixated on author Douglas Adams's answer to the meaning of life (42, in case you're wondering). We're discussing it. Mum turns her left shoulder and asks: "What *do* you think the meaning of life is, David?" (This is a difficult question for a 10-year-old, even a bookish kid like me.) I pause, give it my best shot, and reply: **"To be happy, Mum?"** Mum looks in the rear-view mirror and smiles, indulgently: **"Oh, I don't think so David; it's more complicated than that."** For 30 years, I thought Mum was wrong. (The car started on the next go and the conversation moved merrily on, but my memory didn't.) Happiness is all, right? Everyone deserves to be happy. And logically, if you think about it, being happy is the only thing that matters. Lately, since turning 40, I've begun to question this steadfast belief. **Was Mum right after all?** Part I will explore why we shouldn't confuse happiness with pleasure. Why fears are standing in the way of fulfilment. Why life is a struggle, and it's only through getting to know ourselves, our values and our purpose, that a measure of happiness will ensue. It's about finding out *what matters to you.*

CHAPTER 1

Happiness

> *Happiness, happiness, the greatest gift that I possess*
> *I thank the Lord I've been blessed*
> *With more than my share of happiness*[44].
> **Ken Dodd, *Happiness***

I DISAGREE WITH THE late great British comedian Ken Dodd. I've yet to meet anyone who's been *blessed* with happiness. Dig into the life of a seemingly serene person you point to as happy and, like a gliding goosander on the silvery Spey, there's hard work going on under the surface. Happiness doesn't just happen; you have to work bloody hard at it. Sorry, Doddy.

The corollary of that is a harsh truth: if you're unhappy, there's usually something you can do. It's down to you to choose your actions. If you think happiness is the result of thousands and thousands of tiny actions over weeks, months and years, it follows that taking the *right* actions will make you happier.

Happiness and pleasure

So why do we take the *wrong* ones?

Because we confuse happiness with pleasure: we want to feel good because we're worth it. We are so busy, so put upon at work, that when we come home at night, we need the quick fixes of TV, smartphone and junk food to restore harmony in our lives. Sure, we try to do something wholesome at the weekends, but this revolves around de-stressing from the workweek's activities; and the evenings are a write-off once that first glass of vin rouge floods our gullet like a soporific cure-all.

Even the wholesome activity, spending time with our families, involves throwing money at the problem *we* have created. For parents, it's a trip to the soft play with the accompanying lattes and cake, scoffed down while "liking" people we never see's fake Facebook lives. For the unencumbered, other pursuits open up. Meals out three times a week, a weekend away at a restaurant with rooms every few months and a two-week luxury all-inclusive in Cancun twice a year. Meanwhile, most of our life, what has become our real life, is a sea of 8–6 mediocrity, battling made-up conventions and contrived language to pay for that de-stressing.

And the guilt, the self-loathing; the hideousness of the hamster wheel.

This cannot be good for our mental health. According to the World Health Organisation, 300 million people worldwide live with depression, while 800,000 people a year die due to suicide. In addition, there are indications that for each adult who dies of suicide there may have been more than 20 others attempting to kill themselves[45].

And this doesn't include the problems associated with what us midlife careerists ironically refer to as "living the dream": paranoia, relationship breakdowns, poor memory, angriness, fitful sleep, physical ailments and the years we're taking off our life expectancy through infrequent exercise and poor diet.

Not just feeling good

If we pursue only this version of happiness – the instant gratification, no-effort-required one – well, we only have ourselves to blame. There's nothing wrong with a latte, watching television, enticing people to say how smart or funny you are on Facebook.

This fleeting sort of happiness is good. But don't make it your life's work.

Because there is a different meaning of the word, one that the Dalai Lama was, I'm certain, thinking of when he said: "I believe that the very purpose of our life is to seek happiness. That is clear. Whether one believes in religion or not, whether one believes in this religion or that religion, we all are seeking something better in life[46]."

The second, true, pure, meaning of happiness is living a life in line with your purpose and values: being a good person. And the only way to do this is by showing up and doing the work; taking the right actions, day after day after day.

The pursuit of this version of happiness is at the heart of *RESET*. *What's stopping you?*

CHAPTER 2

Fears

FEARS, THAT'S WHAT. THE biggest thing stopping you leading a happier and more meaningful life is your fears. Here are a few: fear of being different, fear of not being able to pay the bills, fear of the sack, fear of not having enough money. Want some more? OK then:

- Fear of having to start over.
- Fear of your partner stopping loving you.
- Fear of people laughing at you behind your back.
- Fear of making mistakes.
- Fear of standing in front of an audience and being found out for not knowing what you're talking about.
- Fear of investing time in something, doing everything right, and still failing.
- Fear of having to go back cap in hand after mustering the courage to follow your dreams.
- Fear of depression.
- Fear that your judgement pushes you down the wrong route.
- Fear of social ridicule. Fear of people looking down on you.
- Fear that you're being selfish, sacrificing your family's wants and desires for yours.

These fears manifest themselves as thoughts that hold you back:

- I'm too lazy.
- I'm too boring.
- I'm too slow.
- I'm too fat.
- I've not got any willpower.
- I'm too shy.
- I'm not intelligent enough.
- I'm such a loser.
- I'm not competitive enough.
- I'm too worried.

The myth of conquering your fear

What to remember here is every single person you admire has these doubts and fears.

Fears are good, doubts are good (even pain can be good). Everyone has them. As Alberto Salazar, the three-time New York marathon winner (who went on to coach Mo Farah), once said: "I had as many doubts as anyone else. Standing on the starting line, we're all cowards[47]." Without fears and doubts, you won't get far in life. And you won't get rid of them. Instead, you'll learn to use them positively.

In *The War of Art*, a book tackling the most debilitating of all non-medical afflictions, procrastination, author Steven Pressfield said: "The amateur believes he must first overcome his fear. The professional knows that fear can never be overcome. He knows there is no such thing as a fearless warrior or a dread-free artist[48]."

I accept fears, and I accept that I have to live with them. However, I have a golden rule: I never let fear stop me doing anything. Stop me from being myself. I do battle with my fears every day because it's worth the struggle. As US poet E.E. Cummings said: "To be nobody-but-yourself – in a world which is doing its best, night and day, to make you everybody else – means to fight the hardest battle which any human being can fight[49]."

Glossophobia

Let's take public speaking, a common pastime for midlife careerists who are often called on to dig out the PowerPoint and present.

Glossophobia is our number one fear, above death. "If you go to a funeral," US comedian Jerry Seinfeld quipped, "you're better off in the casket than doing the eulogy[50]."

Warren Buffett, Eleanor Roosevelt, that British prime minister Harold MacMillan again, Julia Roberts[51], Jackie Kennedy, Princess Di[52], Mahatma Gandhi all hated public speaking, for one reason or another, before tackling their fears to convey their message.

And if you're still thinking that's fine for them, they come from a background of wealth and privilege; millions of people, normal people such as you and me, overcome this fear every day, every week, every year.

They come to realise that all they need is a good grasp of their subject matter and an intense desire to share their passion (admittedly difficult when you're presenting the monthly sales figures, not freeing a nation).

The Big Daddy fear

But the greatest, the worst fear of them all, the fear that's holding us back, is the Big Daddy of all fears. Steven Pressfield identifies our biggest fear as the: "Fear That We Will Succeed. That we can access the powers we secretly know we possess. That we can become the person we sense in our hearts we really are[53]." Inside all of us is something itching to breathe, to be recognised, to exist without being smothered. Hiding, like Harry Potter, in a locked broom cupboard under the stairs. And only you have the magic key.

Your mission

All these fears lead to an insidious permanent sense of worry that paralyses the psyche.

It causes indecision and prevents us doing the only thing that will make a difference: more small everyday actions.

Do you need to be a confident high-achiever or trick your mind with the power of positive thinking to reset your life? No, on both counts. All you need to do, as the super-motivating T. Harv Eker states in *Secrets of the Millionaire Mind*, is: "practice acting in spite of fear, in spite of doubt, in spite of worry, in spite of uncertainty, in spite of inconvenience, in spite of discomfort, and even to practice acting when we're not in the mood to act[54]."

CHAPTER 3

Life's a Struggle

SOUND HARD? IT IS. Life is hard; let no one tell you otherwise. No amount of positive thinking will change your lot. We have all these fears to quell for starters. Flick back a few pages and look at them all; it's a miracle we achieve anything, aside from breathing and finding the remote control.

We've already established that *Homo sapiens* arrived at 23:53:36 in the timeline of planet Earth. What about the Industrial Revolution? It only came along half a second ago at 23:59:59[55]. Is it any wonder we've had no time to adapt? We're hard-wired to satisfy our appetites, to pursue pleasure, to reproduce and survive. As Pete Adeney – aka Mr. Money Mustache, we'll come to him later – says: "Ancestors of ours who were insatiable, and always wanted more mates, more children, more food, more social standing, and more security against predators and enemies were quite simply the ones who got to produce the largest number of surviving children. But while insatiability did historically lead to more children, it does not lead to more happiness in a modern life[56]."

Which means life's a struggle. A struggle that we must battle every single day of our lives if we are to live a good and meaningful life.

Dedicating time and summoning mental energy to live a good purposeful life is not an easy choice. Yet, if you're reading this book, the thought has occurred to you that the easy option isn't panning out the way you thought it would.

We can control our actions, not our thoughts

First, don't beat yourself up. The brain is a complicated, self-limiting beast. Many of us, myself included, have spent the best years of our life trying to control our thoughts (those fears again).

Yet as we grow older and wiser, many of us accept that pain, doubt, fear, are not signs of weakness, more by-products of a healthy, fully functioning mind.

No one ever makes a 12-egg family omelette without dropping shell in it. If we try to overcome negative feelings or remove memories with the power of positive thought – *coughs loudly* – all we do is end up feeling inadequate when our attempts to control our thoughts and feelings fail. We can't control our thoughts and feelings any more than we can control other people. What we can control is what we do.

The value of struggling and striving

Now we know our mind's not defective, how do we attain this elusive happiness?

It's almost mandatory for self-improvement books to cite Victor Frankl's unique work *Man's Search for Meaning*[57], and this one's no different.

A survivor of Auschwitz and other Nazi concentration camps, Frankl's writing on life's meaning, at the time of his death in 1997, had given more than ten million people speaking 24 languages hope. I've read it a few times and always felt a fraud afterwards. Because how can I compare my life, my trivial struggles, to that of someone who lived through one of the worst periods in history.

People often use Frankl to support the value in "suffering". If you ever read the book, you will gain an insight into the immense degradation humans can endure, and how our will, and mind, can triumph over all, finding meaning.

But *RESET* is not about embracing unimaginable inhumanity in pursuit of happiness – there's no purpose in that. There must be an easier way.

Desires

One thing's for sure: pursuing desires is not it. When you achieve one desire, it's soon replaced by another, then another. Buy that new car and the first six times you drive it, you will experience happiness. Give it a week or two and you'll be comparing it to the next vehicle in the car park, and soon it will become an expensive millstone around your neck.

Instead, such diverse thinkers as Baron Pierre de Coubertin, British 1980s marathoner Charlie Spedding, endurance sports expert Brad Stulberg, jazz saxophonist John Coltrane and Roman emperor Marcus Aurelius agree it's the struggle, the journey, that's important. The struggle towards a worthwhile goal in line with your purpose and values.

"The real risk is not changing," said Coltrane. "I have to feel that I'm after something. If I make money, fine. But I'd rather be striving. It's the striving, man, it's that I want[58]."

Be brave

There's a saying in marathoning: "Well, I'd better zip up my man suit and get out there." (It's probably sexist, running is the sport where we have "ladies" races that are shorter than men's.)

What I take from this phrase is that I have to be brave, consistently, every day. I'm at my proudest as a parent when my kids are brave; ditto myself. For me, and I owe it to them. When kids go outside and practise bravery, they learn valuable life lessons. I want my kids to skateboard, climb mountains, volunteer, compete.

If you apply the lessons in this book, bravery will light up your life. It's not easy to *get out there* whatever the weather, putting into practice your key principles in the form of a plan. It's stressful not taking the easy way, not obeying that emotion-led Chimp that lives inside our brains. But as Victor Frankl wrote: "What man actually needs is not a tensionless state but rather the striving and strugg-ling for a worthwhile goal[59]."

It needs "the endurance of pain or hardship without the display of feelings and without complaint[60]." It needs stoicism.

Lean into your problem

This is the advice of author Ryan Holiday and others. Life is one endless set of problems. Our job is to find the problem we enjoy (or cannot function without) solving.

On one side, in his book on Stoicism, *The Obstacle is the Way*, Holiday advises people to: "Lean into their problem or weakness or issue[61]." To triumph over adversity, to conquer their biggest fear. Even though you don't always overcome the obstacle in the way you intended, you emerge a better person for the journey.

On the other side is superstar blogger and author of one of the books of 2017, Mark Manson. In *The Subtle Art of Not Giving a F*ck*, he writes: "Happiness comes from solving problems... To be happy we need something to solve. Happiness is therefore a form of action; it's an activity... True happiness occurs only when you find the problems you enjoy having and enjoy solving[62]."

RESET's advice? Try a mixture of the two: problems you dread and problems you relish. Both involve struggle, striving for a worthwhile goal; neither is easy.

Enjoy the effort and the ride

Last year, I read Roald Dahl's childhood autobiography: *Boy*[63]. Every summer, his single mum used to take him and his siblings to her childhood home. The journey (from Wales, in the 1930s) took a couple of days and involved trains, boats, ferries and coaches. Destination? An obscure Norwegian island. On a smaller scale, but in a similar vein, the Family Sawyer drove six hours last year, from Glasgow to the north-westerly tip of mainland Britain. We stopped at McDonald's in Inverness. Just 53 cars passed us in the last two-and-a-half hours. We stayed a few miles from Cape Wrath (you know, the shipping forecast). One morning, we went to the beach, the only ones on a mile of shimmering sand apart from a young couple. The man proposed. The woman said yes. It's that kind of place.

And like most things in life, the more effort it takes to reach somewhere, the better the experience when you arrive.

* * *

Life might be hard for you now. Perhaps your folks have just moved into an old person's home and most of your Saturdays are spent on the three-hour round trip to see them. Maybe your teenage daughter's going off the rails. Perhaps your boss makes a habit of upbraiding you in front of your staff. The lot of the midlife careerist is hard: following the steps in *RESET* will not be easy. Life is a struggle.

But if I can give you one piece of advice. Once you have your early retirement plan in place, once you've rediscovered who you are, please, I beg you – enjoy the ride.

Take it from one who knows. Or listen to Mark Manson, who perhaps knew *me* in a previous life: "[Marathons, raising a child, starting a small business with friends]...involve pain, struggle, even anger and despair – yet once they're accomplished, we look back and get all misty-eyed telling our grandkids about them. As Freud once said, 'One day, in retrospect, the years of struggle will strike you as the most beautiful[64].'"

He should have added that if you want that beautiful feeling you'd better pick a struggle that's worthwhile (that bloke Freud has a lot to answer for).

CHAPTER 4

Finding Meaning

HAVE YOU EVER ASKED yourself what is the meaning of life? This question has exercised the greatest minds throughout history: Plato, Schopenhauer, Nietzsche; and lately, bloggers the world over (on their own journeys of self-discovery).

Ever since reading *The Hitchhiker's Guide to the Galaxy*[65], I've wanted to know, too. And it's only this last six years, when I've started learning again, that I've reached a conclusion.

The answer: there is *no one*. Douglas Adams was a comedy genius, but the answer is not 42. It's not finding unconditional love. It's not achieving fame and fortune. There is no universal truth because we're all different.

My six-year perambulations have, however, not been in vain. I've discovered that you don't need to *know* the meaning of life to live a life with meaning.

What do I mean?

We've already found that to achieve that second version of happiness (the one we want), we need to live a meaningful, striving, action-filled life.

That's our quest. That's the reason we want to reset our lives. For example, a meaningful life could involve:

1. Hard work and generosity (Adeney[66]).
2. Creating a work or doing a deed, finding love, turning disaster into triumph: finding meaning in suffering (Frankl[67]).
3. And my favourite, from The Happy Philosopher (a blogger): "Find a good partner/spouse and network of friends. Find the community that has the right feel. Develop healthy life habits and get your finances in order. Nurture relationships and find a community that makes you happy. Figure out the big things first and the little stuff falls into place[68]."

To do this, we need a vision and a purpose. In a minute, I'll show you how to find it. Before I explain how, let's go deep, the deepest we'll go in this book. Are you up for the challenge?

Deathbed regrets

For any culture which is primarily concerned with meaning, the study of death – the only certainty that life holds for us – must be central, for an understanding of death is the key to liberation in life[69].
Stanislav Grof

We know that life's a struggle and that the lot of us midlife professionals is to hulk our degenerating bodies out of bed every day to do *battle* with partners, children, bosses, nagging memories, a plethora of fears and that old woman in front of us who's driving slowly (*it's a 40mph speed zone for Pete's sake*).

The thing about *battle* is that when you're in the trenches, it's hard to see the bullets for the barbed wire. That's why soldiers have generals (hold on a minute... I'm not sure Field Marshal Haig's men would agree here). It's only after the battle finishes, and time is made for a post mortem, that perspective and insight are gained.

Sometimes, we glimpse this wisdom: little shafts of sunlight penetrating the workaday fug. Perhaps it's your parent saying they don't miss their job after a lifetime's hard, fulfilling work. Maybe it's a teacher who takes you aside and imparts the knowledge banked from 30 years' teaching secondary school kids. For your ears only.

Last year, I saw one at *TEDxGlasgow*[70]. The best talk was by David Eustace[71], then 55, an internationally renowned photographer and director born in Glasgow's impoverished East End. Reflecting on a 30-year career, he talked of a sliding-doors moment and urged us to seize the day; seize the moment, just as he had. To never let fear get in the way. To always act on the "what if"; never be left thinking "if only".

But these are sunbeams, they pierce the gloom and make us think, but nothing changes and really, we rationalise, it's only one person's worldview.

That's why the findings of Bronnie Ware, an Australian nurse who spent 12 years working in palliative care, are so illuminating. She asked patients in the final 12 weeks of their lives about "any regrets they had or anything they would do differently." In her blog post "Regrets of the Dying" (which also became a best-selling book), Ware identifies five common themes:

1. I wish I'd had the courage to live a life true to myself, not the life others expected of me.
2. I wish I hadn't worked so hard.
3. I wish I'd had the courage to express my feelings.
4. I wish I had stayed in touch with my friends.
5. I wish that I had let myself be happier.

Ware's patients regretted unfulfilled dreams, missing their kids growing up, working too hard, not saying what they thought, not spending enough time nurturing friendships and not realising there was another way. That happiness was, in fact, a choice[72].

* * *

Imagine yourself in the future: old and grey (er). Do it now.

You're 84, living in sheltered housing. You're in an armchair looking back on your life. What advice do you think you'd give your current self? Do you want to be full of regrets? Regrets that you didn't do what you wanted with your life, buffeted by external forces like a sailboat in a gale. Regrets that you didn't find time to love those you loved. Regrets that you spent every single day fretting over those worries that never happened, and those people who didn't care about you, anyway.

If it's true, as psychiatrist Stanislav Grof and philosopher Arthur Schopenhauer might say, and Victor Frankl asks: "Doesn't the final meaning of life, too, reveal itself, if at all, only at its end, on the verge of death[73]?", let's not wait 40 years to find out. Bronnie has done that for us.

Anonymous – she gets everywhere – once said: "Someone once told me the definition of hell: the last day you have on Earth, the person you became will meet the person you could have become[74]."

Don't be Anonymous's mate. Don't let the hopes and dreams you had as a kid – that are still there, somewhere, buried deep in your soul – be cast to the wind. Be brave, stand tall, reach for the tiller and make that one life of yours count.

I leave you with US author Mark Twain's wise words: "Twenty years from now [when you've retired, hopefully] you will be more disappointed by the things you didn't do than by the ones you did do. So throw off the bowlines. Sail away from the safe harbor. Catch the trade winds in your sails[75]."

If you don't do it, someone else will, and before you know it, you'll be halfway to the inappropriately named Cape of Good Hope – or even worse, the Bermuda Triangle – without a paddle.

Stripped bare

Often through looking at the experiences of people on the edges of life, the purest insights emerge. It's these morsels from the ends of the earth that give us hope. For instance, the power of Victor Frankl's book is that the life he recounts in the Nazi death camps is human beings stripped literally and figuratively bare. It's life at the absolute extreme. When Frankl finds that those who survived in the concentration camps of the Nazi empire were often not the fittest, as Darwin's research suggests, but those who had a purpose, a *why* to live, we listen.

As we sit in our comfortable houses and air conditioned offices, living our satiated lives – full of artificial constructs and inflated egos – it's hard to strip ourselves back to our essence, to find who we are. But we must, even without the external force (divorce, breakdown, losing our job, the death of loved ones) that commonly leads us to re-examine our lives. We must find our purpose, however prosaic it may be.

CHAPTER 5

On Purpose

WHAT'S YOUR PURPOSE? DO you know? Or is that like finding a toaster in a twister? A *Wizard of Oz* tornado containing kids' toys, parental expectations, six smartphones and the Maniacal Manager of the West. If you're thinking *why do I need to do this? It's so difficult,* let's get some perspective. Some hope.

- Business is hard. Life is hard. But if you don't have a purpose, it's even harder.
- Everyone is searching for something. It's a human being thing. Everyone wants to be somebody. Social scientists at Johns Hopkins University asked 7,948 students across 48 countries what they considered "very important" to them now. Sixteen per cent said "making a lot of money", whereas 78% answered "finding a purpose and meaning to life[76]". *Ha, students,* you might say, *always the idealists.* Well, if we're going to play that game, let me respond with – students are not known for their dislike of the green stuff.
- German philosopher Friedrich Nietzsche said: "He who has a why to live for can bear almost any how[77]." If money is your only end – money to pay the bills, to finance your lifestyle that is trapping you, suffocating your soul – no wonder you're un-happy. That's not to say money is an ignoble goal. But without

changing the way you think about money – we'll come to that later – and having a vision and purpose underpinning that money goal, you're on your own. Or look at it like this: if you're in a high-paying job that's sucking the life out of you, buckle up. As long as it fits your purpose, and you take steps to make it better – we'll come to that later, too – you don't have to ditch it. Stick with it, use it for what it is: a means to an end. As Darren Hardy writes in *The Compound Effect*: "The power of your *why* is what gets you to stick through the grueling, mundane, and laborious[78]."

- Frankl wrote: "everything can be taken from a man but one thing: the last of the human freedoms – to choose one's attitude in any given set of circumstances, to choose one's own way[79]." It's not "*Que sera, sera.* Whatever will be, will be." You're in control. Your destiny is yours alone. You have the freedom to be yourself. One thing's for certain, though: you ain't "going to Wembley" if you don't *snap out of it* sometime soon.

How do I find my purpose?

It's surprisingly easy to find your purpose – it reveals itself as you go along.

If after reading the next few pages you're still none the wiser, don't worry.

I was rubbish at running at school, didn't have a clue what I wanted to do when I left university, fell into PR, shambled into digital marketing and discovered the financial independence movement via a circuitous route.

Everything's clear now, but if I'd done this exercise six years ago, it would have scared me. (In fact, I wouldn't have known where to begin.)

But I didn't, and if I had been interested, I would have had to search high and low for the advice that follows.

So, after reading what the best philosophers, self-help and business minds have to say on the matter, and coming to my own conclusions, here's how *you* can find *your* purpose.

Start with the vision

In common with most midlife professionals, **my vision**, my dream, is all to do with early retirement. I call it financial independence, "getting F.U. Money". That's enough money to live off forever, so if someone asks me to do something I don't want to do, you guessed it, I can say: "Fuck you."

(F.U. Money is nothing to do with a man wearing a tracksuit top and snow wash jeans plucking a wodge of bank notes from his back pocket, waving them in your face, and shouting "loadsamoney[80]!")

But that vision, though vivid, is not strong enough. My true vision is my wife, Rachel, and me, sitting in one of those white towns in Andalusia, in the hills. It's an Airbnb: we've been there for two months now. We're in comfy chairs on the roof terrace, reading; her David Nicholls's latest novel, me *Crime and Punishment*. There's a glass of red nearby. As the sky turns crimson, we look at each other and smile. Then I rise, stick on my trainers, and go for a run.

I have that mental picture in my head. Others have one on their screen saver at work. *What and where is yours?* Wherever you place it, having a vision of where you want to go is vital if you are to follow it up with actions. Knowing your destination will keep you going through the hard work it takes to reach it. For, as author Mason Currey discovered in *Daily Rituals*, which looks at the everyday lives of history's greatest creators: "grand creative visions translate to small daily increments[81]." That's where the magic happens.

Ten ways to find your purpose

Let's bring together everything we've talked about in Part I. Here are ten techniques you can use to find your purpose and be happier.

1. What matters to you?

Everyone's heard of the NHS (National Health Service), one of the greatest achievements in Great Britain's history. In Scotland, there is a movement called *What Matters to You*[82]. Hospital staff ask patients to fill in a simple sheet with the three things in their lives that matter to them. They attach it to the end of their beds along with their clinical notes. It helps doctors see the person not the illness, and transforms patients' sense of well-being and inclusion when in hospital. It's now commonplace in children's wards across the country. Imagine a world where we walked around with the three things that matter to us pinned to our chests. What conversations we'd have.

Ask yourself, what matters to you. Write them down (no more than three).

2. Wisdom from a pub near Newcastle train station

Charlie Spedding is a pharmacist by trade, living in north-east England. He's also the author of the most inspirational and insight-ful book I've ever read, and a decent bloke, according to my mate John Paul, who's dealt with him in his job. In *From Last to First,* Charlie charts his running development, from a teenager who was last boy home in the 100 metres on school sports day to winning club races in the north-east. In his late twenties, and by then a good (but not great) distance runner, he had an epiphany[83] while enjoying a pint, waiting for the train to Durham.

"What do I want? Why do I want it? How much do I want it?" became the creed by which he lived his life. Having decided the what – to finish his running career feeling he had fulfilled himself; and the why – to avoid having regrets for the rest of his life had he just tried harder; he then answered his "how much". One hour and a pint of Eureka later, Spedding left the pub and caught the train home. In the weeks that followed, he sold his car, rented his house, resigned his job and moved to Boston, Massachusetts.

Four years on, he won the marathon bronze medal at the 1984 LA Olympics. Twenty-five years afterwards he recalled what it felt like: "I am left with a deep contentment because I got close to the limit my talent would allow," said Spedding. "The greatest moment in my two decades of running came 22 miles into the Olympic mar-athon when I took the lead and pushed the pace. After all my setbacks, injuries, failures, I was living the fantasy that every distance runner has on a long, cold, winter run. I had the initiative, I was calling the tune. I was grasping the opportunity with both hands. I was taking part in Olympic proportions. I was running as fast as I dared. I was trying my utmost to fulfil my wildest dreams. Today was indeed the day. I was doing it. I was flying and I felt absolutely fantastic[84]."

Sometimes inspiration strikes at the weirdest times. There was no external event, nothing special about that pub; Charlie just took decisive action.

But he credits jotting those thoughts in his notepad as the transformative moment in his running career.

It's amazing how your life can turn on a sixpence, supping a jar of real ale in Newcastle.

3. Minus the money

Here's a question for you. Say you were loaded and had enough to live on for the rest of your days. If money were no object...what would you do with your life?

Not Bill Gates-loaded. Just enough to live a comfortable lifestyle, with a soupçon of cattle-class international travel.

If you never had to work for money ever again, what would you do?

4. Let's professionalise this

I know, this is hard. Let's frame it in a work context. How about a family mission statement, one that is clear and measurable?

One that passes *Essentialism* author Greg McKeown's test of: "When will we know when it's done[85]?" One that focusses on one thing, the one most important to you and your family. One that defines what success will look like.

Write it down.

5. Channel your death fear

Say you were given a year to live; what would you do with those 365 days? **Make a list and see what themes emerge.**

6. The power of three

Triangles, Billy Goats Gruff. Little pigs; gold, silver, bronze; red, white and blue – there's a power in three. Once you realise, you'll notice it everywhere.

Ask yourself these two – yes, two – questions:

What are the *three* activities you love doing the most?

What are the *three* activities you want to be doing but aren't?

Rate them on a scale of 1–10.

In his 1959 book *The Magic of Thinking Big*, David Schwartz has a similar idea. He has three questions: "What do I want to accomplish in my life? What do I want to be? And what does it take to satisfy me[86]?" He then splits it into three: "Work", "Home" and "Social". A useful exercise, but don't forget that *RESET* is about looking at your life as a whole. Everything's interconnected. It's your life that concerns us, not your work.

7. Future-gazing

There's much to admire about China.

I used to have friends who lived in Hong Kong. We visited 15 years ago and I remember a conversation in one of those exclusive westernised Thai restaurants. Our mates talked of rich Hong Kong residents' admiration of the Chinese economy and the country's five-year plans[87]: I listened, googled it, and my logical brain agreed. And I wondered why we didn't do the same in the UK. (This was partway through a time when one political party enjoyed 13 years of government with a large majority in the House of Commons.)

To apply this to our lives, those of time-pressed midlife professionals, how the hell are we going to achieve anything if we don't have a plan? Even if, unlike most, we have a destination in mind, we ain't going to reach it without looking to the future.

To devise a five, ten or 15-year plan, we must ask ourselves where do we want to be in five, ten or 15 years' time. For instance, my wife and I are 45. When we hit 50, our kids will be 12 and 14. My family are what matter to me. Once 50, to celebrate our birthdays (which are ten days apart), we want to go on another "holiday of a lifetime", when the kids are old enough to enjoy it and before our family disperses through education, marriage, etc. So we're squirrelling away money every month to pay for it.

Where do you want to be in five years' time? What do you want to have achieved? Write it down, bring it to life, be ultra-specific and make it memorable and motivating. Then work out what you need to do to get there.

8. Past-gazing

When you were little and someone asked: "What do you want to be when you grow up?", how did you answer? How did you answer when you were six, when you were 12 and when you were 15, as your education began to specialise?

Do you remember? How did it change? **What did *you* dream of when you were young?**

9. Listen

Turn off the internet and TV. Listen to what's in your heart. When it's silent, what do you feel? What is it that brings you joy? Or, leave the city, find a mountain and start ascending. When you near the top, turn round, sit on a boulder and listen to the silence. **What do you love doing?** What are you best at? Listen to your soul.

10. Enter the dark side

OK, all lovely and life-affirming so far, but what of your negative thoughts, the ones you try to suppress: jealousy, envy, inadequacy and your feelings of low self-esteem?

This is fertile ground for those in search of purpose. Think of the people in your life and focus on the three you're most envious of, whose success and acclamation you covet. Think good and hard, be angry, go "aargh".

Now calm down. **What is it they've got that you haven't?**

Finding what you desire most is the ultimate shortcut to finding your purpose. Making it a good and meaningful one is the logical next step.

Two examples

Robert Kiyosaki

If you're interested in personal finance or even financial independence, you may have read Robert Kiyosaki's anecdote-laden 1997 book *Rich Dad Poor Dad.* It's sold over 32m copies in more than 51 languages across 109 countries.

He talks about his reason for wanting to be rich, as a combination of deep, emotional don't wants and wants.

First, the don't wants: "I don't want to work all my life. I don't want what my parents aspired for, which was job security and a house in the suburbs. I don't like being an employee. I hated that my dad always missed my football games because he was so busy working on his career..."

Then the wants: "I want to be free to travel the world and live in the lifestyle I love. I want to be young when I do this. I want to simply be free. I want control over my time and my life. I want money to work for me[88]."

A simple purpose, underpinned by reasons that connected with his soul. Kiyosaki got his F.U. Money aged 47, free to do what mattered to him.

David Sawyer

I've asked myself these questions and had plenty of late night discussions with my wife. Neither of us wants to retire too early: we love our jobs. But we don't want to *have* to work (there's a big difference) – we want F.U. Money.

Yet we want to enjoy the journey, too, and *what matters to us,* what we want out of life, is similar now to what it will be when we reach our goal.

That's family and close friends, working for bosses we admire, adventure, off-the-beaten-track holidays, the coast, walks, running, respect and recognition, stimulation and learning.

But it's the vivid vision (Andalusia) and a clear family mission statement that powers us through:

ON PURPOSE

Achieve a stash* of £855,000 before the age of 60 through living a good and meaningful life that matters to us.

Simple, measurable and all down to us: just as we like it.

*See Glossary of Terms.

CHAPTER 6

Values and Your Worldview

WE'VE DISCUSSED HOW TO find your purpose. Now, we come to who you are. What are your beliefs? What is your unique worldview? Everyone has one. What are your "red lines"? Be honest – what are your principles? To take ourselves seriously – and we must, if we are to live a good and meaningful life – we have to believe in something, stand for something, let it define us. That something must whistle through us like the sound of sea through a conch shell.

Before the pursuit of fame and fortune and the culture of personality became a defining force from the 1920s onwards, we lived in the age of character where morals, manners, honour and good deeds done without expectation of anything in return, were prized above all else.

That I think this is a shame is immaterial. What is important is you do the soul-searching to know what *your values* are (tip: pick three and stick to them), *then* let them define your vision and your purpose.

This is the key to living a life with meaning: no cognitive dissonance (saying or thinking one thing and doing another).

As Darren Hardy writes, values "define both who you are and what you stand for." He adds: "Your core values are your internal compass, your guiding beacon, your personal GPS...nothing creates more stress than when our actions and behaviors aren't congruent with our values[89]." Values are a motivating force. When you're going through difficult times, it's acting in line with values you hold dear, in the pit of your stomach, that pulls you through. They're what you stand for and what you stand against.

Think of them like obituaries and gravestones. If your obituary appeared in the local paper, that's where we'd learn about your achievements, your claims to fame.

Your values would go on your gravestone. How proud would your son be if he went to pay his respects and read "'Here lies David Sawyer, devoted son and father. Believed in keeping up with the Joneses. What he didn't believe in was himself.'"

No interest in death? How about mantras? Before every marathon, I write three words in black ballpoint pen on my left wrist. When I enter the second half of the race (after 20 miles), and every muscle in my body is telling me to slow down, that my time target is unrealistic, that the training session I missed seven weeks ago and those four days off through injury are going to start coming home to roost, I glance at my wrist. It's then, when times are toughest, that my three-word mantra, which I start to chant in my head, comes into its own.

Values are similar: they're what power you through to the finish, help you achieve your goals, keep you striving, struggling and toeing that start line. The difference is that marathons finish; whereas life, it continues. Strong values that underpin your purpose will help you achieve that lucid vision, whatever it is. They're what keep you putting one foot in front of another when your body and mind are begging you to stop.

Choose whatever values you want; these will come from within you. But choose them wisely.

* * *

I went through this process four years ago when I set up my company. During a month of soul-searching, I realised that what mattered to me was my family. And, having asked 15 close friends what they thought about me – and racking my brain, heart and soul – I discovered that I stood for three values: trust, integrity and results (I find that any more than three values and you struggle to remember them). I called my company Zude PR (after my sons Zak and Jude) and embedded those three words in my logo. It's those values that have guided my business, and me, ever since.

Last, if you've never considered this, or think you've lost touch with your values over the past 20 years, don't worry. To lose your values is impossible. They're there somewhere; you just need to find them.

CHAPTER 7

Plan and Goals

YOU'VE DONE ALL THIS thinking. You have a vision; you're clear on your/your family's purpose, which flows from your values. How do you turn theory into practice? In one corner of the ring is those that think you need habits, not goals. Others think systems are more important than goals. After reading about and trialling every system known to man, here's my advice:

- Set a clear and measurable goal (it must fit your purpose and align with your vision).
- Make sure it complements your values (or you won't see it through).
- Make a plan.
- Make sure your plan is flexible (this only comes through discovering the behaviours you need to follow to achieve the goal). If you need to, modify it.
- Follow the plan. Complete each line item in the plan (no more no less).
- Measure your success against your goal.
- Apply what you learn.
- Set a new goal.
- Repeat.

For example, in 2012, approaching my fortieth birthday, I decided to start running. I was two stone overweight, and couldn't jog round the block. After three years of hard work, I became good at it, so it was particularly disappointing that 2015 and 2016 were lost to injury. I thought I'd never run again. Around Christmas 2016, my troublesome left Achilles abated, and I was able to start training. I set a difficult goal and devised a plan based on my body, injury record, family and work schedule.

Along the way, kids' classes, work commitments, minor injuries all made demands on my time. I adapted the plan but tried to stick to the original as much as possible.

On Sunday September 24th 2017, I clocked 2:40:36 at the Berlin Marathon, missing my goal by 37 seconds. My three big learnings?

1. Make your plan flexible, adaptable. As Mike Tyson said when reporters were magnifying one of his opponents' strengths in a pre-fight press conference: "Everyone has a plan until they get punched in the mouth[90]."
2. Make your plan short. Anything more than a couple of pages is not worth the paper it's written on.
3. Set one goal. Make it tough but achievable.

And if you don't attain it, don't worry; what's a few seconds between friends?

CHAPTER 8

Part I Index Card

- Choose the meaningful happiness, not the pleasure-chasing, self-indulgent one.
- Act despite your fears.
- Life's a struggle: lean into it and enjoy the ride.
- Get a clear, memorable vision.
- Discover your purpose.
- Be true to yourself.
- You need a plan, but expect to be punched in the mouth.

And finally...

For me, all this came last not first; I discovered it along the way. Apart from a nagging desire to prove my doubters wrong, there was no method at all. As Anne Lamott writes in her book about life and writing – *Bird by Bird*: "What people somehow (inadvertently, I'm sure) forgot to mention when we were children was that we need to make messes to find out who we are and why we are here[91]." Don't worry if you can't make sense of this now. Take inspiration from me. Before I did any of the above, I created one hell of a mess. Beginning by tackling *my* biggest fear – digital.

PART II

Going Digital – How to Future-Proof Your Career

WHATEVER INDUSTRY YOU WORK in, digital is transforming it. Name me one part of your job that hasn't changed through increasing digitisation. The pace of change is at once bewildering and exhilarating. As Wikipedia has it: "The transformation stage means that digital usages inherently enable new types of innovation and creativity in a particular domain, rather than simply enhance and support traditional methods[92]." That's all very well. However, for the midlife careerist, who's already *busy*, such innovation is seen more as a threat than an exciting opportunity: the last thing they have time to do is "get with the digital programme". Whether you're a lawyer, accountant, PR, chief executive, engineer or scientist, the fundamentals of your job haven't changed. You still have to hire and fire people, motivate your staff, hit targets, be good at maths, be able to state your case, be able to lead. But digital has given those who have grasped them, opportunities to do many tasks quicker and better. Yet it's in the field of personal reputation and profile that digital change has had most impact. And it's this aspect of digital that creates the most threats and opportunities for the midlife professional. It's not enough any more to do a good job and be rewarded for it. You've got to tell people you're doing it, too. Part II will explain how to harness technological change to build your reputation, raise your profile and future-proof your employment. I shall share what happened to me, how digital first threatened then reconstructed my career. Then outline 25 actions you can take to enhance your influence and boost your earning potential. A F.U. profile for F.U. Money: I'll drink to that.

CHAPTER 9

Trapped in "Digital or Die" Land

EARLIER, IN STATUS QUO, we found that great leaps forward in technology have brought new ways of working. With universally available wifi and reduced costs associated with running one's own business, many people are choosing portfolio careers, diversifying their income streams, designing their working lives. These people have one thing in common: they have grasped the enabling opportunities of digital, set up on their own and transformed their work and life.

Yet for most, drawing a single wage (a salary) is the default choice. For example, data from the World Bank estimates that in the UK, wage and salaried workers make up 84.5% of the population, rising to 90% in the US[93].

Risky business

This is a risky situation in which to find oneself. Many midlife professionals do not realise how dangerous it is having one job, no external profile and not a clue how to make digital work for them. Here's what can happen:

- You're sacked.
- You're made redundant.

- You're manoeuvred out of your role.
- Organisation goes bust: don't think because you work for a big corporate you're immune.
- Organisation closes your office and asks you to move.
- Organisation merges with another organisation and you're surplus to requirements.
- Something happens in your personal life that means you need to change jobs.

Your life can change overnight and you need to be ready.

Four things

What follows in Part II is a tried and tested prescription to build a F.U. profile that will de-risk your career and make *you* relevant for the next 20 years. There's no reason, whatever your profession, you can't be the one who works more efficiently, is invited to speak at industry conferences, suggests new systems and processes, shimmies up that greasy pole and is noticed by people they respect. If you choose to roll up your sleeves, this plan could be one of four things for you (or all four):

1. **Your ticket to promotion.** The better you become at your job, the more you can do, the more confident you are in your digital abilities, the more your star will rise. You'll restore pride and be more strategic as you regain calm and perspective. Your value to the organisation and the people it services will increase immeasurably.
2. **Your insurance policy.** The higher your external profile, the more Zero Moments of Truth[94] (ZMOTs) you achieve, the more people will notice you, the more desirable you'll become to other employers. This might not be your intent, but it's good to have in your back pocket. By going digital, you will de-risk your life.
3. **Your happiness-at-work pill.** Fifty per cent of every waking weekday is spent working, so no one should be doing a job they

hate. If you're one of the 87% of the world's population who dislikes their job or is disengaged, taking these steps will, over time, make you happier at work. If you do it for one reason, do it for this.

4. **Your escape plan.** (Keep this last one a secret, because you don't want to be doing your digital enlightening in your own time; it benefits your work, so persuade *them* to finance it.) If you're past the point of no return in your salaried employment, and you want to escape, this is a great medium-to-long-term plan to smooth your exit. As soon as you know all this, you'll start seeing ways to escape and, just like the insurance policy, maybe employers will come aknocking.

The 25-step plan I'm going to share with you can be applied whatever your field of work. But first, I'm going to explain the business of PR. My business. And how technological change has both transformed it and my place within it.

CHAPTER 10

PR: a Case Study

IT WON'T HAVE ESCAPED your notice that as the years tumble by, you do less dancing in nightclubs with old friends and more dinner parties with your kids' mates' parents. There's a line I like to trot out at such soirées, which I nicked from somewhere: "No child ever asked their dad to read them a press release for their bedtime story[95]."

After I've finished reading a quote from a press release (which starts with "I'm delighted"), I add: "And no kid has ever answered the question 'what do you want to be when you're older?' with 'I want to be a PR man.'" (Apart from my sons, who are still young enough to believe that when *they* grow up they want to be like their father.)

PR gets a bad press, often undeservedly. I don't help matters.

My favourite movie clip about PR is from the 1962 Blake Edwards-directed *Days of Wine and Roses*. Towards the start, the Jack Lemmon character is sitting around the kitchen table with his future father-in-law for the first time[96].

"What kind of work do you do?" asks the Lee Remick character's dad. "Well, er, er, public relations." Lemmon replies. After his fiancée struggles to explain, Lemmon resumes: "Well, er, I suppose you might say my job is to sort of help my client create a public image. For example, let's say my client, corporation X, does some good, something of benefit to the public, or something that could conceivably be conceived as benefit to the...well my job is to see that the public knows it."

"So if your X corporation makes a mistake, and the thing turns out bad?" says the father-in-law to be.

"Well, theoretically they don't, well part of my job is to help my client to think of ways to operate in a way the public would approve."

"But if your X corporation makes a mistake, and the thing turns out bad?"

"Well. I guess I try to make it look not quite so bad...but there's more to it than that..."

To which Dad replies: **"I don't understand that kind of work."**

Do I think I'm changing the world? No.

Would I do PR if I wasn't paid for it? No.

Yet I love the work, love doing a great job for my clients, helping them achieve their aims. I love writing, telling stories and helping people communicate.

It's important to me that I excel at this job, which has given me so much over the past 20 years. I may not be saving lives but, when earning a crust, *PR* is what matters to me: there's nothing I'd rather be. And it matters that I'm damn good at it.

My story

It was mid-December 2013; I remember it vividly. The sense of elation coupled with overwhelming fear. Writing on that napkin, or was it the back of an A4 menu card, what I was (could, just maybe) going to do. For that afternoon, sitting in an anteroom of House for an Art Lover in Bellahouston Park, everything was clear. I felt like Atlas must have when he got that weight off his shoulders. On a billowy and unsupported, cloud nine. Why the sense of relief?

Because that morning I'd decided, in six weeks' time, to leave my job leading the Glasgow office of a big PR firm. At first glance, this was strange. I had no plan. Big clients, a great little staff team of committed individuals, the support of talented peers, a cracking pension, a great agency that I believed in and a stable pay packet at the end of the month.

But was I happy? To misquote magician Paul Daniels: "Just a little, not a lot."

I'd fallen into that trap of many a middle-class midlifer who's spent a generation in corporate life climbing that greasy pole. I'd got farther and farther away from what I loved about my profession. Concerned more with HR, exceeding "the numbers" – at which I excelled – and managing work, not doing it. My practice, what I'd made my name on, was stagnating. I talked a good game, but wasn't so adept at playing it anymore.

I was anxious as my industry – once media relations with a few bells and whistles – was changing before my eyes. I had the fear. The world was going digital. And I was expected to go with it.

At first, I raged against this dying of the light. Media relations wasn't about to cop it yet. There'd still be demand for someone good at getting their clients into the papers or keeping them out. But I thought I'd toe the party line. After all, digital was here to stay. So I started dabbling in social media and did a passable job jazz handing clients' communications campaigns. I was better at it than most. But I knew I didn't understand the broader picture and, what with one thing and another (the demands of running a profit centre), for a few years, I didn't have or make the time.

Somewhere along the line, kids came along; now, I really was *too busy*. Once, in my eyes, one of the best in my field, I increasingly felt a fraud, making it up as I went along when it came to digital.

That was my work life. What of my home life?

A similar story. Beautiful wife and young boys, foreign holidays, meals out, lattes, cleaner, Montessori nursery, great friends and a comforting house 100 yards from a top primary school. On the face of it, one to envy.

So why did it feel like it was all going to come crashing down any minute – some fears, it turns out, have a basis in truth – and that somehow I didn't deserve it?

Unhappy at work with no financial or life plan, the lattes were not helping the daily work dread.

The stress-related scab on my left elbow wasn't going anywhere. And I kept having nightmares where the head of marketing at whatever big client my team and me were presenting to asked me to explain the whizzy digital "wheel of content" slide I'd glossed over in the pitch deck. For someone so competitive and proud of excelling, digital was doing my head in. It was digging my PR grave.

An insanely brief history of public relations

Let's rewind 16 years.

My public relations career began in 1997. Back then, we posted press releases. My boss and I agreed, as we drove back from Livingston to Dundee, that email would never catch on as a press release delivery mechanism. And if, in the future, one were to email this crucial precision-guided PR missile into the newsrooms of Scotland and the UK, it would need to be backed up by a fax which had by then supplanted the posting of releases as the modern, if expensive, way of delivering the news.

For most of its hundred or so years – particularly after the second world war – public relations has been, as an ex-colleague used to say, a limpet on the media whale. The idea being like so:

- Josephine Public receives most of her information through the mass media.
- Mass media – especially when I started out – is trusted.
- To reach the people they want to reach (we call them audiences or publics), organisations use the press to get their points (we call them key messages) across.
- To do this, organisations need people who can write like journalists, can tell a story and have the experience to advise them how to show themselves in the best light while maintaining their integrity.
- They hire these people from outside the organisation (consultants or contractors) or employ them in-house (employees).

For the first ten years of my career, this was the status quo for me as a PR consultant working in Dundee then Glasgow: Scotland's largest city and the fourth most populous in the UK. Yes, the internet and social media existed and people were beginning to discover different ways of getting the information they desired; yes, this is a gross over-simplification of PR (what about public affairs, newsletters, public meetings, investor relations?). But day-to-day, week-to-week, year-by-year, this was the PR I knew and loved and what clients hired me for: to help them clarify what they wanted to say and to whom they wanted to say it. And help them broadcast it through newspapers, radio and TV.

T'internet

Slowly but surely, the internet changed my job. The past 20 years have seen an often-baffling transformation in how people communicate and are communicated with.

For example, in 1997, Britain's best-selling newspaper, *The Sun*, sold 3.87m copies a day. In 2007, this was still a healthy 3.21m. By 2018, circulation had more than halved to 1.55m[97]. Closer to (my) home, the picture for print media is even starker. In 2003, *The Scotsman* sold 71,000[98] copies a day; the latest figures show sales of just 15,870[99] (except *bulk,* eg, giveaways to airline travellers[100]).

With a combination of Facebook and Google stealing their advertising spend, and an old and ageing customer base, the future is bleak for newspapers the world over. The decline in traditional media has complicated matters for public relations professionals. Whatever organisation a PR woman or man works for, the people they want to reach have dispersed to far-flung corners of what we used to call the information super-highway. Their choice of how they receive their information is bewildering. Here are a few examples:

- TV, radio, print media.
- Blogs.
- Email newsletters.

- Online news sites such as *BuzzFeed*, *Huffington Post* and, often, electronic versions of traditional media, eg, *The Guardian*, *The New Yorker*.
- Google.
- Video (whether YouTube, Facebook, LinkedIn).
- Facebook feed.
- Facebook groups.
- Other social networks (Instagram, SnapChat, Twitter, LinkedIn, Messenger, WhatsApp).

Because people are going elsewhere for their news (leaving aside the insidious "fake news" that has diminished trust in journalism, a vital part of society), the PR industry has had to change with the times.

A new breed of digital PRs has sprung up, urging traditional practitioners to "get with the programme". They share what they know, for the benefit of others (and themselves, of course, *coughs loudly, again*).

Meanwhile, most senior PRs are still struggling to come to terms with the new paradigm, getting by on Twitter and Facebook ducking and diving while remaining in their comfort zone of media relations and crisis management. For them, the drive to digital is unwelcome and threatening. Few people in senior positions want to appear weak, to ask for help they need. Studies show a dearth of digital experience and knowledge among older PRs: 12% of PR practitioners in the UK with more than 21 years' experience feel confident in their social and digital skills[101].

Still, not to worry, they think, *although traditional media is dying there'll always be a place for it, and demand for my specialised skills.* Just how much of a demand and will it be enough to see them to retirement, is the primary concern of most PRs in their mid-forties upwards.

Digital is at the same time the single biggest challenge and opportunity facing the PR industry today. In agency land, digital marketers, influencer marketers, bloggers, content marketers, search engine optimisation (SEO) experts and even management consultants, are staking a claim on the digital communications mishmash, and even beginning to eat PR's media relations lunch. Name me a decent-sized SEO agency now that doesn't have a PR person on staff.

Not having to reach people through the filter of press and television should be liberating for PRs who are, at their core, frustrated writers (just ask the late great Terry Pratchett[102]). Digital should be a chance to learn new skills, a chance to write creatively, not in the style of a press release.

But stressed to the nines, too busy at work and at home to understand *why* they need to learn digital (never mind *how*), too many midlife practitioners ignore the changes; while little by little, year upon year, digital is hammering nail after nail in their PR coffin.

What makes PRs tick?

Before we head into the universal advice on what *you* can do as a midlife professional to future-proof *your* career, master *your* digital fear and bag *your* insurance policy/escape plan/promotion ticket/happiness-at-work pill, a final word about what makes PRs tick and the prevailing culture in which we work. You're sure to notice similarities with your own profession:

- **More than 80,000 PR people work in the UK**[103]. There's a historical culture of not sharing expertise and knowledge. This is changing.
- **We like to navel-gaze**, spending lots of time redefining ourselves with words and feelings, instead of learning from related industries and redefining ourselves with our actions. Particularly with digital.
- **Few understand what the future will bring**. As entrepreneur Gary Vaynerchuk has written, progressive firms seeking to raise their profile should be thinking: "less about having a PR person and more about building a modern production company around that person[104]."

- **Pride and image are important to most PRs**. Which is why digital is such a threat to the senior PR's psyche. Deep inside we know we're failing our clients and employers by not understanding the best way of reaching people in this modern world. We're not only doing ourselves a disservice but also our paymasters.
- **The industry is taking too long** to realise that communication nowadays is no longer about being polished and controlled. It's about authenticity and having conversations – not broadcasting to people but, instead, speaking with them.
- **Being a public relations practitioner is a tough gig**, given it ain't *life and death.* It ranks in the top ten of the world's most stressful jobs[105]. This is because, in the words of a friend of mine, PRs are always in the middle of a "shit sandwich". With our client, line manager or chief executive at the top, and the journalist/influencer/gatekeeper-to-that-information-being-published at the bottom. Our job is to chop the lettuce, arrange the pastrami, layer the sauce and sprinkle enough garnish to make it palatable for the person who's ordered it.
- **We're bright**. Degree-educated. Ambitious. Often extrovert.
- **Women dominate the lower echelons** whereas men are disproportionately represented in senior roles.

A statistic to finish: Glasgow City Council, one of the UK's largest local authorities, reported that in the financial year 2014/2015, 27% of its "customers" received information digitally. By December 6th 2017[106], this had risen to 56%. The pace of change is unbelievable: it's transforming my industry (and how we all communicate) in the evolutionary twitch of an eyelid.

CHAPTER 11

How to Master Your Digital Fear: a 25-Point Plan

I HOPE THAT USING my profession as a case study has made you think about the parallels with your own. Now for the universal bit: what follows is a 25-step influence-raising plan any midlife careerist can and should use.

This chapter was easy to write: all I had to do was imagine someone who couldn't insert a hyperlink, hadn't a clue how to work wirelessly, had never read – never mind written – a blog post and knew not how to find a wifi hotspot on their phone. In short, me, five years ago.

If you work for an organisation – whether public or private sector – it's your promotion ticket, insurance policy, escape plan, or happiness-at-work pill. It will help you escape from the shadows to become a person of influence and future-proof your career. This part is aimed squarely at you. If you work for yourself, it's a set of skills that you *must* have.

Is following the advice in Part II mandatory for all midlife careerists seeking to reset their lives and make a fresh start? No. Is it more relevant to some professions than others? Probably. Will your personal digital transformation happen overnight? Unless you spend eight hours a day on it like I did, no, it'll take years. Yet I can't think of one profession whose members wouldn't benefit from the advice below. Like hundreds of people I know, and millions of people I don't, implementing these steps has future-proofed my career and transformed my life.

Many will read Part II with interest, but think – *It's not for me. I don't like drawing attention to myself. This stuff isn't going to make me money.* Few will devote the hard hours of reading, writing and tinkering needed to effect this change. And that's great for you, the committed reader; because this stuff will give you an edge...differentiate you from the crowd.

Remember the subtitle of this book: "The *unconventional* early retirement plan for midlife careerists who want to be happy"? Becoming expert in digital communications might not make it into most self-help personal finance books, but that doesn't mean it shouldn't.

Without further ado, here are my 25 top tips. I hope you have as much fun implementing them as I have. (If you're expecting a plan that tells you how to build a landing page, how to set up a LinkedIn profile, or which online tools you can use to do what, you've come to the wrong place. Such a plan would soon date. This one will not.)

#1 Make technology work for you

Let's start with the basics. No one is asking you to become an IT boffin overnight. However, a rudimentary understanding of how technology works, and a simple system for making your work life more efficient, is crucial.

What system you choose will depend on (a) what you're used to and (b) what your work uses. Here's what you need:

1. A fast laptop with a long battery life and a keyboard that can withstand serious punishment.
2. A fast smartphone with a good camera that can take high quality video.
3. A file storage and synchronisation service embedded in your laptop and smartphone.
4. A linked internet browser and cloud calendar.

5. Email.
6. A work IT department, speedy-service warranty, or a computer specialist who lives locally.

That's it.

When you're linking this together, you have three global behemoths vying for your attention: Microsoft, Google and Apple.

Which you pick is up to you. I'm a Google man myself, with an Android smartphone and a subscription to its "brand of cloud computing, productivity and collaboration tools, software and products", G Suite. I avoid Apple. Microsoft's Office 365 cloud service is now good and by far the most widely used cloud-based productivity software.

If you have neither G Suite nor Office 365 at work and are still storing everything on servers or your computer's hard drive, speak to your boss and ask them to remedy this dysfunctional situation. In the meantime, make sure you have access to a file-sharing service. Dropbox is the one most people opt for (I use Google Drive).

The above sorted, the world is now yours. You can work anywhere, any time. You're a productivity machine.

One final thing: wherever you go, if you're using your new productivity machine, make sure you sign in to the wifi. Either by finding the password or logging in using Facebook if it's a cloud service.

If all else fails, go off the wifi hotspot (found in "settings") on your phone.

#2 Tools

Online tools, apps, extensions, add-ons increase your efficiency. Find ones you like – only one for each need – and enhance your computer and smartphone.

For example, discovering Chrome extensions, spending time learning the intricacies of Google Docs and maximising the functionality of both Google Calendar and Gmail means I am able to do things quicker and better, leaving more time to do creative work.

#3 Read

The more that you read, the more things you will know. The more that you learn, the more places you'll go[107].
Dr Seuss

Before heading off into the big wide online world and making a fool of yourself, you need to go back to school. First, online school. Everything you need to master digital is now available online free. You just need to know where to find it.

Blogs

There was a time back in 2014 when I read blogs all day. Regularly, even nowadays, I'll spend a happy two hours gorging myself on the collected wisdom of a worldwide diaspora of online writers. Like your favourite author as a kid, a particular blogger's writing style will appeal and you'll eagerly await their next missive. You'll look at the people they reference, those they admire, and find new bloggers to follow. This will take you deeper and deeper into whatever topic you are reading about. Blog posts have immediacy: you don't have to wait a year until an author publishes a book anymore. Blog posts are unfiltered, often raw, and don't cost a penny. You'll learn from bloggers: I did and still do.

Email newsletters

When I started on my digital odyssey, I devised elaborate systems to stay on top of the bloggers from whom I was gleaning this amazing free knowledge. The likes of Neil Patel[108], Jeff Bullas[109], Brian Dean[110] et al. I used a blog aggregator site called Feedly and came up with an elaborate bookmarking system (now unused) in Google's Chrome browser.

This was until I read the Facebook post a *digital* friend had written asking people how they found their *best* information. Buried towards the bottom of 70 responses (he's a popular guy[111]), was an urging to simplify the process and have the best writing come to you, direct to your inbox, through the humble email newsletter.

Three years on, and thousands of subscriptions later, that's how I receive my news and views. And if someone becomes boring, I unsubscribe.

I've found that people share their best thoughts with email list subscribers. Gather round, they say; it's story time.

Books

It's like a sliding scale of insight. In blog posts, people give their immediate take on topics, often with self-promotion jimmied in at the end. Newsletters are more akin to a fireside chat – less bombast, more reflection. Books, though, are the writer's best shot: something they'll be proud of for the rest of their lives, something they've edited and re-edited to ensure a smooth read. If I think someone's worldview is worth exploring, that what they have to say is consistently valuable, I buy their book. The best are timeless and you can refer to them repeatedly.

Part II is about teaching yourself digital to future-proof your career, but the advice below on reading is universal. I want to give particular thanks here to Ryan Holiday, whose blog posts[112] helped me rekindle my love for reading. Here's how I now treat books, one of the key planks in my journey from digital ignoramus to digital hippopotamus:

1. **Spoil the ending.** With business books, I read the table of contents, introduction and end first. I also google the author. I then go to Amazon and read the top- and bottom-rated reviews. My purpose when reading a book is to glean wisdom – I don't want to waste time trying to work out what the author's big idea is.

2. **Deface it.** Not one mint condition book sits on my bookshelves. Every one I've read in the past three years is curling at the corners, has colour-coded Post-it notes protruding from it and

pages turned over at the edges. Inside, passages are highlighted, with scrawling handwriting in black biro (mine) on most pages. I want to work out what the author is saying and do I agree with it. Then how does that contribute to or change what I think? How does it add to my worldview?

3. **Just buy it.** If you see a book that tickles your curiosity, either buy it or make sure you record it somewhere for future purchasing. (I use Amazon's Save for Later[113] facility.) The financial independent in me says "order it from the library", but my rational head knows that I may want to refer to it later (and defacing and repeat-hiring library books simply will not do).

4. **Footnotes and sources.** The book's author always quotes and cites people. I find other books to read by following the writer's interests.

5. **Read with intent.** I pay attention to the way the author joins the clauses, and pieces the sentences together, how they punctuate and use alliteration. Not just the message but how it's crafted.

6. **Take a book everywhere.** Whether going shopping, attending the dentist's or visiting a client, I always clutch a book. You never know when you might have a spare five minutes to read.

7. **Return in two weeks.** I revisit books two weeks after reading and, from my notes in the margins, write up what I've learned. I transcribe the main insights on to index cards (more on that below). Then I explain them to others before I forget: the Feynman Technique[114].

#4 Index cards

Talking of index cards. I've trialled all sorts of digital and analogue methods of plucking thoughts out of my head and into order. Evernote, swipe files, Word docs for this, Google Docs for that.

Along the way, thousands of insights, and an untold amount of calmness, have been lost through complicated systems that, although started with best intentions, have fallen by the wayside after a few weeks. This all changed when I discovered the bulldog-clip-and-ruled-index-cards approach.

I have plastic (and shoe) boxes[115] full of index cards for: life in general; *RESET*; and getting with the digital programme, complete with index-card-size subdividers. Now, whenever I have a thought worth capturing, I write it on an index card in either marker pen or biro (depending on the length of the thought), and place in the relevant box.

I use index cards for books, blogs, conversations I overhear at the club, memories, etc. They're in my coat pocket when I fetch the kids from school. I leave them handy in the locker at the swimming pool (where I do much of my best thinking). And I run with them.

Sound weird? Well, I'm in good company. Ryan Holiday[116], Anne Lamott[117], Robert Greene[118], Oliver Burkeman[119], Ronald Reagan, Vladimir Nabokov[120] and Ludwig Wittgenstein[121] all use (d) the humble index card to catalogue and organise their thoughts.

If you're serious about embarking on this digital journey, buy a hundred-pack of 127 x 76mm ruled index cards for less than a pound, rescue a shoebox from the attic and stick a few marker-penned notecards on their end to act as dividers. Write a "My Digital Box" label on the top of the shoebox, and you're off.

Index cards capture what you think about the world and leave your mind clear to do things. The secret to going digital: index cards.

#5 Listen

As a midlife professional, what is your biggest life-energy-leech on a weekday? Granted, there's a long list to choose from. Still, most would agree, the daily commute sits at the top.

On the rare occasion I take public transport, I'm flabbergasted by the number of people glued to their smartphones either playing games or on social networks.

Make better use of the time by listening to podcasts or audiobooks. Hundreds of podcasts are dedicated to all aspects of digital communications, including how to use social media, set up a website and blog. In the same way, there's nothing I like better on car journeys short and long than a good audiobook. Driving is dead time, time you'll never recover. Cranking up your car stereo, Audible[122], or LibriVox[123], and imbibing the collected wisdom of Seth Godin[124] or Gary Vaynerchuk, is much better than sticking on *BBC Radio 2*.

Like books, blogs and email newsletters, my taste in podcasts and audiobooks is not confined to the subject of digital communications. Whatever your area of interest, these media are great sources of learning. I discover the people whose views I respect, then see if they've appeared on my favourite podcasts as guests. Podcasts such as *The Tim Ferriss Show*[125] or *Freakonomics*[126].

#6 Obscurity and the introvert's advantage

So you've started to learn. You're gobbling up this information with the zeal of a convert. But you realise – you're a bright midlifer – that this will only see you so far. Real knowledge comes from active learning, from tinkering – getting out there and making a few mistakes along the way. Yet you're afraid, a mixture of chastising yourself that you never cottoned on to this opportunity ten years ago, and a belief – founded on fact – that other people are that far in front you that it's pointless trying to catch up. A fear that you'll make a fool of yourself.

Here are three things I wish I'd known five years back that will make you feel better, *before* you stick your head above the parapet:

1. **No one's listening.** When you make it, when you're beating back the interview requests and have to employ an assistant to deal with your newsletter subscribers' replies, when the "as featured on" bar on your website homepage counts the *New York Times*, *The Atlantic* and *Forbes* among its shiny logos, you'll look back on your early, halcyon, days with fondness and regret. As Jason Fried writes in *ReWork*: "Obscurity helps protect your ego and preserve your confidence... Now's the time to take risks without worrying about embarrassing yourself[127]."

2. **The introvert's advantage.** It's ironic that when building your online reputation, it's the qualities associated with the third to

half of the world's population who are *introverts* that come into their own. Qualities like writing ability, original thought, introspection, focus. Don't believe me? *#AskGaryVee*, someone most would place at the opposite end of the introvert/extrovert spectrum: "We are in the glory days of the introverted entrepreneur...social media and technology have put the whole game in your favor[128]." If you're an introvert, or even hovering somewhere in the middle like me, it may seem anathema to tell the masses what you think – the preserve of those self-aggrandising blowhards you detest. But rest assured, you'll be good at it, and you'll meet fantastic new people along the way, too.

3. **You don't exist.** As a one-man band high-value consultant – don't call me a freelancer – it didn't take me long to realise that without a digital presence I may as well not exist. No one's going to take you seriously if they haven't been able to google you from the comfort of their living room first. If all they find is an out-of-date LinkedIn profile, or an old Myspace page, they'll move on. *Not* learning digital, as a PR practitioner and small-business owner, wasn't an option for me. If you're salaried, like most of the modern workforce, it is an option for you. You don't need to do this. But know one thing: to the rest of the world, if they can't google you and find between eight and 11 things that tell them something about what makes you tick, it's much more difficult for them to place their trust in you. You may exist but only within the four walls of your stultifying office.

#7 Pick your platforms

In my home life, I tend to avoid social media like I avoid forty-degree temperatures and sand. Nevertheless, in my business life it's a must.

A social media presence is crucial for the modern professional or anyone who wishes to make their mark on the world. Work out who you're trying to reach, then set up your social media profiles, and tell stories/have conversations where they gather. Focus on one or two social networks and do them well. Make one of them LinkedIn and read a few up-to-date blog posts on how to set up a profile before you begin.

#8 Before you create, comment and curate

Once you've embarked on your digital learning and established what common themes, threats and opportunities your niche is experiencing, the best way to turn thinking into action is to share what you've read and watched with others.

You're starting to give people an idea of what you like, what you don't like, what you stand for. You'll begin sharing obvious stuff, stuff that everyone either read yesterday or wouldn't be seen dead sharing, such is its obviousness. But as you go on, your tastes develop, and your interests and desires take you down all manner of rabbit holes, you'll emerge clutching the odd hare or two. And people will start to take notice.

Maria Popova, whose curated every-Sunday newsletter *Brain Pickings* is a worldwide phenomenon, describes curation thus: "a drive to find the interesting, meaningful, and relevant amidst the vast maze of overabundant information[129]."

Share these treasures on social media (add in your own viewpoint) and the conversations will start. You'll meet new people and some of them will know what they're talking about. If nothing else, you're reading all this good material anyway, so you may as well derive extra benefit.

One thing to remember though: give credit where credit's due. Artist, poet and author, Austin Kleon, calls it leaving "a bread-crumb trail[130]". For example, a few years ago I grew obsessed with search engine optimisation. For six months in 2014, I was across every development in every facet of the field. Through sharing his writing with my network, I got to know, online, Cyrus Shepard, then an important figure at SEO industry bible Moz. A year later, when he left Moz to strike out on his own, he said the tone of voice of his new venture would be somewhere between *Mr. Money Mustache* and *Wait But Why*, two blogs I'd never heard of at the time. That bread-crumb trail helped me discover the predominantly US financial independence movement, the teachings of which have improved my life.

Crediting who inspires you is not only the right thing to do but also may get you chatting with them, too, with sometimes life-changing consequences.

#9 Writing (and reading)

Now seems as good a time as any to mention the importance of writing to this whole profile-raising endeavour. No one is born a writer. You learn how to write over the years and, as every writer will tell you, that learning process never stops.

Take me for instance. I've been writing my entire life: first at school and university, then throughout my career as a PR person. Along the way, I've picked up a rudimentary grasp of grammar. (Anyone who was educated in a comprehensive school in the 1970s and '80s will know that learning grammar was considered passé at the time.) I can spell, write a press release, pen a business proposal; but until five years ago, creative writing was something I didn't do.

Hundreds of self-penned newsletters and blog posts later, I've added new weapons to my writing armoury. Through reading then writing. For example, faced with a new challenge (writing a book), I read: *The Economist Style Guide*[131], *English for Journalists*[132], *Waterhouse on Newspaper Style*[133], *Eats, Shoots & Leaves*[134], *My Grammar and I*[135], *On Writing*[136], *Perennial Seller*[137], *Essential Law for Journalists*[138], *Bird by Bird*[139], *The Elements of Style*[140], *On Writing Well*[141], *Draft No. 4*[142] and *The Writing Life*[143]. Then I wrote *RESET*, learning, obsessively, as I went.

My points?

- "Writing is the primary basis upon which communication, history, record keeping, and art is begun[144]." Twas ever thus.
- Good writing shows clear thinking. People listen to clear thinkers.
- To be a good writer you have to read.
- Writing takes many forms – you must be an eternal student and work hard to grow proficient at each one.

#10 Blog

So you're set up, you've learned heaps, your name is out there. It's about time you started contributing. Here's where you need to play to your strengths. If you're good in front of a camera, do videos. If you're a whizz at designing infographics, go for that. If you've an artistic bent, make stick drawing or cartoons your thing. However, I'm not here to advocate any of those as your main creative outlet, your means of sharing what you've discovered with the world.

The best decision you can make to accelerate your digital learning and start making an impact is to set up a blog. Here are my 11 pointers from five years of online scribbling.

1. **Start with a free service** that makes it easy to format and publish. I used Blogger. Two good ones are LinkedIn Pulse and Medium.
2. **Once you get going, choose WordPress.** Twenty-seven per cent of the world's websites are built with this software[145]. And if it breaks or you want to add functionality, the answer's only a google away.
3. **Learn the rudiments of SEO.** Writing a blog is the single best thing you can do to teach yourself how to rank highly on search engines when someone types in, for instance, "Glasgow PR company". But don't write with SEO in mind. Share your best thoughts with the world and build a community around them: you're writing for readers, not Google.
4. **Spend time on your headline.** I write ten then test them using a website[146]. Your headline – just like a newspaper's – has a huge impact on whether people will read your blog post.
5. **Find a few image libraries** and help yourself to free-to-use[147] or OK-if-you-credit[148] pictures to add zip to your online articles.
6. **Learn how to format a post properly.** It helps people read it.
7. **Write in short sentences and paragraphs.** Does it surprise you that some of the world's best writers wrote for primary school-children? Clear writing encourages. Academic writing befuddles. Go on; write for a 10-year-old.

8. **Link out, to authoritative sources**, and in, to other posts on your blog.
9. **Don't worry about the length**. Sometimes you'll write a thoroughly researched epic. In others, you'll have one thought to express.
10. **Learn from your favourite bloggers**. Then create something that is your own.
11. **Don't be obsessed with frequency**. Of course, it's best if you blog every few days, but don't worry if you don't. Sometimes life gets in the way.

Then what?

Well, for most of us, blogging is a long hard slog with a few agreeable comments to keep us going. We don't do it for fame or fortune; we do it to work out what we think, to learn. Nevertheless, there's always a longing, deep inside, that one day, we'll get our just deserts, be heralded as the geniuses we know ourselves to be. Take succour from Gary Vaynerchuk's observation that: "you're always one great piece of content away from changing your life. Everyone you know started off as an unknown until they did the thing that made them known[149]."

If you do prove interesting, and people dig your worldview, consider making money from it[150]. It's hardly passive income (blogging is hard work), but money earned from limited display adverts or affiliate marketing on your blog is not to be sneered at. Financial independence bloggers are funding their early retirement, without touching their capital, by following this route[151].

Last, try different tactics. If you're serious about going viral, write 30 blog posts, your best work, then release them every two days for two months. Or, like Tim Urban[152] does, spend two months writing a blog post the length of this book.

#11 Build your list

You're now contributing. Catapulting your unique take on life into the ether. What's next for the midlife professional intent on transforming and de-risking their career by harnessing the perplexing technological change happening all around them?

Every single true expert on digital marketing and personal branding agrees on one thing: if you want to future-proof your means of communicating with people you want to reach, build your email list.

You know why? Because with an email list, you're in control. What if Facebook decided overnight to make you pay to reach anyone on your Facebook page (what if, eh)? What if Twitter went bust?

What if you lost your job?

Email is more than 50 years old and ain't going anywhere. I don't know about you, but I've always considered email my inner sanctum; I run my life from there. If I'm inviting someone in, I want to hear from them, which is what makes *your* email list such a powerful tool.

The people on your list have asked to be there and unless they hit unsubscribe, you can send them as much or as little communication as you want.

Here's how you can get started:

- Sign up for a free account with a cloud-based email marketing system, such as MailChimp[153]. It's simple to use, easy to understand and you don't have to pay a penny until more than 2,000 people subscribe to your list. Trust me, that will not happen quickly.
- Tweak the preset templates and decide a name for your newsletter. Add branding or a picture if you have them.
- Work out what you want to do with the newsletter and don't make its production a chore. I have three templates. Every time I write a blog post, I send it to my subscribers (15 minutes). Occasionally I send a reading list email, profiling the best four books I've read over the past month or two (half a day). On Thursday nights I send a newsletter sharing the best four or so articles I've read that week, and what I think about them (1.5 hours).

Simple. If you join my list[154] at zudepr.co.uk, you'll see what I mean. I've subscribed to and unsubscribed from thousands of email lists, and I've operated one for more than three years. Here's what I've learned:

1. **The best source of new sign-ups is word of mouth.** That's what you're after. People you trust and respect talking about you. You want them to be excited enough about what you write to tell their friends to sign up. Not as a favour to you, but because it reflects well on them.

2. If you want more people to join your list, **give them something in exchange.**

3. **Make it easy for people to sign up.** Whatever your view on pop-ups, they work.

4. **It's not quantity but quality that counts.** I'd rather have a hundred people who love my work than a thousand or so who open my emails only to clear their inbox. Unsubscribes are tough to take at the beginning, not any more.

5. **It ain't complicated.** As artist-and-author Austin Kleon writes in *Show Your Work!*, when talking about people he knows who run million-dollar businesses through their email lists: "The model is very simple: They give away great stuff on their sites, they collect emails, and then when they have something remarkable to share or sell, they send an email[155]."

6. **Giving creates trust and triggers the law of reciprocity**[156]. For example, in three years sending weekly emails to the Zude PR community I've never once asked for a thing. I hope this will mean when I do want my email subscribers to tell their friends about *this* book, they'll be glad to oblige.

7. **Let your voice and passion shine through.** That's why people signed up and that's what they want from you. For every person that unsubscribes in a fit of pique, there's another that likes you more.

8. **Show up at the same time every week.** The best email news-letters arrive in my inbox on the same day at the same time weekly. They have three things in common: the author's on a

voyage of discovery, bringing me back gold nuggets from her or his adventures; they speak to me in a consistent way; and every week I know them better.

9. **You need a testing routine.** There's nothing more annoying than sending a newsletter with broken links, then having to rush out *that* correction email. Avoid mistakes by developing a testing routine, involving your computer and smartphone.

10. **When you go to a networking event, make it your business to return with something concrete.** If you like someone you meet, ask them if they'd like to join your email list. Encourage them to sign up. Two years later, they could be a new client.

11. **Read up on GDPR.** Enable double opt-in and make sure you know everything there is to know about how the EU's new privacy law – General Data Protection Regulation (GDPR[157]) – affects your list.

Last, stick with it: it's a long game. In *Perennial Seller: The Art of Making and Marketing Work That Lasts*, Ryan Holiday shares the statistics on *his* list. In 2008, Ryan knew he wanted to write a book, but didn't know how to tell readers about it. So he started a list. Over the course of four years, by writing a monthly reading list email, Ryan grew his list from 90 subscribers to 5,000, in time for the launch of his first book. Fast forward a few books, plus five years, and by 2017, Ryan had 80,000 subscribers to his list, including me[158]. As of June 2018 he had 90,000[159]: that's a lot of book sales – more than a million, and counting.

#12 Learn how to measure

You've got your WordPress blog, you're rocking LinkedIn and you've set up your newsletter list. But just how effective is all this bluster? What are you setting out to do? And what will it look like when you achieve your goal? A good start is installing and linking Google Analytics and Search Console on your blog. But the purest measurement? The humble email subscriber. And the more you amass, the more you're doing something right.

#13 Learn how to promote

There's no point creating blog posts if no one sees your work. Learn how to promote them, get to know influential individuals, find where the people who might appreciate your writing gather, gorge yourself on posts about paid social media promotion. Have a dabble.

Remember, this is about raising your profile, increasing your influence, building a community that you can take with you whatever your means of paid employment. In short, future-proofing your career. Yes, promoting your work on social media is a faff, but the prize is worth it: the mountain did not come to Muhammad.

#14 Get obsessed: be committed

The word obsession has negative connotations in modern life. Anyone of a certain age – that's you and me – will remember Glenn Close in *Fatal Attraction*, which gave rise to the phrase "bunny boiler".

I don't see obsession like that. When it comes to the ever-changing landscape that is "digital", there is no substitute for reading lots, doing lots and getting involved. You need to be obsessed with topics to discover something new, separate the corn seed from the bushel, and share it with the world. Whether it's SEO, email marketing, building a website, or getting the most out of social media, the details of the matter are its most problematic aspect. And it's only through understanding the devilish detail that you realise how all this interrelated digital mishmash fits together and can benefit you.

#15 Tangents

When I learned piano growing up, I used to marvel at kids who rocked up at a baby grand and performed with no sheets to read from. And adults who could find their key and make music appear as if by magic, they were like gods to me. I try to apply this approach now as I navigate life. Although I always have goals in mind, I enjoy riffing, making my own music. If I hadn't taken this approach, I'd not have discovered SEO, rediscovered reading, established a newsletter, or been turned on to the life-changing learnings of the financial independence movement.

Riffing is spiffing.

#16 Don't worry about imposter syndrome

"Fake it until you make it" is not an approach I recommend. On the flip side, imposter syndrome ("the psychological phenomenon whereby people are unable to internalise their accomplishments[160]") is one of the biggest threats to creativity and achievement I know.

If you're a midlife careerist, you've been on this planet for between 35 and 60 years. You may not have done digital for too long, but it's only a set of skills, a new approach to life. What you do have is a lifetime of experience, a wise head, something worth sharing with the world. The fact you started blogging yesterday doesn't mean you don't have a valid opinion. Maybe it'll be even more valid than others who've been round the digital block a few times. Imposter syndrome stems from comparing yourself to others. I have it every time I write a blog post on a topic that better bloggers have covered, hundreds of times before. But it doesn't stop me sharing what I think, and it mustn't stop you.

#17 You'll meet me on your way back down

Don't listen to the haters or feed the trolls. Once you start raising your profile by sharing what you know, people will start holding an opinion about you. Some people will like you, some won't. That's life. Every time an "influencer" tries to undermine something I say in a public forum, I exit stage left, thinking – *karma, mate. I'll meet you on your way back down.* Constructive criticism I love; the other kind – often motivated by insecurity – I leave well alone and focus on my work. I also keep a document where I cut and paste written praise I receive. In moments like these, I take a look; it helps.

#18 Mentors

Luckily, most people aren't like that. Along your journey through life, you'll meet individuals who have a profound effect on your development. I call these people mentors and split them into three types:

People you've met

These are mentors in the conventional sense of the word, "believing mirrors[161]", as *Artist's Way* author Julia Cameron calls them. They don't need to be your designated mentor although that can happen.

At school, there was Mr Hulson, who taught me to draw what I saw.

I've had a couple in my corporate career: my first boss and my second. When I set up in business, I had an official one, the former head of the local chamber of commerce; we met every so often and chewed the cud. He listened, I learned.

Partway through my digital journey, I met Stephen Waddington, then president of my UK trade body, the CIPR. Here was someone who spoke my language and articulated what I thought and where the profession should be going. Four years on, I'm still in touch with Stephen and follow his writing. Not an official mentor, but someone who was instrumental in my transformation from analogue to digital PR.

People you've chatted with

Next are people you've chatted with but never met. In my case, we've exchanged emails (I'm on their lists), we've spoken on social media, or I've asked for their contribution to a blog post I've written. If you've interacted with someone, you're more invested in them, you learn more from them and sometimes you'll become friends. Here are a few of mine[162] (all experts on one or more facets of increasing your online profile):

- Cyrus Shepard.
- Andy Crestodina.
- Ann Handley.
- David Meerman Scott.
- Ted Rubin.
- Doug Kessler.

People you admire from afar

Then there are those whose work you admire above all others. You hang on their every word, try to find out how they did things, follow their recommendations. Mine are:

- Ryan Holiday.
- Pete Adeney (aka Mr. Money Mustache).
- Tim Urban (of *Wait But Why*).

My wife thinks I'm mad

She playfully pokes fun at these friends and mentors, most of whom I've not met, and some of whom are 15 years my junior. "Age is no barrier," I reply, "and the internet has changed everything." I have up to ten mentors on the go at one time. I can understand what goes on in their heads, meld it together and create something special of my own. One last thing, they say never meet your heroes. I've ditched a few mentors after listening to podcasts or watching videos of them online. Seeing them in the flesh, observing a slip of the tongue, a loss of poise that has shown me a different side of their personality, has often turned me off their teachings. Sometimes it's better to read what they write and admire from afar.

#19 Circle of friends

I have two circles of friends in my professional life: an outer circle I exchange advice and information with and an inner circle I trust.

At the centre of my inner circle are what Austin Kleon calls "knuckleballers[163]" – it's a baseball term, buy his books – and you don't pick them for what you can gain from them, you pick them for who they are.

Going digital is hard work, disconcerting and exhausting, along-side the everyday pressures inherent in middle-class midlifer-dom. So it helps to have people you can share your successes and failures with. People who hold you to account, whose opinions mean some-thing to you. I have two digital knuckleballers, with whom I con-vene monthly. They're an invaluable source of advice and firm friends. You should get some, too.

#20 Communities

I used to work for Prospect PR when I was starting out. It was brilliant: a great boss and colleagues. But the website...well, suffice to say, our main strapline was "don't hide your light under a bushel", which might have worked well in Shakespearean times but not in the late 1990s. Harnessing the power of communities is a great way to bring your light from beneath a bushel and into the open.

Since turning 40, I've become involved in three communities: the Glasgow running one, the tiny-Glasgow-suburb-where-I-live one and the UK/US digital PR/marketing/SEO one. All have had a positive effect on my life and spurred me on to greater achievements.

Studies consistently show[164] that being part of a community is a key factor in happiness. Being part of my industry (PR) in Scotland has always been important to me. But as I grasped the digital nettle five years ago, I realised there weren't a whole lot of people doing what I was doing. So I looked further afield for support.

Step forward, eventually, #PRstack, a crowdsourced UK-wide attempt to catalogue the online PR tools that had sprung up over the past few years. I made friends for life, got to know influential industry people, bagged a few clients, and built my reputation through getting involved. As anyone who volunteers at their kid's sports club or helps at their local school can confirm, getting involved in a community is one of the best ways to find out what's going on. Find a meaningful digital community that is welcoming and get involved. It'll make you – a little – happier.

#21 Social proof

As you develop, soon you'll want what Robert Cialdini calls *social proof*. You'll want to reach a wider audience than your WordPress blog or email list. This social proof will boost your street cred and lead to more people reading what you write. Some will sign up to your newsletter. Social proof: it's what I've been providing clients for 20 years when one of my press releases leads to an article in the *Financial Times.* I can recommend two tactics that will boost your credibility, spruce up your CV and increase your influence:

1. **Write guest posts/articles.** I've written articles on PR, digital marketing and SEO for publications ranging from *Social Media Examiner* to *The Guardian.*
2. **Write a book.** But do me a favour, don't write a business card book. Write something you're passionate about – the book you'd want to read.

The first is easy once you pass the pitch stage. The second is the toughest thing I've ever done.

#22 Be an early adopter

Gary Vaynerchuk was an early adopter of Google Ads when he ran Wine Library and made a small fortune shaking up the vino industry. And he was in there experimenting at the birth of Snapchat a few years back, now head of his huge New York media organisation: Vayner Media.

I remember being an early adopter of LinkedIn Pulse in 2014. I garnered more than four thousand views and hundreds of comments after a blog post I wrote about the business lessons you can learn from caravanning went viral.

Everyone was asking me jealously: "What's the secret? How did you do it?" It reminded me of folks that wish they'd been early retail investors in Amazon, Google, Facebook and the like: "if only" syndrome. The difference is I did something. And got the rewards of increased profile and business. As you make your digital journey, don't be afraid to experiment.

(It doesn't need to involve caravanning.)

#23 Be nice

As a student of history, I've always been fascinated by tales of what happened on the Western Front on Christmas Day 1914[165].

Anyone who's read *Birdsong*[166] or studied the first world war will know what a horrific, senseless waste of human life it was. So the tale of German and British soldiers disobeying orders and emerging from the trenches to play games of football in no-man's land appealed to the young me. That sworn enemies could cast aside their differences and act humanly, even in the heat of battle, now wouldn't that be something.

For some reason, throughout the noughties and onwards, the CIPR PRide Scotland awards – my industry's annual gathering, populated mainly by PR consultants – reminded me of this. It was the one time of the year us protagonists met for a big jolly – leaving aside all those lost pitches, rejected proposals, gossiping – and had a good time.

It always struck me as a real shame that the other 364 days didn't feel that way.

For PR, read the business culture in Scotland, the UK, the world over. One where we cradle secrets close to our chests, lest a competitor gobble them up. And this doesn't just apply to companies; it's a mood still prevalent in the public and charity sectors today.

Until 2014, little did I realise there was another way. One where the more truthful and honest you are, the more you enjoy your work, the more money you make. "Give it all away for free. Reveal your secrets. Share without expectation of anything in return." Whatever you want to call it, if you're nice to people they'll be nice back and good things will happen.

Yes, on occasions you will feel like you're urinating in the proverbial force ten.

But if you can embrace this new way of thinking, give it a year and you'll start to see the benefits. Here are a few observations on this crucial new internet-driven way of working I adopted in early 2014, which is good for your soul:

1. **It's a virtuous learning circle.** The more you teach those who want to learn, the more you learn yourself.
2. **Give, give, give**. Remember Ryan Holiday? He spent four years sending a monthly email before he asked his subscribers for anything. To build your audience (your community), and reach a point where people are recommending you to their friends, you have to spend a long time building trust. So they can discover the real you. And when you do ask for something in return that's when Cialdini's law of reciprocity[167] kicks in (google it).
3. Ever heard of the term **enlightened self-interest**, a phrase popularised by the UK's leading 19th-century foreign secretary, Lord Palmerston? Wikipedia has it as a "Philosophy in ethics which states that persons who act to further the interests of others (or the interests of the group or groups to which they belong), ultimately serve their own self-interest." Giving it all away for free is it, with bells on.
4. **Whatever you do, be honest.** Tell the truth as you believe it to be. The times you connect with people will be when you show them how to do something they want to do or inspire them to be brave and become better versions of themselves. Lead by example. As Anne Lamott writes in *Bird by Bird*: "When people let their monsters out for a little on stage interview, it turns out that we've all done or thought the same things, that this is our lot, our condition. We don't end up with a brand on our forehead. Instead, we compare notes[168]."

Codicil

See this karma thing, it's like kids and Father Christmas, it only works if you believe. Unless you embrace this karmic concept – being nice without expectation of receiving anything in return – it's going to seem artificial to you. And the act of being nice will not create that nice happiness-inducing feeling inside you.

So break out of your box, reveal your secrets – not all of them – without fear or favour, and see your influence soar.

A warning: there is no such thing as a selfless act. Don't be carried away with your niceness. Every act is selfish. Even when being nice without expectation of reciprocation, you're still gaining that warm fuzzy feeling in return. For example, decorated surgeons who spend sabbaticals in war zones[169] – a selfless act par excellence one would assume – admit that part of the attraction is "the buzz" – they feel a heightened sense of being alive.

In your professional life, keep your wits about you. Yes, be nice. Enjoy sharing what you know. But don't be a mug. If someone is all take and no give, avoid them like a scabby-spotted toddler in a public pool.

#24 Be real

Write for one person as if you're talking to a friend. Don't use brand speak. Ask yourself the question: does what you're saying online sound as it would if you were talking to someone? Reveal what you think; give away your secrets. And whatever you do, keep it real. Last year, I read a post by blogger Jon Westenberg entitled "The Success Bloggers are Selling you Bullshit[170]". Someone should take Jon Westenberg back home to meet their mother and wash his mouth out with a pumice stone. Barely a heading goes by without a profanity. I enjoy the ones where he gets something off his chest. Jon's all about "keeping it real". I quote: "I don't wake up at 5. I don't float through life on some kind of cloud, where my existence buoys me up and I can see the threads of humanity...success comes from luck, timing, hard work, perseverance..." And you just know the ellipses I've inserted cover words with four letters. But Jon's right isn't he. Which is why I wonder what people are doing wasting their lives on Facebook when they'd do better putting in the hard miles that turn Jon's "6/10 days" into "9/10 days". The world needs more people who tell it like it is. More Jons (unless you're a monk, or a nun).

#25 Be you

Most of all, be yourself. Cos if you ain't being you, then what's the point?

CHAPTER 12

Part II Index Card

- Don't hide your light under a bushel.
- Build your F.U. profile to future-proof your career.
- Transform existing skills and experience by going digital.
- Write as if you're in a coffee shop, talking to a mate.
- Get obsessed: read until your eyes bleed.
- Build your list.
- Find a mentor or ten.
- Index the experiences and thoughts that create your worldview.
- Be nice, especially to your knuckleballers and circles of friends.

And finally...

Tackling my digital fear head on began for me way back in January 2013 (secretly, a year before I left the corporate world). It restored immense pride in my job and improved my life. Whatever field you work in, change can happen overnight, when you least expect it. It's the modern way. If you follow this 25-point plan: you'll be less exposed should the worst happen, your career star will rise, you'll be much happier at work and you'll take a giant leap towards maximising your earning potential. Your new F.U. profile will help you get your F.U. Money so you *never* have to "suck it up" *ever* again.

PART III

Declutter Your Life

NOW YOUR WORK LIFE'S sorted, let's turn our attention closer to home. At this juncture, you may be thinking, *what the hell does clearing your house have to do with getting an early retirement plan?* At first glance that's a good question. However, I never claimed this book offered a conventional route to financial independence, and – as we'll discover – there's a life-changing magic in tidying[171]. Before we begin, let me give you an insight into our home life a few years ago, that of a married-with-two-children, early-forties couple living in an upmarket suburb of Glasgow:

1. Two hours' non-work-related social media use a day, while limiting the kids' screen time.
2. An inability to either do meaningful work or be present in the moment through digital-distractedness. This led to cognitive dissonance: a dad who extolled the virtues of reading to his kids – and himself – but rarely read a book.
3. A fairly tidy house but with ever-growing piles. Exhibit A: kids' art corner. Exhibit B: two of those 12-hole IKEA units housing rattan cubes, in which lurked a multitude of plastic.

4. We could never find anything we didn't use every day, leading to stress and precious hours wasted.
5. We had a cleaner who spent half the time clearing our clutter into a tidier version of the same clutter (shoes, kitchen surface adornments, the piles on the floor in every room) and the other half cleaning the house. And that was after we thought we'd done a passable job tidying the house to make our clutter presentable to our cleaner.

All this physical and digital detritus was cluttering our minds, decreasing the sense of calm needed to make informed decisions that weren't based on habit. An inefficient way of living, in a life, with two young children, that was busy enough. First, Part III will show you how to digitally and mentally declutter your life. Last, it shares a step-by-step process, based on the teachings of Marie Kondo. It shows you how you can alter your relationship with your home and free your mind for more important stuff. This part's about efficiency, minimalism, simplicity, systems and hard work. Wiping the windscreen of life on a winter's morning so you can drive without crashing into anything.

CHAPTER 13

Digital Declutter

ONE OF THE MOST-SAVED long-form articles[172] to Pocket[173] in 2017 was "Have Smartphones Destroyed a Generation[174]?" Six months on, it had been shared 750,000 times on social media.

It painted an expertly researched, terrible picture of a generation of teens hooked on smartphones and social networks, leading to unhappiness, depression and suicide.

The average person touches their telephone 2,617 times a day[175]. We know it's no good for us, yet otherwise intelligent professional people the world over are at a loss what to do about it.

For the midlife careerist it's a problem of time, focus and happiness. Smartphones are addictive and eat our precious lives in ten-minute chunks, leading to feelings of stress and despair. They make us chase that pleasure version of happiness based on short-term hits of dopamine, a *reward molecule* released by the brain that makes us seek good experiences.

The internet and social media allow us to do this from the comfort of our own armchairs. We don't have to meet anybody or speak to anybody; our social interaction is online. With a smartphone at our fingertips we're the boss now; we're in control. The world is our domain.

The problem with that is we don't need to do much to access that immediate happiness. So we become mired in endless dopamine loops, addicted to the damn things like crack addicts – without the restraint imposed by the danger and effort involved in sourcing our next fix.

How many times have you started on Facebook looking for one thing then caught yourself a minute later ogling a school friend's latest supercar, having forgotten what you went on to search for in the first place?

And that's action you've taken of your own volition. Don't start me on the alerts. *Ding, ping, whoosh: where's my phone, someone's contacted me, someone likes me. I'm going to get a doggie treat. Give. Me. That. Phone...*

A mistake this ain't. Smartphones and apps are designed that way to exploit our weaknesses. In a 2016 blog post[176], ex–Google design ethicist Tristan Harris revealed ten hijacking tactics technology firms use to play on our human psychological vulnerabilities, including controlling the menu, providing intermittent rewards, making us fear we're missing out and playing on our need to belong.

He finishes by saying: "The ultimate freedom is a free mind, and we need technology that's on our team to help us live, feel, think and act freely. We need our smartphones, notifications screens and web browsers to be exoskeletons for our minds and interpersonal relationships that put our values, not our impulses, first."

This has led many to call for a digital bill of rights to protect us against this global assault on our thinking and help us do meaningful work.

The internet and social media's addictive nature, played out in our super-sophisticated smartphones, does nothing for our long-term memory – you know, the place where we store our experiences and learnings to create our worldview. No one suggests we shouldn't learn maths and instead rely on calculators. But we're more than happy to outsource our knowledge to a smartphone because we know the answer to everything is only an "ok Google" or Alexa question away.

In our careers, the continual interruptions of our connected world stop us dedicating the hard concentrated hours to do meaningful work, work we cannot achieve in the state of permanent distraction brought on by checking our smartphone hundreds of times a day.

Benefits of digital decluttering

Until a global effort is mounted to restrict the addictive nature of the internet and smartphones – ie, never – we're going to have to take matters into our own hands.

Here are the benefits of digital decluttering (one of the quickest and simplest series of actions in *RESET*):

- Get more done.
- Be calmer.
- Spend more time with friends, family and your community.
- Be a little bit happier.
- Be more confident.
- Have more sleep, more sex and be less lonely.

There's no doubt that the internet is amazing; and the irony of someone who makes their living from digital communications bemoaning social media addiction is not lost on me.

As, no doubt, it was not lost on Steve Jobs, or the host of Silicon Valley tech entrepreneurs who place strict limits on *their* kids' screen time[177].

But if we don't take control of our own performance that little beeping flashing minicomputer charging on the arm of our sofa will run the show for us.

Prescription

Here's how you can say F.U. to Zuckerberg, Gates, Cook[178] and Horvath[179], and wrest back control of your life.

(It's a good idea to set a calendar reminder to repeat this process every six months. I have.)

#1 Track

Install a time-tracking app that works across your devices. A good one right now is RescueTime[180]. Set it up, let it run for the week and see how bad the problem is. I guarantee your jaw will drop.

#2 Remove apps you don't need

You don't *need* most of them. You hardly *use* any of them. They won't come in handy: they're just clutter. If you ever need them again, you can download them in a jiffy or just go in through your internet browser. When you've stripped back your apps, spring-clean your home screen. Only keep apps on there that you want to use daily.

#3 Disable notifications

I'll decide who and what I want to interrupt what I'm doing. I'll decide their importance. Now you've culled your apps, go into your mobile and laptop and remove all smartphone and desktop notifications.

#4 Empty email inbox

I run my life from my email inbox and online calendar. There's no bigger source of low-level anxiety than a sea of marked unread emails in your inbox, distracting your focus and decreasing your Zen-like calm. Practise the ancient art of empty-inboxing by checking your email at set times each day, deleting emails you don't want, dealing with easy requests at once and diarying everything else.

If you can swing it, stick an out of office on, stating when you are checking your emails, and telling people not to expect a response outside those times (*they* can ring you if it's urgent; *they* rarely do). It's much easier to deal with emails in batches, instead of when they come in. Otherwise, how will you do any proper work?

#5 Unsubscribe from mailing lists

Empty-inboxing will be easier when you undertake the next task. If you're as big a fan of email newsletters as me, you'll be subscribed to a few hundred – a thousand even – email mailing lists. You'll have forgotten why you signed up to half of them and spend 15 minutes a day either deleting emails as they come in or leaving them marked unread. This takes time and two unread emails soon become ten. Before you know it, more than a hundred of the blighters are staring you in the face, daring you to delete.

Every six months, prune your subscriptions. You can use services like Unroll.Me[181] that speed up the process. Then stay on top of them. If someone goes off the boil or your interests change and you don't want to hear from them anymore, when their next email plops, just unsubscribe.

#6 Social networks

If you must have a social media profile (kind of important if you want to future-proof your career), don't have more than two. Just don't spend too much time on them – life is best spent elsewhere.

#7 Charge your phone somewhere you're not

Why do 99% of us take our mobile everywhere? I love the idea of a wooden bowl by the door where guests place their smartphones when they come in, but I've never seen it in action. When you enter your home, charge your smartphone in the room next door. Close enough that you can hear it ring when someone calls you, but far enough away that the temptation to check it every five minutes is removed. On the other hand, if it's before eight or after six, charge it in the farthest away place in your house. The only person that rings you nowadays is a spam caller, and no one wants to speak to them. What about the third of the day we spend asleep? Do you have it on your bedside table like 55% of us, under your pillow (13%), or in your hand when you doze off (3% of people[182])?

We have to get a grip on this malaise. It's neither good for our sleep nor our minds. A trick I use is to charge my phone downstairs when I go to bed. This saves me being tempted to check it before I go to sleep or, heaven forbid, if I wake up during the night.

#8 Read a book, do something, anything

If you're checking your smartphone every five minutes, there's a void in your life. The only way to combat this addiction is to take action. So go for a walk, take your kids swimming, meet a friend for coffee, bake bread, have a bath, light a candle, read a good book. Please don't stare at a screen. You'll also find that when you have a purpose, goals and a concrete plan you're working towards, your smartphone addiction will become manageable.

#9 Cold turkey

If all else fails, you can always go cold turkey.

For us midlifers, not versed in the wiles of Snapchat and the like, it's Facebook that has us in its thrall. I have nothing but admiration for the two-thirds of adults who aren't active Facebook users[183]. I shed a tear when a running friend sets up a Facebook account purely to join the running club Facebook group I administer, and honk with *brio* when they persuade their Facebook-using partner to become a group member instead.

Try ditching your Facebook account for a month and see what happens. See if you miss anything. See if you're unhappier. If that works, extend it to six months. If you miss it, reactivate your Facebook account. But remember: you're an addict, and if you're not careful, you'll soon revert to the self-loathing status quo that is swipe-time.

A call to arms

I grew up in a world where the telephone was attached to a wall and you had to turn a *whirry-clicky* dial to patch yourself through.

I grew up in a world of books where the only thing resembling a computer was the local library's microfiche (until Binatone tennis came along, damn you Binatone).

I grew up in a world that valued having facts and experience in your brain – not at the click of a button – to help you *form* your worldview.

The internet is a positive force, giving instant access to friends and information that it would have taken me weeks to order from the library as a kid growing up in 1980s northern England. It's transformed my life and many of the tactics in *RESET* are not possible without it.

However, the web clutters our minds, makes us unhappy and stops us fulfilling our potential. It bewilders us with too much choice, forcing us into the sticky tentacles of social media.

Facebook lets you keep in touch with old mates, have a chuckle, hear about local events. But does it make you happy, fulfilled and successful? Or do the many negatives outweigh the benefits? Once we find our purpose, set goals and hash out a plan of how to achieve them, is playing on our smartphone for two hours every day helping?

As midlife professional people, we owe it to ourselves to do battle with this self-inflicted, dopamine-fuelled, smartphone-enabled, attention-deficit epidemic.

The nine points above will give you the weapons.

CHAPTER 14

Mental Declutter

I can see clearly now the rain has gone. I can see all obstacles in my way...[184]
Jimmy Cliff

OUR PRIMARY PROBLEM AS midlife careerists is that we are navigating on autopilot, taking the lane of least resistance, sleep-driving our way through the best years of our lives. It's raining and we can't see the yellow brick road for the munchkins.

In Parts V and VI, I outline 11 core principles and 12 do's and don'ts to live your life by. All of these will help you battle through that mental fog to live a life of purpose. What follows now are five tactics I've specifically used to declutter my mind, so I can achieve what I want.

A: Journaling/Morning Pages

I first read about Morning Pages in Oliver Burkeman's column[185]. I then bought one of author Julia Cameron's spin-off books *The Artist's Way for Parents*[186]. For one year, every morning I got out of bed, sat on the toilet, opened my – inevitably – Moleskine notebook, and wrote whatever was in my head until I'd filled three pages.

It clears your head "as if you're sending a telegram to the Universe[187]". No, I didn't think it'd be my cup of tea either. But trust me, it works.

The key is to do it immediately after you get up, when you can still remember who you are. Looking back, my pearls of wisdom involved all sorts of banalities such as: "Why the hell am I doing this?" And: "I'm never going to fill three sides." Plus: "What's the point in breakfast, anyway?" On the other hand, it helped me root out what was bothering me, work through work and life dilemmas and clear my mind of mental clutter to focus on what was important that day. Fifteen minutes of *me time* every morning before responsibilities kicked in.

Morning Pages is a type of journaling, and Cameron's *The Artist's Way* has sold more than 4m copies worldwide. On my recommendation, friends and family have started their own Morning Pages, and never looked back.

I've moved on to index cards as a way of capturing and cataloguing what I think. But I return to Morning Pages, or journaling, every so often, when I have something important I'm working on. It clears my mind and helps me focus.

You should try it.

B: The great outdoors

I read a Facebook post the other day (yes, I know, naughty me). Someone I met last year when spectating an ultramarathon with the kids had posted a picture of himself up a mountain. I read the accompanying text: "This is my church."

When you leave the city, you notice the seasons, you hear the air and the birds, your thoughts take flight and you're in the moment. Even a trip to your nearest park or a walk along the cycle path in your lunch break is a worthwhile investment in thought.

When writing *RESET*, my communing with nature was confined to swimming breaststroke in an outdoor pool. I cleared my emails, read the past chapter, read my notes for the next, then did 30 lengths. Those 15 minutes of rhythmic zoning out were the most important of my day, like an aquatic Morning Pages. They helped me think about what I wanted to say, reconnect with the book's purpose and inspired new ways of telling the story. They also helped rationalise the high price of our low-opportunity-cost-and-lovely health club membership: a win-win situation.

C: Mindfulness

Mindfulness is popular. Everyone in the charity sector raves about it. Interest has grown over recent years and millions of midlife professionals the world over use it as a stress-busting technique. "The quality or state of being conscious or aware of something." And: "a mental state achieved by focusing one's awareness on the present moment, while calmly acknowledging and accepting one's feelings, thoughts, and bodily sensations, used as a therapeutic technique[188]." When I'm swimming, I sometimes use mindfulness to help stop worrying about things the rational part of my brain knows will never happen. For example, certain worries pop into my head regularly, causing mental fug. If I feel one coming, I'm ready for it. I use two techniques, gleaned from Russ Harris's book on mindfulness: *The Happiness Trap*[189].

1. I have a fun-poking name for the worry/fear. When I sense it insinuating its way into my mind, I dream up a story and set it to the tune of a favourite song (in my case, a northern soul[190] track or *New Order's* "Love Vigilantes[191]"). Soon I'm grinning at the ridiculousness.
2. I use the daft voice technique. I imagine the worry wittering on like the alpha dog in the Disney Pixar film *Up*, whose electronic voice box malfunctions causing him to speak like a kid who's inhaled helium from a balloon. Soon I'm smiling and see the worry for what it is.

Mindfulness is based on the premise that we can't change our thoughts – research shows that 80% of them are negative. Again, it's to do with evolution[192]. We can't stop our minds being mini Chicken Littles[193], worrying that the sky will fall on our heads. And if we try to combat this with the power of positive thought, telling our brain that we don't have this or that feeling, we just feel inadequate and weak-willed. We need to accept that we're going to have negative thoughts, but not let them stand in the way of what we *can* control: our actions.

If you don't want to practice mindfulness, you don't need to. If that's you, I hope these few paragraphs at least effect the same lightbulb moment that happened to me. Having negative thoughts doesn't mean there's something wrong with you: it's natural, you're only being normal. But if you *are* able to learn a few mindfulness techniques, you'll be better equipped to treat these never-going-to-happen worries with the disdain they deserve. Your mind will be less cluttered and you'll get more done.

P.S. Mindfulness (being present in the moment and aware of what you're thinking and feeling right now) is like Buddhism. I'm not religious but have a friend who's a Buddhist – a rarity in the west of Scotland – and have seen the positive effect it has had on his life. He says the best book on Buddhism is not the Dalai Lama's but Richard Causton's *The Buddha in Daily Life*[194]. It's worth a look.

D: Breathing (and meditation)

I have mates in business who meditate. I don't. Perhaps I'm not doing it the right way, but it doesn't work for me. I do, however, sometimes, if I'm battling distraction and can't focus, just breathe. I slow my breathing for a minute and say the words "and relax". I've done it right now, writing this passage. It helped.

E: A problem shared is a problem halved

If you're stuck, and your mind is so cluttered that it's making your blood boil, nothing beats offloading on your partner or a good pal. After all, as author James Altucher says: "The 'worst thing' is the clogged artery of your soul[195]."

CHAPTER 15

Physical Declutter

NOW FOR THE REALLY important bit. If you're looking to reset your life halfway through, if you're seeking practical steps you can take to transform your family's future and rediscover who you are, this chapter is a must.

It may seem counterintuitive that decluttering your home will have a profound effect on your life – after all, it's only tidying, and you have a cleaner for that – but it will.

If you undertake this one-off herculean (physically and mentally) task, you'll have more time, more money and less stress. It will also help you look back and forward at your life, reconnect with your values and find your purpose. It's worked for my family and millions of others across the world. Let's root around.

Public information notice

Before we start, I owe a debt of gratitude to Marie Kondo, the Japanese tidying sensation whose *The Life-Changing Magic of Tidying* has sold 4m copies in 30 countries. Marie's book, complete with copious marginalia, was a constant companion during the two months I spent gutting our four-bedroom family home. Her teachings – along with the scores of blog posts and books I read on the topic – form the core of the process I advocate below. Though I don't agree with Marie on everything (socks!), if you do decide to embark on this transoceanic voyage – it belittles the scale of the task to call it a marathon – you must buy her excellent book on decluttering your home. All 240 pages of it.

Why you hate your house

Did you know that the average American consumes twice as many material goods as they did 50 years ago? That the size of the average American home has almost tripled during those years and contains roughly 300,000 items? That 25% of people with two-car garages don't have room to park their cars inside; or that one in ten Americans rent off-site storage to stash their belongings[196]?

A 2008, US National Association of Productivity and Organizing Professionals (NAPO) survey of 400 consumers in the US showed that 65% of respondents noted that their household was at least moderately disorganised. Seventy-one per cent said their quality of life would improve if they were better organised and 96% of respondents indicated that they could save time every day by becoming more organised. I doubt things have improved[197].

In the UK, it's well known we're a nation of hoarders, with a recent survey finding one in five households have enough clutter to fill a whole room[198].

If you're a midlife professional, I guarantee your home is not a clutter-free zone. Yes, it might be neat and tidy – if so, you're one of the lucky few – but clutter-free it will not be.

This is because no one taught you how to tidy. As the products of middle-class-dom we're taught how to swim, play tennis, learn a musical instrument, eulogise Tebay Services and trade used Isla-bikes on eBay. But no one, at any time, gives us a single lesson in tidying. Yet we spend our whole lives doing it daily, inefficiently, and costing ourselves a small fortune in stuff-purchasing in the process.

No one's saying we didn't receive on-the-job training from our parents. But who did they learn it from? Their parents. And who taught them?

It's no wonder that we let our homes/belongings rule us rather than serving their purpose: to make our lives a happier and less stressful place. Here are the drawbacks of having a cluttered house:

- Clutter causes family arguments.
- Clutter always leads to one room in your house being a dumping ground for unclassified objects. Like a lurking basement monster who won't stop growing.
- You waste ages trying to find your belongings. NAPO reports we spend one year of our lives looking for lost items[199].
- Clutter overloads your senses adding to your stress levels: it distracts you from thinking clearly.
- Clutter is sentimental and makes you live in the past.
- Clutter is catching. If you have a cluttered house, it's likely you have a cluttered approach to food, and waste money each week throwing it away.
- It costs money through buying duplicate items *you* don't need and paying penalty charges on bills you've forgotten about.
- It's overwhelming. (Every so often, for instance, you tidy the kids' art corner, but within a few weeks, it's back to where it was: a mess.)
- Clutter can prevent you moving house, such is the scale of the task involved. And it's a huge sentimental heartache for those you leave behind when you die.
- Clutter makes you feel as if you're not in control: that your house is a hopeless case.

In short, clutter is inefficient, preventing us taking action to meet our goals. It hinders us living meaningful lives and exerts a subtle stranglehold on our personal development.

Benefits of decluttering

If you want to take control of your house but don't know where to start, here's some motivation.

First read the disbenefits again, then think of the exact opposite. But I'm not finished there:

- If you complete this process, you'll learn more about what matters to you.
- You'll feel lighter.
- You'll be more efficient when you work from home.
- You'll make money selling your possessions on Gumtree and eBay and feel good when you give the rest to friends who need it, or charity shops.
- In a study by IKEA, 31% of those surveyed reported more satisfaction from clearing out their closet than after sex[200].

Most of all, decluttering will give you a new lease of life. Marie Kondo reports possible effects of radical decluttering as **quitting your job, getting divorced, increasing sales and losing weight.** As she puts it: "When you put your house in order, you put your affairs and your past in order, too. As a result, you can see quite clearly what you need in life and what you don't, what you should and shouldn't do[201]."

Still not persuaded?

Still don't fancy it? Think you're above tidying? Think you can outsource it? Allow me to make an intellectual case for a once-in-a-lifetime super-spring-clean of your humble abode.

Writing in the *Washington Post*[202], Valerie Peterson cites Randy O. Frost, a professor of psychology at Smith College and co-author of *Stuff: Compulsive Hoarding and the Meaning of Things*, as saying that people have three basic reasons for stockpiling items in their homes: sentiment, utility and aesthetics.

For instance, I have a full rack of summer and winter climbing equipment in the eaves of our bedroom. I can't bear to part with it because of the ten years of happy memories (plus I paid a fortune for the gear). Before our big clear-out, I had 15 years of bank statements because they might come in handy someday. And we had four wooden vases we received as wedding presents even though our tastes had moved on.

In an article in *The Atlantic*[203], former staff writer and ex-*Freakonomics* editor Bourree Lam (liberally citing *Financial Times* journalist Tim Harford) argues that the reason Marie Kondo's book is such a worldwide phenomenon is because it highlights human beings' mental fallacies, draws on powerful economic ideas and makes us look at our belongings anew.

Take my climbing gear (don't try, I wouldn't let you). That's an example of the sunk cost fallacy[204]. I paid at least £2,000 for my rack 15 years ago and I'm not giving it away for peanuts, even if I never use it again. No way is that going, Marie Kondo or no Marie Kondo.

Then there's status quo bias[205], which, when applied to your cluttered house (not the rock band, to which I am in no way biased) means that most of your belongings stay because you can't think of a good reason to get rid of them. Marie Kondo turns this on its head by saying only keep something if it serves a purpose. Take my bank statements for instance – too late, they've been shredded – there's no reason I needed paper copies stretching back to the start of this millennium.

How about our wedding vases and the law of diminishing returns? Do we need all those vases or will one do?

As Lam writes in the conclusion to her article: "A rational place to live doesn't sound very sexy, but a tidy place to live is indeed much more comfortable. And now tidying carries a point of pride beyond having a clean apartment: knowing that we're outsmarting our cognitive biases."

Right, I rest my case. If you're not listening now, I give up. Skip to Part IV. However, if you want to: restart your life; stop wanting and buying possessions; and discover more about yourself, allow me to effect a formal introduction to worldwide cult sensation Marie Kondo (a woman for whom tidying is an all-consuming passion). And if I've learned one thing in life: always listen to the most passionate, obsessed woman – or man – in the room.

Who is Marie Kondo?

The chances are you'll know someone – or know someone who knows someone – who's Marie Kondo'd their house.

They're the ones who with eyes aglisten explain how they've discarded everything in their home that doesn't "spark joy" and proudly show you the inside of their chest of drawers, replete with rolled underpants.

The person responsible for these evangelical hordes is a matter-of-fact Japanese woman who in 2010 distilled a lifetime's interest in tidying into a book that has since taken the world by storm. All you need to know now is that people who follow her teaching in full – or as I have, adapt it to create their own version – agree that Marie Kondo has, indeed, changed their life[206].

Principles

Aside from the obvious (discard lots and organise what's left[207]), here are the principles that underpin what you're about to try:

1. **One time only.** This is something you only have to do once. What we are aiming for is one-off near-perfection. Like all the best systems, it's a "set-and-forget". Meaning you can pour yourself into any project for a short period, learn the theory, practise it; then reap the benefits as the system takes care of itself. Just check to make sure you're on track (that the principles still stand firm) and incorporate new behaviours into your family life. This applies as much to finding your purpose and de-cluttering as it does to finding your path to financial independence.

2. **Immersion.** Be immersed in the big clear-out until you've finished. This could mean your partner and you taking two weeks this summer to blitz your house. Or perhaps during a gap between jobs. You could try allocating a few hours every Sunday for six months, but you would make a difficult task near impossible. You'd lose motivation, focus and a grasp of the ideas

that guide this process. Best to do it in a glorious oner – it took me two months between client work.

3. **Excited.** You need to be excited by the process on which you are embarking. You need to believe it can change your life. You need to have faith. I recommend reading Marie Kondo's book from cover to cover, underlining bits you think are important, writing your own thoughts in the margins. You should then carry it around with you when you're undertaking this tidying trans-oceanic voyage. Otherwise, you will forget why you're doing things that seem unnatural to you. You will forget why you're doing them in the order you're doing them. And you will start wondering if you should be spending all this time doing, frankly, weird things on the say-so of a Japanese woman who lives 5,761 miles away. I also recommend reading people like me's take on decluttering, people who have used Marie's teachings as a jumping off point and devised their own system. Remember the beauty of the internet: anything in our minds, any question we might have, is now only a (ok) google away.

4. **Out of sight is not out of mind.** Just because you've tidied belongings away in storage boxes or placed them in the garage, attic or basement where you can't see them, doesn't mean they're not clutter. As Vicki Robin writes in her ground-breaking book on financial independence, *Your Money or Your Life*: "our attics, basements, garages, closets and storage sheds are havens of clutter, filled with projects and products we'll probably never use. Unfinished projects sap you of vitality[208]." One of the key principles underpinning this decluttering method is that every-thing be visible, on show, not stored away in boxes where you never see it. This is some U-turn for most people who like to pack everything away neatly in expensive storage containers.

5. **It'll get bad before it gets better.** This will in turn be one of the most stressful and life-affirming activities you ever do. Be prepared to live in mess throughout this process. But remember, the prize, those benefits, will be well worth it.

6. **A place for everything and everything in its place.** In the end, every single item in your house will have earned its keep and

have a place to live. You won't need to write this down; you'll just know it.

7. **Home as a sanctuary.** I love this concept. When I return to my home now, I look forward to walking through the front door. It makes me feel calm.

8. **Discard everything that has outlived its purpose.** I adopted Jacob Lund Fisker's advice here (apart from seasonal items such as sledges): "I used this today (keep it). I used this within the past week (keep it). I used this within the past month (keep it). I used this within the past six months (get rid of it). I used this within the past year (get rid of it). It has been more than a year since I used this (get rid of it!). I did not even know I owned this?! (get rid of it[209]!!)"

9. **Minimise sentimentality.** This is the hardest and most rewarding aspect of the entire process. As Kondo says: "By handling each sentimental item and deciding what to discard, you process your past[210]."

10. **Does that object make you happy?** Russell Baker said: "The goal of all inanimate objects is to resist man and ultimately defeat him[211]." If you take this view, the task in front of you is easy: chuck everything. Kondo advises to handle an item and ask "Does it spark joy?" I'm afraid this is too irrational for me; I prefer Fisker's more utilitarian approach. However, utility aside, if there's something I use less than once a month, like that beautiful red Alvar Aalto vase on my front room windowsill, looking at it and deciding whether it makes my family happy is a good default choice. Red vase sparks joy – keep; oak wooden vases don't – charity shop.

11. **Remove annoyances**. Before beginning the big clear-out, I walked around our home with my family and compiled a long list of annoyances that perturbed one or other of us. For me, the kids' art corner. For Rachel, the clothes spilling out of every cupboard. For the kids: an inability to find their games and too many "random" boxes (rattan cubes full to the brim with unclassified bits of toy plastic). Removing the many things that annoyed us about our cluttered house became key.

12. **Involve.** None of this works without the active involvement of your family. They – even your kids, assuming they're five or over – need to understand and buy into the philosophy, or at least not fight against it. They need to know the house will be a mess for a while. And you need to seek their approval before you chuck important items away: anything I was unsure about I gathered in a pile every evening for my wife and kids to inspect. And I spent a day each with Zak and Jude, chatting through their belongings and sorting through the "randoms". Last, two things: it helps if one person has done the reading and is in control; avoid tidying one room together, or you'll never chuck anything.

Process

Once you understand the benefits of decluttering and the principles behind it, the actual process is easy. Here's *RESET's* take:

Tools for the job

Before you begin, make sure you have these tools:

- Car with a large boot.
- Heavy-duty refuse sacks.
- Vacuum cleaner.
- Cloth, polish, cleaning fluid.
- Shredder (optional) for confidential paper, eg, old wage slips and bank statements.
- Marie Kondo's book. Preferably a printed copy, but a highlighted Kindle version will do.
- Courage, keen focus and indefatigability.

Order

Discard first then tidy is Kondo's advice. When discarding, start easy. The *best* advice I took from Kondo's book was the order in which I should purge. She says: "The best sequence is this: clothes first, then books, papers, miscellaneous items *(komono)* [such as CDs, electronic equipment, makeup] and, lastly, sentimental items and keepsakes[212]."

This is crucial. Clothes are your practice ground. It's easy to amass refuse sacks of clothes that you know you never use, don't need any longer and will never either "come in handy" or "fit into once I lose weight". It's a whole other thing to chuck what Grandpa Joe left you or that memento from your work leaving do. But when you're all fired up and have already discarded thousands of belongings, tackling the "sentimental items and keepsakes" becomes easier.

Categories

Kondo argues you should sort in categories, ie, all the clothes first, then all the books, then all the papers. This laudable concept held in our house until the end of "papers", when every room was upended and untidy. So much so that we were having to leave the house and spend most of our time at the health club.

We then modified the approach to move room by room from the top of the house downwards, picking the easiest rooms first. If I was ever repeating this process – which I won't be – I'd follow the same approach again. You have to make a huge mess and drag items from every nook and cranny. But not everything, not all at once.

Marie's category-by-category approach allows you to discard all your clothes, all your books, all your papers, before organising them. This avoids attacking each room at a time and wasting days duplicating effort when you find more books/papers/clothes in a different part of the house. It's a holistic method and there's no doubt it makes sense.

Even so, this didn't work for our family: it felt things were getting ten times worse with no end in sight. The motivational uplift of completing a room at a time – after we'd completed half of the work (clothes/papers/books) using Marie's approach – kept us going. And although we lost a few hours later, through duplication of effort, what we gained was equilibrium.

I advise a hybrid. Follow the categories approach for clothes, books and paper. Then switch to room-by-room once you've embedded the principles and are au fait with what's in every room of your home, including garage/attic/cupboards.

One thing though, leave the sentimental items – whether it's photos, climbing gear, your collection of Russian dolls, whatever – to last. When you see an item with sentimental value, whichever room it's in, sweep it up and relegate one room in your house to the status of "sentimental dumping ground". If you try to sort mean-ingful items room by room, you'll become bogged down and lose motivation. Save that until the end when you're a doyen of the decluttering arts.

A word on books

The only books we chucked away were out-of-date university textbooks and kids' hardbacks they'd grown out of (*That's not my lion...*[213], anyone?). When it came to the rest, handling each book and deciding whether it gave me a "thrill of pleasure" seemed wrong. And how did I know if a book excited me by looking at its cover? I bought it and read it for a reason, and that reason was reason enough.

Books are important in our house. They build your mind. I refer to them over and over again. I have books to dip into when I want to find out what I thought of this or that. By all means, chuck a few study books; but keep the rest...they will come in handy – they're what made you.

A word on photos

Again, Marie suggests a thorough and ruthless approach to photo disposal. We decided against this, considering the time it would have taken to go through each one and the small space they took up in our house.

Do I keep it, what should I do with it if not?

I've already talked about the principles behind making this difficult decision. I would add one thing though: be as ruthless as you can. Don't keep an item just because it was useful or meant something to you once. Marie wouldn't like that. Life's about the present and the future, not the past. The intention here is to help you clear your house, so you can focus on what you want, and learn to appreciate the possessions that help you do that.

If you don't want to keep something, place it in one of five piles:

1. Sell on Gumtree/eBay/local-community-Facebook-page pile.
2. Give-to-friends pile.
3. Give-to-charity-shop pile.
4. Recycling pile.
5. Take-to-rubbish-dump pile.

If you're flying solo, seek your family's input on anything you're unsure about every night. But try to make most of the wee decisions yourself; 99% of the time, they'll agree with you. And don't worry that you'll regret chucking possessions away. There's nothing that can't be fixed by an online trip to Amazon.

Organising

After sorting what you want to keep and discard, and disposing of it, organising what you have left is a cinch. Here are a few tips from the frontline:

- **No piles.** Marie doesn't use the word "piles", but I can guess what she thinks of them. If you embark on this process, your job, once done, is never to have a pile in your house again. The most you should have is a paper in-tray. But even that should be dealt with daily, with events marked on your family wall planner/online calendar or chucked in the bin.

- **Nothing hidden away.** Your goal is to have everything on show where you can see it. No items squirrelled away in storage boxes you can't see into, no matter how well-labelled. No boxes of university folders, no shoe collection Imelda Marcos would be proud of, no old carpets or tiles you'll never use. This is a one-off opportunity for you to deal with all the flotsam you've accumulated, holistically, and only keep what matters to you. And when you have, show it. For instance, our camping gear is in a large open IKEA box in my home office. Every day I walk past it and think of the fun time we're going to have wild camping next summer.
- **Shoeboxes.** If you must *contain*, the humble open shoebox (minus lid) is a good choice.
- **Roll your clothes.** Right now, most of your clothes will be stored on top of one another in drawers. No, says Marie, roll them up and stand them on edge. I drew the line at socks: pairing them, like my mum taught, works just fine for me.
- **Every man for himself.** Concentrate your own belongings in one place. That way you will take responsibility for them.

Finish what you started

Don't start this process and give up halfway. You have to commit and see it through to the end. Don't take a break and return a few weeks later. You'll lose your thread, start doubting the principles and when you try to start again, your enthusiasm will have dissipated. Also, the clutter around you will now be doubly stressful. Keep at it, power through day after day to reach the promised land. Marie, who you'll by now have developed an internal dialogue with, would be proud of you.

Results

Kondo states: "The lives of those who tidy thoroughly and completely, in a single shot, are without exception dramatically altered[214]." I followed her approach, with a few tweaks here and there as outlined above, so did it work for me? The short answer is yes. The comprehensive response? Over the course of two months, we:

- Threw out 100 heavy-duty refuse-sack-fulls.
- Sold 50 items online.
- Took 20-plus full carloads of belongings to the rubbish dump.
- Took five carloads of possessions to two local charity shops, one specialising in children's gear.
- Gave away hundreds of books and toys to friends.

Our home is transformed:

- We know where every item is in our house.
- We have removed all annoyances.
- My wife and I can now work from home when we need to. Previously it was impossible to focus because of the thousands of tasks and annoyances everywhere.
- Everything is on show, available to use when we need it. This inspires us to, eg, fly that kite with the kids on a windy day.
- The storage areas, once packed to the gunnels, are almost empty. There are 20 items in the basement and a toolbox under the stairs while the only items in the eaves of our converted attic are those 24 rattan storage boxes that once covered a multitude of sins in the kids' bedrooms.

But the gold is in the more profound effects:

- We're the masters now.
- It feels like someone's lifted a great weight off our shoulders.
- It's so simple to keep on top of things by dealing with them when they come in. We've even developed systems to do just this, such as leaving anything that comes into the house with no obvious home on the end of the kitchen table, so we address it

that night.

- It's easier to make decisions.
- Our eating habits have changed. Because it's easier to *think* in our own home, we have started cooking meals every night and planning our meals a week before.
- We're happier and more efficient; it has made us ponder the drawbacks of consumerism. Chucking away belongings you've spent tens of thousands of pounds on tends to have this effect.
- Last, despite Marie's advice of decluttering in silence, I spent much of the two big clear-out months listening to podcasts or – on those half-hour trips to and from the rubbish dump – audiobooks. This gave me a good grasp of an idea related to financial independence (FI) and decluttering: minimalism.

In short, one of the key planks of resetting your middle-class halfway-through life is Marie Kondo'ing your house. Read my principles, follow my plan and buy her book. Doing these three things will, *I* guarantee it, make you happier and restart your life.

A few words on minimalism

I watched a film a couple of years back. You might have seen it. It centres on two people who give up high-flying corporate careers to live a meaningful life for less. *Minimalism: A Documentary About the Important Things*[215], it's called.

The idea behind minimalism is that we should concentrate more on who we are than what we own. It's about simplifying our lives, so we can focus on what's important. As Vicki Robin writes: "People who've simplified their lives...are happier than mainstreamers. They are less materialistic, less status conscious, more interested in personal growth, friends, family, and participating in the life of their community. Happiness studies confirm again and again that these are the elements of a fulfilling existence[216]." The more stuff you have, the more attention it demands. As the Dalai Lama has said: "Simplicity is extremely important for happiness."

Decluttering your house is a great practical introduction to the joys of simplicity and minimalism. It not only clears your mind but also reduces the choices you have to make on what to wear and where to store items. For instance, much like Mark Zuckerberg and his grey t-shirts[217], I have a small range of clothing. I don't have to waste time choosing what to wear every day – because I don't have much choice.

Also, I have a versatile holdall[218] that can double as a suitcase, briefcase, rucksack, running emporium. I don't need to spend time deciding which bag will meet my needs the next morning – because I have one I love that covers every eventuality. Incidentally, the life-in-a-bag holdall tip came from author Tim Ferriss's *5-Bullet Friday*[219] newsletter after *The Minimalists* had turned me on to the concept of one-bag-to-rule-them-all through their new Pakt One venture[220].

Six years ago that sentence wouldn't have made sense to me; it does now. Are you beginning to see how everything in *RESET* is interlinked?

CHAPTER 16

Part III Index Card

- Social media apps on phones are the devil: do battle with him.
- Disable all notifications.
- Try Morning Pages.
- Be mindful (not empty).
- Marie Kondo – Family Sawyer variation – your house.
- In a oner: it's a transoceanic voyage, not a sprint.
- Simplify to make clearer, better, fewer choices.

And finally...

Decluttering allowed me to see clearly, without filter, what was important in life. It's a crucial step in the *RESET* process. But it was the next stage of my family's journey that gave me a hook to hang this new learning on, when I grew obsessed with the US-based financial independence community and completed the reset of my young family's lives. Gradually, all this learning was beginning to pay dividends. Now the bit you've been waiting for. Without moolah, none of the self-actualisation in Maslow's famous pyramid is possible. What follows in Part IV is a comprehensive, long-term, life-changing plan to reset your relationship with money and knock years off your retirement date. The entire book's been building to this point. Excited? I am. I can't wait to *share it with you.*

CHAPTER 17

Halftime Downer Interval

THE FIRST FILM I watched was *Superman*, with my dad, at Northwich Odeon, in 1978. Back then, you always had to endure a ten-minute "short". Then, happily ensconced, halfway through the main feature there'd be an interval where two dimly lit ice-cream sellers would stand at the bottom of the aisles with wooden trays around their necks. To me, this always felt like a grim but necessary pause in proceedings, whetting my appetite for the best part of the film: its second half. So before you remove the cardboard cover from your ice-cream carton, let's remind ourselves why we're watching this movie.

- Too many of us think the world owes us something when the only people who care are our close friends and family.
- Too many of us are trapped in a job we hate.
- Too many of us earn loads of money, but have no idea what's in our pension or when we can retire. We employ cleaners and childcare providers and skip the queue with private healthcare. Either our kids are at private school or we pay £100k more on our mortgage for a good catchment area: same difference.
- Too many of us are so beaten down by an always-on working culture that we spend half our free time de-stressing.
- Too many of us like what we do, but don't like our boss.

- Too many of us take the occasional Monday or Friday off sick because we ~~have a bug~~ just can't face going in.
- Too many of us have problems sleeping or wear gumshields to stop our teeth grinding during the night.
- Too many of us joke about that Monday morning feeling. We post sardonic memes on Facebook implying we hate our jobs then hover to see if anyone likes or comments. And a comment's better than a like. Course it is.
- Too many of us have lost pride in our work, plodding along in a state of unproductive but hyper-vocal busyness, accepting that in the modern workplace, "playing the game" is all-important.
- Too many of us, whatever we earn, think doing the lottery is our best chance of making a million.
- Too many of us never defrost the freezer, have a third-drawer-down in the kitchen that is overflowing and buy items on impulse that we already have.
- Too many of us throw away a third of the food we buy every week because we never plan our meals and can't stomach the healthy kale and mushroom risotto when we get in from work, opting instead for comfort food.
- Too many of us spend too much time worried about what the future holds and going over past mistakes. Instead of living in the present, the now.

OK, enough already, and sorry for that rather rude slap in the face with a Lyons Maid Strawberry Mivvi[221]. The ice-cream sellers have disappeared through their fire exits. Dad's back in his seat. Let's slide back the curtain and settle down for the most exciting bit, the second half.

PART IV

Getting F.U. Money – a Plan

FIRST, CAN WE SKIP back to Part I? Remember my vision? That sundown glass of red with my wife, watching the white houses turn pink, the Mediterranean in the far-distance, as I transport myself to the snowy and desolate St Petersburg of Dostoevsky and Raskolnikov. What's your early retirement vision? Is it as detailed as mine? Where do you see yourself sitting, with whom, and why? And remember my purpose? **To amass a stash of £855,000 while living a good and meaningful life.** Now what's your purpose (remember the advice in Part I)? What's your early retirement mission statement? Is it measurable like ours? How do you know when you get there? By now, you'll be scratching your head thinking *yeah, sounds good, I've done that, but how the hell do I go about it? Money doesn't grow on trees.* At the end of Part IV, you will have the tools, and background knowledge, to reset your entire life. And implement an early retirement plan that will see you sipping *your* glass of Rioja years earlier than you otherwise would have. I was going to write "than planned", but if you're anything like we were, you don't have much of a financial plan. *This* plan requires no prior personal finance knowledge or aptitude. *This* plan:

- Is doable by anyone who can work a big button calculator and Google.
- Is a set-and-forget one-off blitz that (aside from adopting a few daily routined habits, monthly checking and yearly rebalancing) you can – and should – forget about for most of your working life.
- Will take you less time than Marie Kondo'ing your house.
- Draws on the advice of the world's leading investors, Nobel prize-winners, personal finance authors and scores of financial independence bloggers.
- Is universal, whichever country you live in. However (unlike most financial independence literature), when it comes to laws, fund choice and tax-advantaged accounts, **it's UK-focussed**. US readers can consult such luminaries as Mad Fientist, Mr. Money Mustache and JL Collins for tips on Roth IRAs, 403(b)s and 401(k)s.

Most of all, it's a set of principles, rules and actions that I not only passionately believe in but also carry out, as do hundreds of thousands of people the world over. I tell you, once you understand the power of all this, it will transform your life, as it has mine. This is my comprehensive attempt to pay it forward. It's an amazing plan that works, even when you are punched in the mouth.

(Warning: this will happen.)

CHAPTER 18

Structure

PART IV WILL START with you, then move on to an explanation of what financial independence (FI) is and the principles that guide this plan. Next, it will focus on the three foundations of FI, which run through this part like fusion rods. They are:

1. **Budgeting** (brief).
2. **Frugality and efficiency** (important but not too long).
3. **Investing** (by far the most detailed and interesting bit).

Before finishing on the macabre topic of legacy, I shall unveil a detailed-yet-easy-to-follow *ten-point investing plan* that any mid-lifer can implement.

A note on the tone and structure. It bears repeating that I've written Part IV for people who have no prior financial or investing experience. If you wish to find out more, consult *RESET's* comprehensive Notes for further reading or buy the excellent books I reference.

I make no apology for the necessary detail, the result of two years' obsessional research. There was no way my family was taking decisions about the wealth we'd spent a lifetime accumulating without being sure first. And it is necessary that you, dear reader, see from where my thinking derives.

Whenever you see an *italicised* sentence beginning with the word *Action*, listen up. This is something I suggest *you* should consider doing.

Last, a repetition of a line in *RESET's* disclaimer: "Although this book makes every attempt to give authoritative and accurate information, I'm not taking any responsibility for what you do with it. None." Eg, don't blame me if the stock market plummets. (Word to the wise: keep your nerve, however long it takes, and hoover up those cheap units...you may even thank me for it eventually.)

CHAPTER 19

You're Not Alone – Money is the Commonest Problem

LET'S SAY YOU'RE THE main breadwinner in your family. What are you on? Sixty thousand pounds? Eighty? Too steep? Fifty? You're a midlife professional. It's difficult for me to guess. Let's say you're at the lower end of the scale. Perhaps you work in one of the caring professions. Or maybe you're a primary school teacher with a few years under your belt. Thirty thousand pounds maybe?

But hold on a minute. That's your salary. What about your take-home pay? That £30k turns into £23,780 after-tax[222]. **Did you know that places you in the top 1.18% richest people in the world?** Let's run that again with a £40k salary (£30,580 after-tax): now you're in the top 0.6%[223].

We're loaded. So why is it that we always feel skint, and we have bugger all savings to show for our decades on this planet?

Well, it could be that since 2008 wages have been static while the cost of living has increased. It could be that interest rates have been paltry for the past decade, discouraging a whole generation of midlife professionals from saving. (For many of our generation, the dot-com bubble of 1997–2001 then 50% plunge in the stock market post-2008 put paid to any lingering interest in shares.) It could be that a decade of low mortgage rates have, instead of encouraging people to pay down their mortgage or invest the money they saved, led them to pour extra money into consumer goods and self-medicating lattes to ease the anguish of a life tied to both-working-full-time salaried employment. Whatever the reason, if you've reached a stage in your life when you're starting to worry that you'll have to work until you pop your clogs, just to pay the bills, you are by no means the only one.

A 2017 large-sample-size study of 13,000 UK adults by The Financial Conduct Authority found that four in ten aged between 35 and 44 have no idea what their company is putting in their pension. Thirty-one per cent of people in the UK will rely solely on the state pension in retirement and most with defined contribution (DC) pensions (a work pension where the employer puts in money every month, and you contribute, too) said they had relatively little in their pot. Around two-fifths have less than £5,000 and only 12% have more than £100,000[224]. In the US, latest statistics show the average (median) net worth (value of investments, cash savings and house equity [what it's valued at minus what you owe on the mortgage]) is $35,000 for 35- to 44-year-olds, rising to $84,542 for those aged 45 to 54[225]. No wonder people are relying on social security to take care of their old age.

So if it's all going to hell in a handbasket, why don't more of us do something about it? I reckon it's the sheer hopelessness of the task, not knowing where to start and that (especially in the UK) money is the last taboo.

Statistics show that the primary cause of most relationship breakups is money[226]. This is because we'd rather discuss our relationship problems than what we earn. After surveying 15,000 men and women, researchers from University College London found that people are almost seven times as likely to tell someone they don't know how many people they've had sex with, or whether they've ever cheated on their partner, than reveal what salary they're on[227].

Objections

We all agree that money makes the world go round. And that having money gives us freedom to make choices in line with our values and purpose. So why don't we take action?

- **It's too late for me.** If you're a midlife careerist, you're wrong: it's never too late to grab hold of your life.
- **We're in debt, never mind saving.** Make changes, pay your debt, unless it's your mortgage, then move on to investing.
- **Every time I make ends meet, someone moves the other end.** Yeah, usually you.
- **I don't have time for all this.** It's a one-off, set-and-forget, investment of time that will see you retire years earlier. You can do it every weekend for a couple of months or take two weeks off and break the back of it in one short burst. You'll thank me when you're 60 and the only thing you've got to worry about is who moved your beach towel from that sunlounger.
- **Scrimping and saving isn't for me: life's too short.** Think of it as being efficient not being tight. My family saved £900 a month and live a much happier life because of it. Instead of going to Starbucks *et al's* coffers, £800 of that £900 a month is invested in our asset column. And yes, you're right, life is "too short", so why are you spending so much of it working in a job that makes you sad?
- **Saving is boring.** Not if you make it a game, have a plan and a clear vision.
- **Can't I get paid more and not bother with all this?** How's that worked for you so far? Have your pay rises gone to building your net worth or purchasing bigger and better motorised vehicles? Or you could spend years learning about how to invest and do it this way (very few succeed). Or you could ditch your career, become an entrepreneur and get your F.U. Money that way (risky and not for the faint-hearted). Or you could just follow the plan below. (Disclosure: I run a small business. This is distinct from being an entrepreneur[228] but bears similarities, such as tolerance for risk. For those seeking FI, it's a path worth considering. However, the plan in *RESET* assumes you're in salaried employment.)

- **My partner and I aren't paid enough to save anything.** Not true, it's possible to become a millionaire on a middling, midlife household income of £60,000 before-tax.
- **The stock market is gambling: I know too many people who've been burnt. Any money I have left at the end of the month, I put in my savings account.** Are you bonkers? Over long periods, the stock market outperforms all other asset classes (savings accounts, gold, property). You just need to know where to put it.
- **Most of the investing suggestions given by the financial independence movement focus on America.** That's why *RESET's* here.
- **We've got two kids: do you know how much they cost to feed?** There's no denying it, kids cost a small fortune. The cost of raising a child in the UK is approximately £230,000[229]. Times that by two and, dependent on your income, you're adding a good five years on to your early retirement date (if you're a doctor, reduce to two[230]). Here's the thing though: it's not kids that burn a hole in your pocket, it's you. You can feed and clothe children without it costing the earth. Aside from that, kids need love, activities, someone to listen and believe in them, to learn responsibilities. Then it's down to you: you can outsource it or do it yourself. Children will add a few years on to your working life. But if you follow this plan, not by as much as they are now, and you'll enjoy the journey more, too.
- **Every time I think about this it makes my head hurt. I wouldn't know where to start.** Oh man, I was that person. Just do it: I'll show you how.
- **We have a financial adviser to take care of that.** Oh yeah, and how much are they charging you? Do you know how that's affecting your investment returns? Wouldn't you feel better if you were in control?
- **The only way I'm going to get rich is by winning the lottery.** Good luck with that: the odds of winning the UK jackpot are 45,057,474 to one[231].

CHAPTER 20

What Do Rich People Look Like?

Us. THOMAS J. STANLEY and William D. Danko know more about the traits of rich people than anyone living or dead. Decades of market research, focus groups and meeting tens of thousands of millionaires across the US led them to a few golden conclusions, which they shared in one of the best financial independence and personal finance books ever written: *The Millionaire Next Door.* Their findings should give every middle-class midlifer great heart. Here's a summary:

- The grades you receive in school have no correlation with your economic wealth and success other than in the medical and legal professions[232].
- And what's more, you don't have to be earning a doctor's salary to amass your "go-to-hell fund", as they call it. Many people they interviewed with a net worth of $2m or even $3m got there on a joint pre-tax annual household income of $80,000 (£56,000[233]).
- Eighty per cent of US millionaires are first-generation rich[234].
- They share seven characteristics: "They live well below their means. They allocate their time, energy and money efficiently, in ways conducive to building wealth. They believe that financial independence is more important than displaying high social

status. Their parents did not provide economic outpatient care. Their adult children are economically self-sufficient. They are proficient in targeting market opportunities. They chose the right occupation[235]."

- The top ten occupations of the adult children of the affluent are: corporate executive; entrepreneur; middle manager; physician; advertising; marketing or sales professional; attorney; engineer, architect or scientist, accountant; college or university professor; and high school/elementary school teacher[236].
- Most don't become millionaires until they're 50. Most are frugal[237].
- They become millionaires by budgeting and watching what they spend[238].

In short, Danko and Stanley found: "Building wealth takes discipline, sacrifice, and hard work[239]."

Are you up for that?

CHAPTER 21

Financial Independence and F.U. Money

LET'S GET A COUPLE of definitions out of the way.

F.U. and FI are like the yang and yin[240] of FIRE (Financial Independence Retire Early). **Financial independence (FI)** is the positive yang: having enough money that you can live off the income from your assets and never have to work again. **F.U. Money** (the menacing yin), as we've discovered, is having enough money that you never have to do anything you don't want to for money ever again.

For example, say you have the perfect job and someone starts picking on you. With F.U. Money, you don't need to be stressed about it. The power is in your hands. And if she doesn't understand, you have my permission to approach your boss, tell her where to stick her job and yell... – you get the picture – "Fuck you!"

FI is about hope; F.U. Money is about pride. Together the yin and yang of FIRE are a powerful motivating force.

A brief history of FI

The chances are you've never heard of financial independence until now, which is why *RESET*'s front cover centres on the phrase *early retirement*. Early retirement means never working again. Financial independence means never having to work again. (Loads of FIers have jobs, but jobs they want to do, not ones they have to do.)

Financial independence is an unconventional, underground cult, without the messianic ruler. Powered by the internet, the FIRE community has mushroomed as bloggers such as Pete Adeney and JL Collins have taken on the mantle of early pioneers such as Joe Dominguez and Jacob Lund Fisker, leading hundreds of thousands of (largely US) people to change their lives.

The past two years have seen hundreds of FIRE converts follow their lead, rustle up a WordPress website and spread the FI gospel[241]. Still an underground movement, financial independence has gone from a term recognised by one in a thousand Americans in 2011 to one in 50 in 2017. That estimate is from Mr. Money Mustache himself, who, such is his popularity, received 8.8m page views on his website in April 2017 alone[242].

The UK

Across the pond, everyone's heard of early retirement, everyone's heard of *Which?*[243] magazine and everyone's heard of *Money Saving Expert* Martin Lewis[244]. Don't get me wrong, there's more to Lewis's brilliant personal finance advice than saving £10 on a pair of pillows. In fact, Lewis has done more to improve financial literacy in the UK than any other person living or dead. If I want to knock money off my car insurance renewal, change utility provider, or learn about inheritance tax, he's my first port of call. But if I want to change my life and bag a holistic early retirement plan, I'll look elsewhere: he's never tied it together for me, like the top US FI bloggers do.

Over the past two years living in Glasgow, I've asked hundreds of people if they've ever heard of the financial independence movement or *Mr. Money Mustache*. Not a single one has answered yes.

I hope *RESET* will change that. Yes, much you will have heard before, no it's not about being tight, and yes, some of it's just common sense. But so's rocket science, when you think about it, and I imagine – unless you're SpaceX[245] founder Elon Musk[246] – you need instructions before you begin.

Benefits

- F.U. Money brings freedom.
- You can live the lifestyle you want.
- It gives you options. As a friend of mine says: "Money gives you time tokens."
- You can work for people and towards goals you like and respect.
- Financial independence gives you the power to lead life on your own terms.

Getting your early retirement plan with a measurable goal will make your journey through life, the struggle, taste that much sweeter. You'll make more time for your friends and family because you'll know what's important to you.

Once you take the first steps towards financial independence, you'll have a mission that necessitates a new you: one more in tune with the *real* you.

12 essential disciplines for FI

> *In this complex world we have created, money is perhaps our most powerful tool. Learn to master it and the world opens before you and the path becomes smooth. Ignore it and the way is littered with jagged stones, sharp thorns and dark, deep pits*[247].
> **JL Collins**

Part IV of *RESET* comprises a plan that will transform your relationship with money and help you retire years earlier. It'll also explain the theory that underpins said plan. Let's start with 12 essential disciplines for those who want to achieve financial independence:

1. **It's your net worth that matters, not your salary.**
2. **Know the difference between assets and liabilities.** Build your assets[248].
3. **Minimise your taxes.** Make money while you sleep by *maximising* your passive income.
4. **Avoid debt,** apart from your mortgage.
5. **Understand consumerism.** Learn the difference between needs and wants. Wants are insatiable.
6. **Take care of every pound.** Keep expenses low and save as much as you can every month.
7. **In your career, seek knowledge.** Take jobs for what you can learn, not what they pay. Work hard to fulfil your earning potential: don't buy more to reflect your increased earnings, save them and invest.
8. **Learn about investing, tax, law, accountancy, the markets and human psychology.**
9. **Don't use investment advisers.** Do it yourself. If you must, pick one on a trusted recommendation who charges by the hour. Never pay management fees to an investment adviser, or commission.
10. **Invest as much as you can.** The stock market offers the best long-term returns for the least effort.
11. **Don't try to pick stocks or time the market.** Keep your costs low and your emotions out of it. Get an easy-to-remember plan, automate monthly investments and never dabble.
12. **Ordinary people who keep their heads win.** Bright people who don't, lose. Be ordinary.

CHAPTER 22

Four FI Fundamentals

YOU UNDERSTAND THE PRINCIPLES now. But what do they mean in practice and how do you apply them to the world of stressed-out midlifer-dom?

I'll now share four FI fundamentals with you before we move on to the **FIRE Triumvirate** of budgeting, efficiency/frugality and investing. Four fundamentals you will refer to time and time again. Four fundamental constituents to this easy-to-remember set-and-forget early retirement plan.

It was learning these four fundamentals, and following **STEPS A-D**, that made me think financial independence was possible for my family.

CHAPTER 23

#1: Stash Maths

ANY FELLOW DEVOTEES OF the cult of Mustache will be familiar with the word *stash*[249].

It's a genius one-syllable way of simplifying the necessary but often-confusing detail around personal finance to focus on one achievable goal.

To achieve financial independence, you need to build your stash until it's big enough to live off for the rest of your life.

This is as a simple or as hard as you want to make it. Let's start with simple (we can do hard when we come to *safe withdrawal rates*).

There are four steps:

- **STEP A:** How much will you need to live on when you become financially independent (five minutes)?
- **STEP B:** What size stash do you need (five minutes)?
- **STEP C:** How much do you already have (15 minutes for a guess, two mornings for a more accurate assessment)?
- **STEP D:** Run the numbers on a website. Based on stash-size required, frugality/efficiency, target FIRE date, budget, how much do you need to save every month (15 minutes, play around with the monthly savings box)?

STEP A: How much will you need to live?

When I was growing up on Wimpey's Hill in the 1980s, two communications of record graced our house: *BBC Radio 4* and *Which?* magazine. Fast forward to today and a world where trust in most media has diminished, these two beacons of truth remain undimmed. So when *Which?* published (first in May 2017, updated February 2018) the results[250] of a member survey of 6,000 retired and semi-retired couples, you can imagine my excitement. I'd long been struggling to work out how much my wife and I would need to live on after reaching financial independence. In one fell swoop, my prayers had been answered.

To live a "comfortable" lifestyle the average couple needs an after-tax income of £26,000 (£26,750 gross).

To live a "luxury" lifestyle the average couple needs an after-tax income of £39,000 (£43k gross).

A comfortable lifestyle includes: £3,870 for groceries, £2,879 for housing payments, £2,489 for insurance, £2,364 for transport, £2,081 for utilities, £1,607 for recreation and leisure, £1,466 for household goods, £1,251 for charitable gifts/donations, £1,236 for health, £1,077 for buying new clothes, £935 for tobacco/alcohol and even £4,491 a year for holidays/European travel.

A luxury lifestyle adds in an extra £7,376 for long-haul holidays over and above the £4,491 already allocated, plus £4,404 for a new car every five years and £1,369 for a golf, health or even yacht club membership.

What about you?

First up, it's important to remember that if you follow the *RESET* process, you and your partner will not be "the average couple". You won't have as many outgoings as "the Joneses", who you will long since have stopped trying to keep up with. That £26k figure now looks high.

That said, remember your vision. Perhaps it's living in Costa Rica for three months every year or treating yourself to three five-star transatlantic breaks? Everyone's different. Or perhaps your vision of early retirement arrives earlier than mine? Perhaps the kids will be at secondary school, so you're going to need to take account of those costs, too?

Eventually you'll need to jettison the big button calculator, close your Excel spreadsheet and make as educated a guess as you can about how much you'll need to live on when you achieve *your* FIRE.

Our figure is **£28,740**[251].

(This figure assumes a 3.5% withdrawal rate: used to work out how much you can take out of your stash, averaged over a long time, without it running out. This 3.5% figure is based on a UK resident investing internationally. If you're a US investor, most FIRE experts, including Mr. Money Mustache and JL Collins, recommend a 4% withdrawal rate, which, in the equation in **STEP B**, would lead to a vastly reduced stash target of £750,000.)

So, **£28,740**. That's how much after-tax cash, in today's money, we will need to live our vision of financial independence, including £10k a year for holidays/living in other places. To do this, we'll need **£30,000** a year (in 2018/19 we'd pay **£1,260** in income tax every year in retirement).

And it's that gross, before-tax, figure that's all-important. **Ours is £30k. What's yours?**

Later you can spend an evening calculating it with your partner. But for now, reread the above, google the *Which!* survey and come up with your own figure, rounded to the nearest £1,000. It's that gross figure we'll require in **STEP B**, when we reveal what size stash you're going to need to set your life on FIRE.

(*Which?'s* survey allows around £250 a month for "housing payments". As a midlife professional, I am guessing this will not cover your mortgage right now. Our £30,000 a year figure is based on our mortgage being a maximum of £250 a month after we achieve financial independence. Our target age for FI is 56.5–60. By this time, our kids will have left home. Either we will have paid off our mortgage, I will continue to take on consultancy work, or we will have enough house equity to move to a smaller house mortgage-free.)

Action
Estimate how much you will need to live on, before-tax (gross), every year once you hit early retirement. To the nearest £1,000.

STEP B: What size stash will you need?

This bit's easy (and helluva complex. If you want the helluva complex bit, flick forward to the bit about SWRs, but make sure you come straight back).

For argument's sake, let's say *you* need **£30,000** a year before-tax. Here's the equation.

$$\text{Gross FIRE spending a year} \times 28.5^{252} = \text{target stash.}$$
$$\text{Or}$$
$$£30,000 \times 28.5 = £855,000.$$

We have your target.

Action
If you live in the UK, use the above equation to calculate your target stash.

STEP C: What size stash do you already have?

You have an idea of how much you'll need to live on when you achieve FIRE. You now have your stash goal. But have you any idea how much money you already have?

Leave the final salary pension (if you're lucky enough to be one of the 1.6 million UK people who still have a defined benefit scheme[253]) and the house aside for a second.

What you need to do now is dredge your memory, ask your partner, dig out that box in the attic (or in your home office if you've already completed Part III) and pour yourself a strong coffee. You're going to need it.

Your mission is to find every pension, Isa, share, trust fund, long-lost savings account, building society windfall, mutual pension windfall, bit of random financial-ness that you or your partner own. Including the ones you've forgotten because you moved house and discontinued the mail redirection after six months.

Your partner and you need to look back through your childhood, university and working life. Think of all the financial organisations you've ever received mail from, emails from, or met. Then contact every one you think might have a piece of your money. Keep your old addresses handy, even your parents' addresses if you ever stayed at home between jobs or after university.

Much of this you'll have. You won't touch it from one year to the next, apart from slinging their annual letter at the top of that box to gather dust.

Next weekend, and maybe the weekend after, you need to block off Saturday morning to ring these people.

Many of the institutions will have changed names since you joined them. Most of them will have outsourced their pension provision to a financial provider. Most will have an online system where you can view your money. Register and root around: the website will answer many of your questions. However, a telephone call is always your starting point.

You'll need your last three bank statements, national insurance number, birth certificate and passport. You'll also need a sheet (or a secure password-remembering Chrome extension) to record your login details. Some prefer to be contacted by telephone, some via email, some by post. I asked one of the providers whether they needed me to write my name in blood after a frustrating game of multicountry telephone bagatelle.

Start with the one that has most of your money and work down. This will probably be the defined contribution pension scheme of the employer you've spent most time working for.

Find out:

1. **How much money of yours do they have?**
2. **What's it invested in**, particularly within your pensions and Individual Savings Accounts (Isas)?
3. **How much are they charging you?** They levy an account fee for looking after your money and the funds they invest in have an annual management charge, too.
4. **Is there an exit fee?**
5. **How much have you contributed and for how long?** This gives you an idea of your return on investment over time, so you can compare.

You're not making any decisions right now. I'm only suggesting asking the five questions at this point because by the time you've navigated the company's queueing system, you may as well get all the information you need in a oner.

All you *need* at this stage is the answer to question one: **how much of your hard-earned cash does each one of these people have?**

Action

Add all these random bits of your money, arrive at one figure and...

STEP D: Run the numbers

You now know how big a stash you need to live a good life when you achieve FIRE. And you'll either have guesstimated (15 minutes) or know (two mornings) the size of your stash right now.

STEP D is the easiest and most revelatory bit. Are you ready for a heart-in-mouth moment? It's time to pop those numbers into an online calculator.

Google "Candid Money How Long Investment Calculator[254]". It's rough-and-ready but simple. (Other retirement calculators exist[255]. If you use them, just switch dollars to pounds and make sure you change the assumptions to those suggested in *RESET*, as US FIRE aficionados tend to take a more optimistic approach than their international counterparts, because of the efficiency, and hence performance, of the US stock market.)

You'll need the following:

A: Target sum (target stash).
B: Initial lump sum (current stash).
C: Annual (predicted) investment return.
D: Annual (predicted) inflation rate.
E: Annual charge.
F: Monthly savings.

You can deal with C, D and E easily at this stage. Tap in **9** for C, **3** for D and **0.5** for E[256]. Now all *you* have to do is play around with F and you'll see when you can achieve financial independence.

Action
Use the calculator to find out what age you'll be when you become financially independent.

Three case studies
To illuminate this, let's look at three fictional middle-class midlife families at different stages of life. For consistency, the FIRE target sum for each family is **£855,000**.

The Baxters

- Age: 35.
- Current stash: £100,000.

- Monthly savings/investment: £1,000 (including the government top-up to their pensions).

John and Yvonne Baxter are 35. They've moved from an apartment to a spacious bungalow in the burbs. After their son, Sam, arrived, the Baxters' lives changed in a flash. Yvonne's part-time now, and John's spending more hours in the office. They're professional people, but neither could afford to pay into a pension when they were in their twenties: they were too busy paying student loans and enjoying themselves. Since turning 30 though, John's been putting into the defined contribution scheme at work. Yvonne's had a few different jobs, but always contributed to her work pension once she realised it was "free money". **It will take the Baxters 22 years and five months to reach financial independence. They'll be 57.**

The Dobsons

- Age: 40.
- Current stash: £250,000.
- Monthly savings/investment: £1,500 (including the government top-up to their pensions).

Cecily and Joel work full-time. He's a supermarket middle manager. She's high up at a recruitment firm. They love children but couldn't have them themselves. The Dobsons live for their holidays and relish spending money on food. But they've always been careful with their money, paying into the company pensions whichever job they've had. Last year they realised they were growing older and needed to start thinking about retirement. They've started saving every month in a cash Isa (they don't trust the stock market: *it's just gambling*). **It will take the Dobsons 13 years and three months to reach financial independence (assuming they stop saving in a cash Isa and follow the *RESET* plan). They'll be 53.**

The Aggarwals

- Age: 50.
- Current stash: £200,000.
- Monthly savings/investment: £2,000 (including the government top-up to their pensions).

Patricia and Sunil had their two kids Joe and Skye early. They've left home now, and it's led the two 50-year-olds to re-evaluate their lives. They're both working full-time and all they can think about is early retirement. They've examined their finances and know they need to make up for lost time. Sunil's quit his job and set up on his own, and they've committed to saving and investing £2k a month. **It will take the Aggarwals exactly 13 years to achieve financial independence. They'll be 63.**

N.B.

(You can reach financial independence sooner than the Baxters, Dobsons and Aggarwals. If you're a professional in your mid-twenties, there's nothing to stop you bagging your stash by your early thirties: just ask Mr. Money Mustache. But for those of us who are married-with-two-children, it's going to take a good deal longer.)

Conservative assumptions

The financial assumptions in Part IV are conservative. This is because:

1. Much financial independence literature you read will have investment returns up at 11% (not nine like *RESET*), inflation down at 2.5% (not three like *RESET*), safe withdrawal rate (SWR) at 4% (*RESET* recommends 3.5%) and no account made for continual investment charges when building your stash. (*RESET* suggests 0.5% when stash-building and 0.3% while living on your stash

post-FIRE). If you apply the non-conservative assumptions, it'll – in theory – knock a few years off your working life. But, particularly if you live in Europe, you may live to regret it. If you apply the *RESET* assumptions, you'll be able to retire early with confidence.

2. The figures above do not include: the effect of your social security/state pension when it kicks in age 67/68, any final salary scheme you may receive age 65 onwards, or any inheritance windfall you get when your folks kark it. This is deliberate: who knows what will happen to the political football that is the state pension in years to come? Only a few lucky people are in final salary schemes, and most probably aren't thinking of retiring early like us. Given medical advancements, you might die before your parents, so if you're fortunate enough to receive an inheritance, it's unlikely to be until you're old and grey. Financial independence is about self-reliance. My path to financial independence relies on my immediate family and me. Not external forces, the timing/amount/existence of which are beyond control. I suggest you do the same. But if you think differently, and want to play around with the numbers, be my guest and google "cFIREsim" and "FIRECalc[257]".

3. Remember that achieving FIRE and getting your F.U. Money is based on the premise you will never work again. You may be one of the almost one in four people who hate their work, in which case this'll suit you just fine. Or you could be one of the lucky 13% of people who love their work (like me). If the three fictional families' examples above look bleak to you at this stage – just look at those savings rates – remember that you can always take a part-time job to either protect your stash once you achieve FIRE or reduce your stash target in years to come.

4. These savings rates are for your household, not you individually, and include any monthly pension payment you may already be paying in through your work. For instance, the Baxters can't afford to scrape together any more than £100 extra a month with Yvonne working part-time and the costs for Sam's two days at nursery every week. The good news is they don't have to.

Between Yvonne, her employer, and the government top-up, she's already contributing £300 to her defined contribution scheme, while John and his employer are socking away a cool £600. One-hundred pounds + £300 + £600: that's £1,000 in total. If they keep that going they'll be retired at 57.

5. When running these numbers, we assume that the amount you save stays the same every month until you retire early – life is different. Remember, one day your kids will fly the coop and you'll have more money to whack away. Or how about that promotion you've had your eye on? If you follow the *RESET* plan, your earnings potential will increase and you can save more every month. (We've already established you're not blowing it on that new Audi Quattro.)

6. It's amazing how addictive this budgeting, efficiency and saving becomes once you get started. The more you save, the more you invest, the sooner you can retire.

Action

Do your stash maths. Realise it's never too late, but the longer you leave it, the higher the amount you'll need to save every month. When do you want to retire? How much do you need to save and invest every month to get there? And remember, a vital part of your monthly savings figure is your partner and you's monthly defined contribution pension payments: that's one hell of a good start!

CHAPTER 24

#2: Net Worth

BACK TO THOSE FOUR fundamentals. Here's the second. *What are you on?* You know, salary-wise? Many love being asked this question, albeit it's a rarity in the UK where your money is, like, well, private. It allows us to self-deprecatingly brag. And for the asker and the answerer it's the ultimate status symbol. The pregnant pause created by the questioner is filled with thoughts, each wondering, in those milliseconds, whether theirs is bigger than the other's.

However, it just happens to be completely the wrong question. There is only one true measure of personal wealth. It's not how big a house you've got, what car you drive, or what salary you're on. The only measure you should be interested in is your net worth. And the problem is most people don't have a clue. When it's one of the most important things about yourself, or your family, that you must know.

Your net worth is your assets minus your liabilities. For most people that's:

- Value of investments.
- Value of cash.
- Valuation of house.
- House equity in rental property (if you have any).

- Transfer value of defined benefit pension (final salary scheme in the UK, if you're lucky enough to have one).

Minus:

- What you owe on your house (mortgage).
- Any other debts (don't forget to include your car leasing contract if you're unlucky enough to have one).

Remember that if you're on a repayment mortgage, each monthly payment increases your house equity (valuation minus money owed) and hence your net worth.

Remember also, your net worth is not the same as your stash. Your stash doesn't include your final salary pension, your state pension or your house. If you were to downsize your house and pocket the proceeds – say, when the kids leave home – then that's different: the money you make would go straight into your stash. The same principle applies to your final salary pension, should you decide to transfer out (we'll come to that later).

Action

Know your net worth to the nearest pound. Track it every month, forever. If you can, identify a net worth partner (mate with a low boredom threshold, mine's called Rob) to email every month and compare notes. It's a powerful motivator.

CHAPTER 25

#3: One Pot

YOU'RE INTELLIGENT. AS YOU learn, your financial awareness will light up like the switching on of the Christmas tree lights in your local town. One after another, garish lightbulbs will snap on in your mind until, before you know it, everything will glow vibrantly in glorious technicolour. Following the principles at the start of Part IV will become as automatic as waking up and reaching for your book (not your smartphone anymore) in the morning.

The single most important thought to remember on your path to financial independence is the concept of "one pot". One of the biggest things holding back your financial literacy is the unnecessarily complex way we manage and track our money, not helped by the opaque financial services industry.

Luckily, government regulation (such as the recent open banking reforms[258] in the UK) and internet-enabled technological advances worldwide are beginning to change this.

We've talked about "the stash" and "tracking your net worth", so you understand why having your financial documents in one place is crucial. But once you've done the detective work, located all the bits of money you've acquired in your lifetime, how do you keep a handle on it? *Imagine* the demotivating monthly chore of having to log in to a plethora of financial services providers to find out how you're doing?

Now, it doesn't have to be this way. You can have all your data readily available in one place: *one pot.*

In the US, services such as Personal Capital[259] get every single one of those accounts (current and investment) feeding into their system. You can view all sorts of amazing figures and graphs – including that all-important net worth – to supercharge your motivation en route to financial independence.

Personal Capital has no plans to cross the pond, but for those outside the US, services such as: Money Dashboard[260]; Yahoo Finance[261]; and Morningstar Portfolio Manager[262], pieced together, fulfil the same role. All are free, no-obligation (not even a free trial in sight) websites.

Our stash is updated real-time in Yahoo Finance. All our different cash savings, personal accounts, tax owed, business accounts, pocket money are consolidated for easy viewing in Money Dashboard.

From this, we discover two things: size of stash (Yahoo Finance), size of cash (Money Dashboard). To work out net worth, we add on the transfer value of a final salary scheme plus our house equity, which increases every month as we pay off the capital.

One pot: a powerful idea, and one that will revolutionise your financial life, as it has ours.

Action

Take control. Sign up to free cloud software that consolidates your umpteen pots and makes your finances easy to understand. If you don't trust this method, develop your own spreadsheet; or google it, find someone else's and modify to suit you. However you do it, the important thing is you track the performance of your stash and net worth forever.

CHAPTER 26

#4: 2015 UK Pension Reforms

FOR MOST OF MY adult life, pensions were things I didn't want to understand. The fact that I would need to pay into something I couldn't access until I was old and grey, and even then need to buy something unfathomable called an annuity, meant pensions never interested me. The reforms of 2015 changed all that. I can get at *all* my money when I'm 55 now – that's only ten years away. Here's what I've discovered about defined contribution pensions (for the lowdown on defined benefit pensions, skip to Chapter 33).

- I can take a 25% lump sum tax-free when I'm 55 (if you were born after 1972, it's 57[263]).
- Even if I have a defined contribution or benefit scheme, I can still set up a Self-Invested Personal Pension (Sipp) and pay into that as well.
- I can pay up to £40,000 a year into pensions. So can my partner. (You can too, unless you earn less than £40k or upwards of £100k, and specifically £150k...it's complicated[264] – check the Notes at the back of *RESET*).
- My wife and I can now pass on our defined contribution and Sipp pension pots to our kids tax-free if we die before 75 (let's hope not).
- As a UK midlife professional aged between 35 and 60, you're

between zero and 22 years away from doing what you want with your entire pension. No longer is pension money something intangible. And the older you are in that age bracket the sooner you can access it.

Action

*Read up on pensions; the devil's in the detail. For instance, although even pre-2015 you could take your 25% tax-free lump sum age 55, you couldn't withdraw it in tranches like you can now. And though it's true you can now get at all of your money when you're 55, think carefully before doing so or you're in for a nasty tax bill. But the big difference – and the move that transformed retirement planning in the UK – was the government's scrapping of compulsory annuities (non-inheritable "incomes for life") for everyone on these isles. With this one reform three years ago, everything changed: power, control and flexibility moved towards you, making the UK system more in line with the US. Last, remember that pensions are just tax-efficient wrappers that invest (usually) in the stock market. **You** pick what you invest in, and what **you** choose right now has a huge impact on **your** early retirement date.*

CHAPTER 27

The FIRE Triumvirate

WHEW, STILL WITH ME? NOW we've covered the four FI fundamentals, perhaps a quick recap of what we've learned so far in Part IV is in order? You have a ripple-less-loch mental picture in your mind of what early retirement means for you. You know what age you want to retire in an ideal world, and you know it ain't 68. You've played around with the figures and know what you need to save and invest every month to get there. You haven't got a clue how you're going to save that much money every month. What you know about investing you could write on the back of a postage stamp. You distrust the stock market and are wondering whether to believe this information I'm giving you. Here's what I think:

- The key to putting this into practice is threefold: budgeting, efficiency/frugality and investing. The rest of Part IV is split into these three sections.
- You need to read each section and turn the *italicised actions* into habits.
- Your aim is to invest the same amount every month. If you ever have more, don't spend it on a house extension or one of those Range Rover Evoques. Make one-off payments into your pension/investment accounts and take years off your working life.

- I'm living all this, like hundreds of thousands of other people across the world. I've also researched the life out of this topic over the last two years. Still sceptical? The next three sections are peppered with advice from experts ranging from academics to Nobel prize-winners through government bodies to the finest investment minds on the planet.

Now sit back and find out how you can carry out each stage of the **FIRE Triumvirate**: starting with budgeting. Remember, it's never too late to transform your life by coming up with a purposeful financial plan.

CHAPTER 28

Section 1: Budgeting

> *Operating a household without a budget is akin to operating a business without a plan, without goals, and without direction[265].*
> **Thomas J. Stanley and William D. Danko (PhDs),** *The Millionaire Next Door*

YOU KNOW THIS, RIGHT? So how come I heard you yawn? Let me tell you a story. When I met my wife, Rachel, she had a ringbinder containing lined A4 paper. In it, she recorded every bit of money she took out of her bank account – cash in those days – and every single item she spent it on.

I used to poke fun at her, but loved the fact she did it. Over the years, as money in and out mushroomed, responsibilities increased and time diminished, this habit fell away. I remembered it when I discovered FI a few years back and eventually took the budgeting plunge. But I don't mind telling you the thought intimidated me. I recalled how much time Rachel used to spend recording. How would I be able to do this efficiently for the rest of *my* life?

Every pound matters

Before I explain how to budget, you must bear three things in mind:

1. Your vision of FIRE. Remember my sundowner glass of Rioja looking down over the tumbledown, chalk-white, hill-clinging villas of Andalusia towards the Med? You'll have your own.
2. Your commitment to take care of every pound that comes your way.
3. That you've earned every pound and that you have traded min-utes of *life energy* for it.

Life energy? Say what?

Life energy[266] is an idea I discovered while reading Vicki Robin and Joe Dominguez's *Your Money or Your Life*. If you measure your life energy in hours and minutes, how much is your one and only life worth? To understand, you need to first work out your hourly wage by looking at your monthly take-home pay and dividing it by the amount of hours you're paid to work every month.

For example, let's assume you're paid for 35 hours a week and take home £2,000:

(£) **2,000** divided by 150 (hours worked per month, assuming between 21 and 23 working days per month) = **£13.66 per hour**.

Then **take off the money** (buying treats, lattes, meals, work clothes, entertainment, fuel) and **add on the time** (commuting, working extra to impress the boss, de-stressing, job-related illness, etc) **you spend maintaining your job.** Let's say:

(real wage "earned" in £) **1,700** divided by (real hours "worked") **225** = **£7.55 per hour**.

That's less than the "national living wage[267]"! Once you realise what your **real hourly wage** is, you'll look at things afresh and be more motivated to find out what you're spending your hard-earned cash on. For instance, say you find out that your real hourly wage is **£7.55**. And you buy a £3 latte – because you're worth it. You have to work for 23.84 minutes to pay for that latte. Put another way that £3 latte costs you 23.84 minutes of life energy (three divided by 7.55 x 60). Now, let's say you buy a latte every day. That's 30 lattes a month. That's a whole 11 hours 55 minutes extra you have to work every month. *Is that worth it when it's the job that's causing you to buy that latte in the first place?*

How to budget

You need two tools to start this process and keep it going:

1. Spreadsheet.
2. Cloud-based website.

Spreadsheet

I use Martin Lewis's. There are hundreds of other free budgeting spreadsheets on the internet, but this is the best one I've found for the UK market. He splits his "Budget Planner" into 13 spending categories and 90 subcategories. I use 12 of the 13 spending categories (we have no loans or debt except the mortgage) and 37 of Lewis's subcategories (plus 28 of my own).

This spreadsheet is my master document. It estimates how much we will spend on what.

Action

Use an existing spreadsheet such as Martin's as a starting point. Download it to your computer or cloud storage (Google Drive/Dropbox). Now, dig out your bank statements, go to your online banking and open your email inbox. Spend the afternoon looking back over the past 12 months and see how much you've spent on everything. Try to break it down as much as possible. If you're self-employed, include your business costs in here as well. Don't fall into the trap of wishful thinking. This is how much you do spend, not how much you'd like to spend. Rope in your partner at the end and ask them any questions. You won't be able to calculate every cost, some will be guesstimates, but be realistic: you're looking for a true picture. Over 12 months where do you choose to spend your money?

Cloud-based software (website)

I use Money Dashboard[268]. It's the best I've found for the UK market. Alternatives are Mint[269], or You Need a Budget (YNAB[270]). But YNAB costs and both are US in origin, so you'll find your bank accounts won't all feed into your "one pot". Depending on when you read this book, I predict there'll be plenty of great UK alternatives in years to come, including the ability to track your investments and net worth. But I've been impressed with Money Dashboard, and it looks as if it's here to stay, hence the recommendation. Here's what you want from a one-pot budgeting tool:

- Sync your accounts to one place.
- Ability to replicate your offline master spreadsheet budgeting categories.
- Once budget categories and subcategories are set, the software allocates spending from shops to subcategories. You don't have to tell it twice.
- Good looking and fun to use.
- Flexibility to tailor dependent on how you want to use it.

And the benefits:

- Real-time one-figure overview.
- Encourages you to take advantage of, eg, one-year savings deals. For example, I have four direct debits to savings accounts bagging us 5% interest by set-and-forget shuffling money around. If it weren't for the one-pot nature of Money Dashboard, this keeping-track-of-all-my-different-pots dynamic would stress me; I wouldn't set up the four direct debits for that reason.
- If I had to budget manually, I wouldn't do it.

- I love the way I can set up "offline accounts" for all our money buckets. There's a "Rach pocket money" account and a "David pocket money" account.
- As a small-business person who owns a limited company, I also love the way I can set up "offline accounts" for value-added tax (VAT), corporation tax, petty cash. A true one-pot approach, instead of life being compartmentalised into work, home, my wife and me.
- To track your net worth, you could set up "offline accounts" for your stash, any final salary transfer value and your house equity. I prefer to keep these separate, however.

It'll take you a day to set this up. And you'll have to check it every few days to make sure everything's been allocated correctly and, eg, split transactions that straddle two subcategories. For instance, you may buy "kids' party prezzies/cards" in the same transaction you buy your "food and household shopping".

Even so, it'll be the best day/ten-minutes-every-few-days you ever spend. It's also particularly important for the first year on your journey towards financial independence: like shining a flashlight in a cellar.

In summary, the biggest benefit is this: by tracking every pound you spend, you establish where you are spending your life energy. You can then make conscious decisions about money and align your spending with your purpose in life.

Action

Sign up for a free account with Money Dashboard, or other cloud-based budgeting software. Set your categories and subcategories, using the same words as those on your spreadsheet. Then assign monetary values to the categories straight from your spreadsheet. You may want to subdivide the categories further if there's an item you want to keep a keen eye on. For my family that subcategory is "food and household shopping". Enable all your bank feeds (including savings accounts, current accounts, business accounts, even mortgage accounts), so every transaction shows up in whatever cloud-based software you choose. Don't worry, your passwords are safe with the likes of Money Dashboard and your bank can't stop you doing this. Then set up your "offline accounts": these are ones you'll have to update manually. That's the hard work done. All you need do now is check every few days to make sure everything's in the right place. Over time you'll see if your spending matches the budget you've set in the master spreadsheet and replicated in the software. Armed with this information, you can make conscious decisions about your money...and your life. (Make sure you update the spreadsheet and the software every time your budget changes. Always use a debit card when you can, it's much easier to track than cash.)

Simple and fun

That's it on budgeting: the simplest section of the **FIRE Triumvirate**. Here are a few thoughts to finish:

- Budgeting is necessary and crucial.
- It helps with Section 2 of the **FIRE Triumvirate**: efficiency and frugality.
- Its purpose is to help you hit your monthly saving goal, the linchpin of any FIRE plan.
- It teaches you the value of money and you start noticing that small everyday expenses become big ones over time.
- Whatever you track becomes a focus.
- Treat it as a game. Once you've done the couple of days' hard work up front, using the system above takes no time. And if you treat it (and Section 2 of the **FIRE Triumvirate**) as a lark, you might even have fun. If that doesn't grab you, think of the sense of achievement. If all else fails, remember *your* Andalusia!

CHAPTER 29

Section 2: Efficiency/Frugality

So, YOU'VE SET UP your budgeting process, and you have an idea of where the money you're paid is going. You now need to have a look at your life and make some changes. I can guarantee that most of my friends and acquaintances will be whispering: **"Dave's written this book. It's all about being a tight arse."** This is an amusing standpoint. I would counter that I've come to realise that there's more to life than work. To make the most of my time on this planet and be as happy as possible I need to be efficient. This section of *RESET* is key, more important than budgeting and even investing. Efficiency is a way of life. It dictates whether you finish the food on your plate, when you wash up that plate and where you decide to place your belongings when you come in from work. Crucially, it dictates what you spend your money on. I'll come to that in a minute, but first I'll reveal *how we slashed £900 from our monthly spend.* Follow these steps and *you'll knock between £500 and £1,000 off yours.* And if you're spendthrift to start with, a helluva lot more.

Case study: The Sawyers' Efficiency *RESET*

Here's how we did it, and you can, too:

- See The LAHs: **£300.**

- Reduce bollocks purchases *(lattes, meals at the health club and work lunches)*: **£200.**
- Ditch childcare *(while both working full-time hours)*: **£150.**
- Ditch cleaner *(DIY: easy after the physical declutter)*: **£80.**
- Ditch shared office *(while retaining an office facility)*: **£65.**
- Renegotiate utility bill *(gaining a smart meter)*: **£35.**
- Renegotiate mobile phone bills *(while upgrading to 4G)*: **£30.**
- Petrol *(through a reduced commute and increased use of our bikes)*: **£25.**
- Renegotiate landline/broadband *(doubling speed)*: **£10.**
- Renegotiate life insurance *(while increasing cover)*: **£5.**

Total Monthly Savings: £900.

Remember The LAHs?

Cuddington and Sandiway – that "double-village" I grew up in – lie halfway between Manchester and Liverpool.

I saw some of the great bands live as a kid, including *New Order* at the then G-Mex...and *Siouxsie and the Banshees*[271] at John Moores. But one of my biggest regrets is never seeing Liverpudlian Lee Mavers's *The La's*[272].

Fast forward 30 years, and it was rediscovering The LAHs that made me confident that this whole financial independence adventure (including a steep monthly savings target) was possible for the Family Sawyer.

Always cost-conscious shoppers, we'd been buying our food online from Asda[273] for the past ten years. We never had time to visit the store and the weekly delivery only took 30 minutes to sort out.

A comprehensive leaf through our financial records (during the initial budgeting phase) revealed we'd spent **£8,000** on food at Asda, Sainsbury's Local[274] and Majestic[275] **over the past year. That's £153 a week or £666 a month** (not including Christmas). A king's ransom.

There must be something we can do, we thought.

Step forward Lidl, Aldi and Home Bargains (The LAHs)

The Family Sawyer now spends **£360 a month** on food and household shopping: that's just over £80 a week, including wine.

On the advice of FI bloggers, I first tried my hand at Costco[276] and Booker[277], then ethnic supermarkets. But the former charge VAT on top of the ticket price and reward bulk buys I don't have room in our kitchen to store while the latter are too far away.

Then I rediscovered The LAHs. Every Saturday morning I pop in on Lidl[278], head over to do the main shop at Aldi[279] then finish with a quick dash around Home Bargains[280]. Sometimes I reverse the order (hell, you have to live a little). Here's what I've observed:

- These three shops are often sited next to one another or a short drive away.
- You can buy everything you need, apart from a few items such as decaf Earl Grey and veggie hot dogs.
- The quality is fantastic. For example, in the case of Lidl and Aldi, instead of stocking 20 different types of tomato ketchup, they offer one. And they make sure that one item is the best it can be.
- Aldi and Lidl sell a similar number of products, at about 2,000. Big supermarkets stock 40,000. Lidl offers more branded items than Aldi, at 330[281].
- Both offer pleasant shopping experiences in the UK[282].
- Choice, and hence decision-making, is reduced. The last thing you want after a hard week at work is more decisions to make. Like IKEA, Lidl and Aldi *flow* you around their stores and, when you want something there's only one of it to *choose* from.
- All three shops have efficiency at their core. From the cracking small shopping trolleys at Lidl, to the almost-identical layout of each UK store, to the fact you never have to queue for more than a minute. The till operators are paid well and are empowered. For instance, in Lidl, when they see signs of a queue they press a button that plays a voice message over the Tannoy asking a colleague to come and open "till three please". The LAHs' checkout

operators also have an approach to scanning of which Quick Draw McGraw[283] would be proud.

- A trip to The LAHs works much better with a weekly main meal food plan – we sit down every Friday evening and spend five minutes on it. We also keep a double-thickness sheet of A4 and marker pen on the kitchen table – if we run out of anything during the week we make sure I buy it at the weekend when I go and see The LAHs.

- Lidl and Aldi rotate the vegetables they discount every week. Once you become a more proficient and efficient cook, you can tailor your meal constituents to the discounted fresh vegetables. And the vegetables: they are always fresh.

- Lidl sometimes holds "super weekends". We stock up on red wine, prosecco, laundry liquid and heavy-duty refuse sacks. For instance, we've just bagged 12 bottles of rather good 2011 Tarragona *gran reserva* for £2.99 a pop.

- The wine choice is good at Lidl and Aldi, with many award-winners[284].

- If you're pushed for time and can't visit all of The LAHs, choose either Lidl or Aldi. I've noticed that they charge the same price on many everyday foodstuffs, so you can't go wrong with either. If pushed, pick Lidl because of the in-store bakery and the fact it stocks Marmite. That said, visiting all three is the ideal for cost-effectiveness and variety: buying the same items from the same shop with a blessedly limited product range can become boring.

- They're everywhere. Off to France for your summer holiday? I'll wager there's a LA nearby. In the US[285], they're expanding rapidly. In the UK, there are more than 700 Lidls[286] and approaching 800 Aldis[287]. And on my yearly trips to Berlin, they're on practically every street corner, as you'd expect from supermarkets of German origin.

- Both Aldi and Lidl have robust ethical sourcing strategies and expect good working conditions for their suppliers and staff, with commitments laid out on their respective websites[288].

- Home Bargains is great for greetings cards, kids' presents and the odd item such as Nespresso-compatible coffee pods, often £1 for ten compared with 30p a pod from Nespresso and 17p a pod in Lidl or Aldi. B&M Bargains[289] is also good. Unfortunately, there's not one near my LAHs, so a B&M trip is a rarity for the Family Sawyer.

I sincerely hope you follow the way of the switched-on middle-class midlifer[290], ditch your natural inclination not to be seen dead in a discount food store and change the way you eat and shop. There's nothing I like better than returning home having saved £70 on the weekly shopping by spending an hour on a Saturday morning treating my family to nutritious goodness...courtesy of The LAHs. With a £300-a-month saving, fantastic food and an efficient, hassle-free shopping experience on offer, why would you choose anywhere else?

Action

Go and see The LAHs. Keep the receipts. Compare the prices of what you want to buy at each. Devise your most efficient LAHs route. Resist the urge to spend the money you're saving on their super-tasty premium ranges. Plan your weekly shop. Learn how to cook a range of easy, fast, nutritious meals using the same ingredients such as olive oil, free range frozen chicken, bacon and fish, lots of fresh veg, spices and pulses. The One Pound [per person] Meals[291] cookbooks by Miguel Barclay are a good place to start.

And the rest of those savings?

That's The LAHs. What about the other £600 a month? Bollocks purchases had to go. For instance, did you know that the cost of a four-dollar-a-day coffee habit over 20 years is $51,833.79[292]? When we had a look through the line items in our budgeting spreadsheet, it made our eyes bleed. Every-day lattes, two café-meals-out (for four) and a takeaway every week – often when we didn't have anything in the house – kids' treats, Clarins products. It soon adds up. We saved at least £200 a month on these items alone.

I changed my working hours to 06:00–14:30 with an hour or two snatched here and there later. Now we don't need childcare because one or other of us can take the kids to school or pick them up. All it takes is a weekly planning meeting and flexibility. The result: no childcare costs and more time with the kids.

Instead of commuting to the city every day, I work from the office space at the health club we were already paying for, saving money on petrol and office costs and upping my real hourly wage.

Renegotiating the *yearlies* was a chore but worth it as we reduced cost and increased cover. Calendar reminders are set to appear well before the yearly premium-due-date so we can rinse and repeat.

The result

My family are healthier, happier and all the better for it. And that £900? Well, we increased our holiday budget by £100 a month – holidays are fun and this allows us to go away for six weeks a year, not five. The other £800 saving, we added to our monthly, automated investment.

That investment, and the positive effect of the changes we have made, are bang in line with our purpose: **"Achieve a stash of £855,000 [in 2018 money] before the age of 60 through living a good and meaningful life that matters to us."**

Redoing your budget

There's administration involved in the Efficiency *RESET*. Contracts to renegotiate, call waiting systems to navigate, new processes to get used to. But after a few months it'll calm down and you'll see if your back-of-a-fag-packet savings calculations and good intentions come true.

You'll know this by looking at your cloud budgeting software, where you've recorded every single item you have spent money on over the past three months. And you'll have worked out the line items you need to keep a good eye on, such as the food and household shopping. *Now for the fun bit.*

Once you're sure you can stick to those grandiose plans, earnestly discussed over a glass of wine with your partner that momentous Saturday night three months ago, that's when you can go into your budgeting spreadsheet, amend the figures and run the numbers. Remember, your first shot at the spreadsheet was based on what you were spending over the past year *before* you decided to reset your family's finances. This is the new you and now you're confident you can stick to it you can start reaping the benefits.

Type the subcategory numbers into your spreadsheet, look at every single line item and estimate a new budget for each one. (Save a new copy of the spreadsheet – so you have a record of the old financial you.) Then click the tab (in Martin Lewis's "Budget Planner" spreadsheet it's called *Check Your Results*) that tells you how much these changes are saving you every month. This is the moment you've been waiting for – the moment of truth. What you now do with this extra money will dictate when you achieve FIRE. And that's where Section 3 of the **FIRE Triumvirate** comes in. In Section 3 (Investing) of Part IV you'll get a simple plan suggesting how to invest your hard-earned savings, and a comprehensive explanation of why.

Action
Go back to your budgeting tools and update them with the new figures. Prepare to swoon. Make sure you update the budget categories in your cloud-based budgeting software as well.

But first this...

> People don't need enormous cars, they need respect. They don't need closets full of clothes, they need to feel attractive and they need excitement and variety and beauty. People don't need electronic equipment; they need something worthwhile to do with their lives. People need identity, community, challenge, acknowledgement, love, and joy[293].
> **Donella Meadows, *Beyond the Limits***

Before we go on to what to do with your newfound wealth, I'll share some of the **principles, the why**, behind this new frugal approach, which could seem alien to you at first.

Without an understanding of the ideas behind this new efficient you, an early retirement 15 long years away – whatever the clarity of your FIRE vision – may not provide enough motivation when the going gets tough.

I will then suggest **bonus tactics** you should consider, in addition to those in the Sawyers' Efficiency *RESET* above, to speed your journey to financial independence.

Principles

Once you appreciate FIRE, you'll spot inefficiency everywhere. You'll look at people driving fancy cars with wry amusement. You'll marvel at friends who buy their weekly shop from Waitrose and your ears will boggle when you hear of people spending an hour driving 50 miles to and from work every day.

It'll feel like you're the only one who "gets it" and you'll wonder why everyone else's world is revolving on a different axis to yours. Especially if you live in the UK where no one's heard of financial independence and most people associate early retirement with *The Good Life*[294].

Here are the principles that guide this amazing approach to life. They'll help you, as we northern soulers say, "Keep the faith[295]."

1. **Every little helps.** Small actions taken daily produce big results in the long run. Don't let money slither through your fingers like egg whites. As Mr. Money Mustache writes: "A millionaire is made ten bucks at a time[296]."
2. **Beware status cocaine**[297]. Don't try to keep up with the Joneses: they're a miserable bunch who smile in public and cry at home. People display their wealth because it's not socially acceptable to have a fight once you've left school. Stop wasting thousands a year trying to impress other people. Remember: it's the size of your stash that counts, *not* the size of your car.

3. **Reject consumerism.** It's not what you own but who you are, what you achieve, that counts.
4. **Don't confuse needs with wants.** Watch out for that unfulfilling pleasure-happiness, itching to lead you astray. Delay that un-satisfying dirty dopamine hit for the clean virtues of a mean-ingful life.
5. **Be efficient in everything you do.** I have boring routines. I use the same locker at the health club every day, shower in the same cubicle and could tell you where every item is in my house, down to the last screw. Paradoxically, this leaves my mind clear to focus on what matters.
6. **You'll have the last laugh**. I imagine even Pete Adeney, before his ascent to FI superstardom, used to receive the occasional funny look when he turned up at his local food store on a bike with a trailer attached to the back, having learned that cycling was the most efficient means of transport when travelling distances of fewer than five miles. And I know that if you pour top-quality olive oil on to your toast every morning because you like the taste (and olive oil is ounce for ounce the most cost-effective calorie-giving foodstuff), even your family may think you're a bit weird. But hey, who cares? And it's worth bearing in mind – you'll have the last laugh.
7. **Set your own goals and measure against yourself, not others**. Don't take your self-esteem from your job. Try different yard-sticks, more in tune with the new efficient you.
8. **Don't outsource your life.** It costs money and, in most cases, it just takes you away from what's important, so you can spend more time working.
9. **Don't borrow money.** If you have debt, aside from your mort-gage, pay it off first before you do anything else.
10. **Disaster fund.** Build an instant access disaster fund (enough to cover six months of living expenses).
11. **Maximise your savings rate.** There's much chat in the FIRE community about what savings rate you should target. What percentage of your after-tax income should you save every month? *The Richest Man in Babylon* suggests 10%; JL Collins,

50%[298]. It doesn't matter. All that matters is how much you need to live on when you retire and how much you stick away every month. As a guide, I know that 25% is neither unachievable nor deleterious for my family.

12. **Enjoy the journey.** No one's suggesting you don a hair shirt, self-flagellate and live a monk-like existence until you retire. Families on the road to financial independence are a lot happier than their non-FI counterparts. You've got to enjoy the journey – just look at the fun I have with The LAHs on a Saturday morning – and the more the FI game excites you, the faster you'll reach your own personal Shangri-La[299].

13. **Experiences.** When my kids are older, will they remember the thousands of pounds worth of plastic toys we bought them or the three-day wild camping trip last summer where we watched in awe as the Harry Potter train puffed its way past Camusdarach beach? Cost: £120 (including petrol), courtesy of Fort William Lidl.

14. **Master your Chimp**[300]. Don't let your emotions run the show. Favour evidence and rational thought over the black and white rushes to judgement and action. We're not still living in caves.

Bonus tactics

That's the principles behind financial independence. And you've read how my family performed our Efficiency *RESET* (the one I hope you're going to do as well). Now follows a list of bonus tactics you can use to increase your efficiency and speed up your journey to early retirement.

1. **Live close to your work.** Remember your real hourly wage? Your commute is the biggest drag on it. Living close to your work saves you money and buys you time, the most precious commodity of all. Drawing on research undertaken by Swiss economists Alois Stutzer and Bruno Frey, author and *Guardian* columnist Oliver Burkeman points to the commuter's "cognitive mistake": "people chronically underestimate the downsides of a

long commute, while overestimating the upsides of (say) a bigger house[301]." Don't be one of those people.

2. **Downsize your house.** Do you need all that space? The biggest drag on most families' household income is their mortgage. Downsizing has the added advantage of living next to new Joneses, with whom you'll have less trouble keeping up. Or, sell your house, invest the money (purchase price minus mortgage) and rent.

3. **Rent a room.** Don't want to downsize? In the UK, you can earn up to £7,500 a year tax-free[302] by renting out an unused room in your home. Not only an extra income but also a great way to meet new people from different cultures.

4. **Ditch the second car.** In 2008, Vicki Robin said: "Midway through the first decade of the twenty-first century, two-thirds of American households own two or more vehicles[303]." Do you need that second vehicle? With more planning, and use of public transport, your partner or you could sell the second motor and save a fortune in car-buying-and-running costs.

5. **Buy two- to three-year-old cars from a trusted dealer**[304]. This is the most cost-effective (time versus money) way of sourcing new vehicles. Get the black book cost, work out the depreciation, pop in and see your trusted dealer (always get a quote from elsewhere, too), deal with the senior sales person (the one you always deal with) and get the best price you can. That's what I do. Never lease; never contract hire. And never, ever, buy new.

6. **Learn new skills.** Rather than "get a man in", learn how to do it yourself. The biggest cost saving is learning how to cook. Your radiators break every two years whereas you have to cook every day (I know where I'd direct my efficiency efforts). If there's something you're no good at or don't fancy, at least learn the basics – so you can evaluate the professional you're outsourcing the work to.

7. **Be involved in your local community.** Aside from making you happier, this simple action will make you rich, too. For the suburban midlife professional, there isn't much in life that can't be enjoyed within a five-mile radius of his or her house. Go to

the park and play, visit friends, do the garden, join online community groups, volunteer at your kid's sports class. Not everything good in life costs money. As the *Beatles* once said, the best things in life are free.

8. **Replace high-cost hobbies with low-cost ones.** Run, take up crochet, join a walking group. Ditch the country/golf club membership and cancel Sky Sports; *Super Sunday* will survive just fine without your undivided attention every week.

9. **Barter/swap.** Yes, that's still a *thing.* If there's not a Facebook group dedicated to that in your local area, set one up.

10. **On yer bike.** It turns out, out of context, Norman Tebbit[305] was right – we should be getting on our bikes. For journeys under five miles, cycling is the most efficient form of transport[306]. Take, for instance, my health club. It's three miles from my house. It takes me 25 minutes to run there, 15 minutes to cycle and ten minutes by car. As opposed to taking the car or running there, cycling costs nothing. You never have to replace bike tyres, whereas I need new £100 running shoes every 500 miles, and short journeys are the root of all evil when it comes to car maintenance. Also, I get exercise, time to think and it brightens my day. I'd have a bike trailer to carry the food shopping if it weren't for the seven precipitous steps to our front door.

11. **Practise minimalism.** But spend good money on items you use, such as a frying pan, stockpot, or kitchen knife, for instance.

12. **Find good-value-and-quality shops/brands.** I've talked about The LAHs. Does it surprise you that we drive Skodas[307] and buy clothes at Decathlon[308]? I'm a big fan of quality reverse brands (they say what I don't stand for).

13. **One-month wish list.** If you want something, stick it on a one-month wish list. If you still want it after 30 days, research it and buy the quality version. Many times, you will find that the perceived need has evaporated.

14. **FIRE community.** I've never met anyone in the FIRE community. This is deliberate: I didn't want this book to be swayed by meeting my heroes; I wanted to plough my own furrow. Yet I couldn't have reset our financial future without the support of

these hundreds of people I read about but don't know. Hundreds of people enacting the same principles in their lives as we are in ours.

Do you see the potential?

Can you see the green fields now? Can you taste the air there?

The steps outlined in the Efficiency *RESET* are all choices you can make.

Sections 1 and 2 of the **FIRE Triumvirate** have shown that with initial hard work, plus adopting new ways of thinking and routines, you too can grasp the potential financial independence has to offer. For the first time, can you see how your early retirement is no longer a pipedream but a brilliant achievable vision?

Now for the super-interesting bit, what you're going to do with your newfound monthly moolah. In Section 3 of the **FIRE Triumvirate**, I reveal the secret weapon in your journey to early retirement. A simple, transparent, set-and-forget approach to investing that allows you to focus on what's important in life: being happier.

CHAPTER 30

Section 3: Investing (Options, Interest and the SWR)

IT'S TUESDAY FEBRUARY 7TH 2018. I'm writing this sentence after the bitcoin bubble has burst and our portfolio has dropped 7% in the space of a week. I have friends who have converted their defined contribution pensions to cash and are running for the hills. Panic reigns.

Yet I'm saying you should consider placing your life savings in the stock market. *Is he mad?* you're thinking.

In Section 3 of Part IV, you will see why what looks like folly is in fact perfectly sensible. We'll consider the other options for investing your money, look at the personal attributes and behaviours you'll need to stay the course and detail what steps you should take to turn theory into practice.

If you want the practical, the how, skip a few pages to the ten-point investing plan where you'll find a step-by-step guide to how I've invested our money and you could, too. But if you're anything like me a few years ago, without a bit of context, it'll be like reading Mandarin.

To get the most out of Section 3 of the **Fire Triumvirate**, you need to understand the *why* first. I'll keep this as simple as I can while answering your inevitable questions as we go along.

I can't wait to share this with you. It will blow your mind.

Quick recap

Before we explore the principles behind the *RESET* wealth-amassing method, let's recap.

First, you've gathered all your bits of financial information in one place. You know how much you have in each little pension, Isa, building society windfall account, long-lost uncle inheritance. You know how the different bits are invested. If monthly payments are going in, you know what they are, and you know what you need to do to get that money out. Likely, the paperwork is in piles on your bedroom floor, complete with Post-it notes.

Second, you're either confident you can stick to your new budget predictions or you're (preferably) a few months down the line and have proof-of-pudding.

Third, you've worked out when you want to retire early, and have a realistic monthly savings figure to achieve that aim.

All you need do now is decide how and where to invest it.

Hold that thought, have it in your mind as you read the rest of Part IV.

Over the next up-to-25 years, what's going to be the best way of making that money, that asset, work for you...efficiently?

The options

There will be midlife professionals reading this with a special interest or expertise in one or other of these options. *RESET* assumes you are not one of them.

RESET assumes you have enough going on in your life without taking the often years of daily actions required to become expert in some of these areas.

RESET assumes that you are busy enough without this extra burden and are looking for advice that is easy to carry out and non-memory-taxing.

So, let's say that your hard work in Sections 1 and 2 of the **FIRE Triumvirate** has led you to find an additional **£800** to invest every month. Remember, it's likely you have a defined contribution pension as well, the contribution to which forms a key part of your monthly savings target. We'll come to what to do with that later.

What are you going to do with that extra £800? Let's assess your options.

(The maths below assumes a rate of inflation of **3%**[309], a good conservative starting point for retirement planning. Why is allowing for the effects of inflation important? Because when you reach your stash goal in up to 25 years' time, you want it to have the same purchasing power as it does now[310].)

Option 1: stick it in a savings account

You could do this. It beats storing bank notes under your mattress. But what a risk. What a price to pay for cast-iron certainty. For the past ten years, UK savers have seen an average 2.25% return on their investment[311]. Meaning your stash would have dropped by 0.75% year-on-year[312]. A real (after-inflation) rate of return of **- 0.75%.**

Option 2: buy a bigger house

The historical return on investment on property is 3% a year[313]. Which means your investment is treading water: your real rate of return is **0%.**

Option 3: buy a house that needs doing up and sell it for a profit

I like this as an idea. In the UK, profits on property sales are free from capital gains tax and if you time the housing market right, big money can be made. Nevertheless, the learning curve is steep, skills need to be acquired and if you're living in the house you're doing up, your next year will not be an unstressful one. You're looking for an easy-to-implement system not a hard one. And for that reason, **this option is out.**

Option 4: rental income

We're getting warmer now. I have friends who buy properties in local areas they know, renovate, then rent them. Purchasing houses (when it doesn't involve the house you live in), together with the rental income it generates, can be a good long-term play. But it ain't passive. You have to build years of experience in property investment, do the administration, attend to the repairs, collect the rent; it's hard work that takes a lot of trial and error to master. On that basis, **I can't recommend it.**

Option 5: pay down your mortgage

I'm not going to lie: most of my life, this always seemed the safe and sensible option to me. And it may become the best investment you can make, in the future[314]. But for the past five years, this would have been an inadvisable course to take. To pluck a year at random, in 2017, the average five-year fixed mortgage rate hovered at about **2%**[315]. That's a real rate of return of **-1%.**

Option 6: invest in the stock market

Over the long-term, ten years-plus, the stock market is *the* best place to put your money. The average market return in the US and UK (with dividends reinvested), historically, is a staggering **9–10% (let's say 9% to be on the safe side**[316]**).** That's an after-inflation rate of return (with dividends reinvested) of between **6 and 7% (let's say 6% to be on the safe side**[317]**).**

Action

Let's look at option six in more detail.

The life-changing magic of compound interest

In retirement planning, percentages matter. Hell, tenths of percentages matter. When it comes to growing your stash, year in year out, the difference between a savings account returning even an impressive (in 2018) 3% and an investment portfolio averaging 9% a year is eye-watering.

It's obvious but doubly so when you consider the life-changing magic of compound interest.

US investor Warren Buffett likens compound interest to a snowball that gathers more snow as it rolls down a hill. It's interest earned on interest. And the longer it rolls down the hill the bigger it becomes.

An illustration

Let's run some numbers, using the Baxters, our one-kid **35-year-old** couple with an existing stash of £100,000.

Let's assume they ditch the planned £1k-a-month savings plan and just rely on the growth of their £100k to finance their retirement.

- If they invested their £100k in a savings account paying 3%, by the time they were 50 they'd have £155,796. If they invested their money at 8.5% (allowing for a maximum – under *RESET* – 0.5% investment charge during the wealth-amassing period), they'd have a cool £339,974. Not enough to retire on, especially after you've taken into account the ravages of inflation.
- Now try that over a 25-year period. Here the magic starts to happen. That savings account will have returned £209,377 now, doubling the Baxters' money. But if they'd invested it, they'd have £768,766, over three-quarters of a million pounds. Even in 2033 money, a sum not to be sniffed at[318].

What happens if we add the Baxters' £1k a month (including the government pension top-up[319]) on to that £100k existing stash?

- Over 15 years, a 3% rate of return will see the Baxters amass £385,679. At 8.5%, they'd have £707,538.

- Over 25 years, a 3% rate of return will leave them with £660,014, whereas 8.5% will see John and Yvonne turn 60 with a tidy stash of £1.792m.

Beginning to see why this stock market malarkey makes sense?

The huge complicated elephant in the room

Let's recap the maths because it's super-important to understand all this before we talk about investing in general. To make the best use of those hundreds of pounds you've saved, the *RESET* path to financial independence is based on investing in the stock market. It predicts long-term investors (10–15 years and over) will generate average stock market returns (assuming dividends reinvested) of 9%. It allows for 3% inflation. It assumes investment charges of 0.5% during the wealth-amassing period of your life, and 0.3% after you've reached FIRE[320]. Surely, under *RESET*, it's safe to withdraw 5.7% a year from your stash once you retire? (Based on 9% return minus 3% inflation minus 0.3% charge.)

Why then does *RESET* suggest a 3.5% safe withdrawal rate or SWR (the percentage of your stash you can live on every year after retiring early without your money running out)? Why such a conservative approach? What effect does this have on our pre-FI lives? And why is this important right now?

Why this is important now

Your safe withdrawal rate (SWR) – that elephant – is fundamental to your retirement planning. Let's flick back to **STEP B** where we worked out that to live on **£28,740** a year we'd need **£30,000 a year in 2018 money before-tax.** Here's the equation we used:

$$\text{Gross FIRE spending a year} \times 28.5^{321} = \text{target stash.}$$
$$\text{Or}$$
$$£30,000 \times 28.5 = £855,000.$$

Examine that 28.5 figure (take a look in the Notes).

The small print reveals the 28.5 figure is based on a 3.5% **SWR** (100 divided by 3.5). Now let's run that equation again, this time with a SWR of 5.7%.

Gross FIRE spending a year x **17.54** = target stash.
Or
£30,000 x 17.54 = **£526,200.**

That's a whole lot less money to amass. Now let's try that 5.7% SWR with our three couples:

The Baxters (age 35, £100k existing stash, saving and investing £1k per calendar month [pcm])

- SWR 3.5%: it will take them 22 years and five months until they hit their target stash of £855,000. They'll be **57.**
- SWR 5.7%: it will take them 15 years and eight months until they hit their target stash of £526,200. They'll be **50.**

The Dobsons (age 40, £250k existing stash, saving and investing £1,500 pcm)

- SWR 3.5%: it will take them 13 years and three months until they hit their target stash of £855,000. They'll be **53.**
- SWR 5.7%: it will take them seven years and two months until they hit their target stash of £526,200. They'll be **47.**

The Aggarwals (age 50, £200k existing stash, saving and investing £2,000 pcm)

- SWR 3.5%: it will take them 13 years exactly until they hit their target stash of £855,000. They'll be **63.**

- SWR 5.7%: it will take them seven years and seven months until they hit their target stash of £526,200. They'll be **57.**

Can you see why the SWR matters to how you plan your retirement? It dictates how many years you need to work to be sure you can live off your stash after you retire.

Can't we just use 5.7% and retire six or seven years earlier?

Now for the science bit. It turns out at first glance even 5.7% is a conservative estimate: that 0.3% charge you'll pay for managing your investments when you reach financial independence only costs you 0.12% in SWR terms[322]. So most of the time, using *RESET*, you'd get away with a 5.88% (six minus 0.12) withdrawal rate.

Over 30 years, real returns with dividends reinvested average out at 6.5% in the US. (*RESET* favours 6% to allow for the reduction in investment performance for a globally diversified UK-weighted investment portfolio by a UK citizen.)

But what happens if you're unlucky enough to retire just before a market correction, crash, or even the sort of 1929 stock market carnage that kicked off the Depression of the 1930s?

Here, I'll hand you over to Michael Kitces, speaking on financial blogger Mad Fientist's podcast:

> *If we just plug in long-term market returns [in the US], you find that the safe withdrawal rates based on average returns should be about 6.5%. And actually, if you just work out all the historical withdrawal rates that would have worked on average, you find that's [in the US] about 6.5%. So, in this world where, on average, 6.5% works, but we have to take out 4% just to defend against the bad luck that we could be on the eve of the next great economic catastrophe and we might happen to be like that 1929 retiree or that 1966 retiree or one of those horrible scenarios, the few that crop up, we take 6.5% all the way down to 4%. But we're still only doing it because*

once every 30 years, we manage to do something that's so
horrible to our economy that we need 10 to 15 years to
recover, and then the good returns finally show up. And once
the good returns show up, the bull market that eventually
shows up is so good, it pretty easily carries you to the end[323].

Aha, got it now. The 4% SWR allows for **worst-case scenarios.** For example, what would have happened if you retired from work in 1929 (the start of the Depression), the bear market of 1966, or the 1973 oil crisis. And even then, over 30 years, drawing 4% from your stash year after year would not have seen your money run out.

Kitces, a recognised world expert who speaks at between 50 and 70 conferences a year on this topic, draws on the work of William Bengen, the person credited with inventing the 4% safe withdrawal rate, after publishing his landmark 1994 paper "Determining Withdrawal Rates Using Historical Data[324]". He also cites the famous 1998 Trinity Study[325] by three professors of finance at Trinity University, Texas, using the same research and coming to broadly the same conclusions, the updated results of which you can find by googling "The Trinity Study And Portfolio Success Rates (Updated To 2018[326])".

His most interesting findings centre on what affects withdrawal rates during the worst-case scenarios (eg, retiring in 1929, 1965–1966, 1973). It turns out the key to it all, and what brings the SWR down to 4%, is the first ten years of retirement. But even if you're unlucky enough to retire at a stock market peak followed by poor investment returns for an entire decade, **in this case**, as Kitces states: "what we find is 4% just seems to be a number that's low enough that, even if you start when valuations are high, and risk is elevated, or returns are likely low, and then you add a whole bunch of bad stuff on top, the withdrawal rate is moderate enough that you can still make it to the good returns[327]." Latest figures based on the performance of US bonds and stocks between 1926 and 2017 back this up, showing that 100% of the time a Safe Withdrawal Rate of 4% would have seen your stash last you the full 30 years[328]. And what about **most of the cases?** Kitces again:

Nonetheless, even on a real (inflation-adjusted) basis, retirees finish with more than 100% of their inflation-adjusted principal 60% of the time, and double their real wealth almost 1/4th of the time, even after supporting a lifetime of inflation-adjusted spending at a 4% initial withdrawal rate![329].

Last, some of Kitces's associates even argue that we can raise the SWR to 4.5% to take into account research that finds people's spending in retirement drops as the years go by[330].

Why 3.5%?

The problem with this research (and the idea of a foolproof SWR of 4%) is that it's based on US stock market returns, a fact not lost on our hero, Dr Wade D. Pfau, CFA®, professor of retirement income at The American College of Financial Services and ex-co-editor of the *Journal of Personal Finance.*

Wade and Kitces know each other, they comment on each other's blogs. They each offer sound advice, backed up by research, cracking data and analysis. They both seem obsessed with the safe withdrawal rate, and if we're going to plan our financial futures around this fundamental concept, we want to listen to the most obsessed, passionate and cited guys in the room.

Although Kitces, Bengen, the Trinity professors, Adeney and Collins focus on the US, Wade takes a more international perspective. And he finds that the 4% SWR may hold true for US investors, but the picture isn't as rosy for their European counterparts. Because for the past hundred years, the US has been the global economic powerhouse with the most efficient stock market, so investors have got higher returns.

The Oracle of Pfau

So, if you're based in the US, you're going to die within 30 years, and your asset allocation is anything between 50/50 bonds/stocks and 100% stocks, you're almost on to a sure thing. I would 100% plan for an SWR of 4%. There's no way I'm arguing with Pete Adeney, JL Collins and Michael Kitces.

However, if you live somewhere else, you need to consult the Oracle of Pfau, by googling "Does The 4% Rule Work Around The World[331]?" When we delve deep into Pfau's research, we discover that the UK SWR for a 100% equity portfolio in retirement is about 3.64%, assuming you're 100% invested in *UK* equities. While a 100% equity portfolio in retirement offers the best returns over time, it also creates the most risk.

So what would happen if after achieving FIRE we switched our 100% equity allocation to 80% equities and 20% bonds (less return but fewer losses if the market falls in our first few years of retirement)? In fact, it turns out that was the ideal SWR allocation[332] in the UK for the period 1900–2015, giving a safe withdrawal rate of **3.77%.** Less risk for a better SWR: don't mind if I do.

Further analysis reveals even on a 50/50 bond/equity portfolio[333], a UK resident investing in global stocks (including UK) instead of 100% domestic stocks would increase their SWR by 0.21%[334]. Now our 30-year SWR is up at an altogether healthier 3.98%.

How do you get to 3.5%?

Well, first subtract the *effect* (remember: the 0.12%) of that investment charge you'd be paying in retirement and we're down at 3.86%[335].

Now let's say you either retire super-early (say 50) or live super-long (into your nineties). What if you need your stash to last 40 years instead of 30? Kitces suggests, in this scenario (40–45 years-plus), allowing for a 3.5% withdrawal rate and that if you live longer than that, the SWR stays broadly the same[336].

SWR summary

In summary, making conservative assumptions, based on someone **living in the UK with a diversified global portfolio 80% invested in**

equities, 20% in bonds, the figure *RESET* is suggesting for an early retirement of up to 35 years, is a **safe withdrawal rate (SWR) of...**

3.5%.

(If you live elsewhere in the world, you can follow the bread-crumb trail in this chapter and devise your own SWR – Pfau's international research looks at SWRs across 20 countries, including the US.)

Do I need to know this right now?

Well, yes and no.

Yes it matters because this is your life we're talking about and it helps if we get the maths right. You need a reliable figure right this minute, so you can start saving and investing, and know (to the nearest month) when you'll achieve your FI. And you need to have the confidence that this figure covers you for even the direst worst-case scenario.

Most people will agree 3.5% is a conservative SWR, especially for a normal 30-year retirement. Many would say too conservative. However, I'd rather be erring on the side of caution when making decisions about money. Better to be safe than sorry, don't you think? **No**, it doesn't, for these reasons:

- You can only go on what has happened in the past for predicting what happens in the future. Use 3.5% as an expertly researched planning guide if you're based in the UK. It's not the be-all and end-all and you may decide to pick anything between 3% and 6.5% depending on where you live and your risk tolerance. All I ask is do your research first, pick a number and reassess every year; the blog *Early Retirement Now* has a 23-part series on the topic, a good place to start[337].
- We've already identified that the biggest factor in *your* SWR is the first ten years after you achieve your stash target. If you

reach ten years of financial independence with half or more of your stash intact you're in clover. No one can predict how those first ten years are going to pan out and I feel sure that when the time comes, you'll be right across "sequence of return risk[338]" (those first ten years of FI). For now until you near financial independence, all you need to know is that it exists.

- Religiously relying on your SWR once you gain financial independence assumes you're an idiot with no control over anything post-FIRE. In practice, you're a hyper-efficient financial independent who reset their life all those years ago – after reading *that* book – and never looked back. If *you* retire, the market dives and your stash with it, you have choices. Are you going to just sit there and watch as your life savings go down the swanny? Or are you going to spend less, take a part-time job, or find other income to supplement your stash?

- All this assumes you won't inherit any money, you won't receive social security and you won't do what most of us do – spend less with age.

Action

In summary, if you embrace RESET and keep your wits about you after you start living off your stash, using 3.5% as an SWR is as near a golden ticket for financial independence planning you'll see without setting foot in a chocolate factory.

CHAPTER 31

Section 3: Investing (Wise Words & the Case for Indexing)

UNLESS YOU HAVE A degree or above in mathematics/financial modelling, you will be glad to see the back of the safe withdrawal rate: I promise not to mention it again.

Before I tell you how you can invest that defined contribution pension and the **extra £800 a month** we're saying you found during your family's budgeting and Efficiency *RESET*, let's take a quick look at the stock market.

First, three definitions:

1. A **stock** is a type of security that signifies ownership in a corporation and represents a claim on part of the corporation's assets and earnings.
2. **Bonds** are loans made to large organisations. These include corporations, cities and national governments. A bond is a piece of a big loan.
3. **Mutual funds** are baskets of stocks. They give more diversification than individual stocks. Humans can manage them or they can be set to track an index, such as the FTSE 100 in the UK or S&P 500 in the US.

We know that the stock market is the most powerful passive wealth-amassing tool on the planet, ideal for us time-pressed midlife professionals. And we've also seen (by looking at the Baxters, Dobsons and Aggarwals) that it's never too late to start. But what do we need to know before we consider trusting our life savings to something we don't understand?

Here are the six things you need to bear in mind when investing in the stock market:

1. Don't base your stash on individual stocks

Few people can pick winning stocks over the long-term. Those who do have spent years reading, investing and making costly mistakes along the way. And have surnames such as Buffett.

Here's Harold Pollack, a professor at the University of Chicago: "This is a completely easy one. There's just a ton of literature that suggests that people chase after shiny objects and the stocks that we buy aren't particularly well-chosen. The stocks that we sell, we're often selling them at the wrong times. Why do you want to get into that[339]?"

Or how about the customer audit by the giant and well-respected multinational investment firm Fidelity, which found that its most successful customers were either inactive or dead[340].

Don't be tempted to base your portfolio on a basket of individual stocks. *It's risky and not what even investing geniuses such as Warren Buffett would tell you to do.*

2. Don't trust the experts

Unless they're gods like Ed Thorp.

Empirical studies find that if you want to make money out of the stock market, do not listen to stock market analysts[341].

As Jim Collins writes in *The Simple Path to Wealth*: "what the media wants from these commentators is drama. Nobody is going to sit glued to their TV while some rational person talks about long-term investing[342]."

Investor and author of *Beat the Dealer*, Ed Thorp, agrees: "Most stock-picking stories, advice and recommendations are completely worthless[343]."

3. Don't try to time the market

To be successful, you need to call the market high and the market low over and over again. Without a time machine, it's impossible. You might try, but you'll end up either missing out on gains or losing your shirt.

Here are some statistics you may find interesting, based on the performance of the S&P 500 index in the US:

- Eighty per cent of corrections (drops of between ten and 20%) don't turn into bear markets (drops of 20%-plus). Only one in five do.
- Since 1900, market corrections have happened, on average, once a year.
- The average correction has seen the market drop 13.5% and lasted 54 days.
- In the average bear market, the S&P 500 index drops 33%. In a third of cases, it drops by more than 40%.
- Over the past 70 years, the average US bear market has lasted a year.
- Over the past two decades, there's been about an 8.2% compounded annual return for the S&P 500, according to the Schwab Center for Financial Research. But if you missed the ten best trading days in that 20-year period, your returns drop to 4.5%, because you miss the magic of compound interest[344].

And the moral of these stats? Selling when everyone's panicking is a recipe for disaster when investing. You only have a one in five chance that you're calling that bear market, and even if you're that lucky one in five, how do you decide when to get back in? But what about those icky bear markets? The really bad ones. Let me introduce 89-year-old Jack Bogle, the person who's done more for the average investor than anyone alive today: "When we get one of these percent declines, I've faced three of them in my career. It's not fun. I get a knot in my stomach," he said. "A lifetime of experience, 65 years of experience in this field, has taught me that emotions are evil and therefore you really ought to fight to keep them out of the equation. Because the day you are most concerned is the day the market hits bottom and that's the day you want to get out. The day you will want to get in is when the market hits a new high. Well, believe me, buying in at the market's new high and selling out at the market's bottom is a very difficult way to make money[345]."

Never try to time the market, however sick-making the lows.

4. Don't let your heart rule your head

You must be impervious to fear.

UK investor and blogger Monevator says: "Our brains are wired against us when it comes to investing. Greed makes us want the hot asset class just as the bubble is about to burst. Fear makes us panic and sell when the market falls, guaranteeing losses. It's human nature. We're a bundle of impulses waiting to run amok[346]."

Even under *RESET*, sometimes your portfolio will drop ten, 20, even 50%. If you can't handle that, and would change course were it to happen, stock market investing may not be for you. (Google "Risk Tolerance Calculator".)

I wouldn't blame you. There's oodles of research showing that the Chimp side of our nature is unsuited to the vicissitudes of the stock market. Nobel prize for economics-winning economists such as Robert Shiller have found that: "Put concisely – it's actually much smarter to admit that you aren't perfectly rational, and to plan and invest accordingly, rather than deny your true nature[347]."

Read up on risk tolerance, take into account *your* circumstances, work out your goals and timings based on how old you are, and see what you can afford to lose. Know thyself. But most of all, don't let your emotions guide your investments: be a rational investor.

5. Invest for the long-term

Think of the past 46 years since I was born in 1972. There's: the recession of 1973–1975; inflation of the late 1970s; the crash in 1987, including Black Monday, the biggest one-day drop in history; the recession of the early '90s; the tech bubble of the late '90s; 9/11; and the 2008–2009 financial crisis. None was good for the markets. But during that time, the Dow Jones has risen from 1,000 to its present 25,108 while the FTSE All Share Index has moved from 218.18 to its current 4,225 (gains of 2,411% and 1,836%[348]).

While there are exceptions (the freak case of Japan since 1989, for instance), typically whenever stock markets have crashed, they've recovered. Always in the US and UK.

This is why (as we'll see later in Part IV), wherever you live in the world, you need to form an internationally diversified portfolio, keep your emotions in check and be in it for the long-term.

6. Good if it goes up, good if it goes down

It's easy looking at the long-term when times are good. But what about when you're mired in the daily 2% hits to your life savings that are commonplace when the market gets the jitters?

I've spoken to scores of people and observed thousands putting these principles into practice, but it's the thoughts of leaders such as Ed Thorp and Warren Buffett that keep me grounded.

Said Thorp: "People say, 'Gee, what if your Berkshire [Hathaway B, Warren Buffett's investment vehicle] goes down?' I say, 'Oh, that's good because now I can buy more'" They say, 'But what if it goes up?' I say, 'Well, that's good too because I feel good because I feel suddenly richer.' So let it go up or let it go down. I don't care[349]."

Said Buffett: "This is the one thing I can never understand. To refer to a personal taste of mine, I'm going to buy hamburgers the rest of my life. When hamburgers go down in price, we sing the 'Hallelujah Chorus' in the Buffett household. When hamburgers go up, we weep. For most people, it's the same way with everything in life they will be buying – except stocks. When stocks go down and you can get more for your money, people don't like them anymore[350]."

Buy the same amount when they're going up as when they're going down. Either way, you're on to a winner.

Action

If you do believe there's more to life than this – that you are the captain of your fate – then a financial independence plan with stock market investing at its core is what RESET suggests. All you need do is settle on a strategy and stick to it.

Mutual funds: actively managed

So, without further ado, let's move on to the *Stakhanovite* workhorse and secret weapon of the *RESET* investing plan: the humble mutual fund. There are two types of mutual funds: actively managed and passively managed. Let's take actively managed first.

When most people refer to "mutual funds" or "unit trusts" or "OEICs", they are talking about ones that are actively managed.

Actively managed funds have these characteristics:

- They are managed by star fund managers, individuals with sometimes-excellent records of generating better-than-average returns on your investment.
- Their aim is to beat the market.
- Investopedia has the average equity fund management fee at between 1.3% and 1.5%[351]. (You are paying for the expertise of your star fund manager.)
- On top of that, they sometimes charge you for the initial fund purchase and for selling parts (units) of your investment.
- And on top of *that*, in common with most investments, you will pay an account fee: the administration charge levied by a financial provider such as Vanguard or Fidelity for investing through their online service.

Until the past few years, actively managed funds were in the ascendancy, and still they remain the default setting for most individual investors and pension funds. For instance, more than 2,000 actively managed funds but fewer than 100 passive funds are listed by the Investment Association. Still, a whopping 71%[352] of US mutual fund investors choose to follow the actively managed route.

If you have to invest in active funds – for instance, your money is in a work pension with no good index fund option – try to pick one with low expenses and high ownership by the fund manager. If you don't *have* to, here are four compelling reasons why you must avoid actively managed funds like a plague of midges in a Highland glen on a windless, sunny day:

- **Few beat the market.** You're statistically more likely to lose than gain on an "average market return" (eg, tracking an index). Research released by Vanguard in 2013 tracked the 1,540 actively managed equity funds that existed in 1998 for the next 15 years. Only 55% of these funds made it to 2013 and only 18% survived and beat the index: a staggering 82% didn't[353]. Other research studies across different countries and periods come to a similar conclusion. If you're a believer in making big decisions on evidence, avoid actively managed funds.
- **We've already discussed that when it comes to your entire portfolio, you shouldn't trust yourself with stock-picking, so why would you trust someone else?** What would possess you to trust your life savings to other human beings who, we know, are hard-wired *not* to make good investment decisions?
- **The cost.** Under *RESET*, our conservative long-term real rate of return (after fees) is 5.5%. If we allow for 2% fees rather than the maximum 0.5% *RESET* suggests in the wealth-amassing period, we're adding years on to our working lives and entrusting even that reduced rate of return to a human being with an 82% (see above) likelihood of reducing it even more.
- **Actively managed funds appeal to our worst instincts.** We love a gamble, we believe *we* can be lucky and we never want to feel like we're settling for average. Who wants average returns when

you can hit the jackpot? So we make investment decisions on Sunday newspaper supplement stock tips and fund managers' past returns, instead of analysing statistics like an economist or scientist would, and investing on facts.

They say

Bob French CFA is one of Wade Pfau's colleagues at Retirement Researcher: any friend of Wade's is a friend of ours. Here's what he has to say: "There is simply no way to consistently beat the market. Identifying the best active manager is akin to finding the best coin flipper[354]."

My hero Wade's mate's advice not good enough for you? How about the Nobel prize-winning economist, University of Chicago professor Eugene Fama, who said: "I'd compare stock pickers to astrologers, but I don't want to bad-mouth astrologers[355]." What about his son, Eugene Fama, Jr? He agrees broadly with Dad: "After taking risk into account, do more managers than you'd see by chance outperform with persistence? Virtually every economist who studied this question answers with a resounding 'no.'"

Or my personal favourite, from *Freakonomics*: "Bottom line: most people who pick stocks for a living do a worse job than a monkey with a dart board – and they charge you a lot more than a monkey would[356]."

Mutual funds: passively managed

No, you definitely don't want to invest in actively managed mutual funds. What you do want to do, what they don't teach you at school, what the world's greatest investors, economists and most of the financial independence community say, is build an investment portfolio with the humble, rational, simple-to-understand, heavy-lifting index fund at its heart. It's the secret weapon I've been itching to reveal since the start of Part IV.

Remember, you've followed **STEPS A-D**, embarked on your budgeting and efficiency odyssey and know how much extra you can save every month. You just need to know where to put it. In a moment, *RESET* will lay out a ten-point investing plan that every midlife professional can follow, wherever they live in the world.

First, let's have a quick look at index investing and discover why it's such a potent force.

Definition

Index funds and Exchange-Traded Funds[357] (ETFs) track stock market indexes such as the S&P 500 or the FTSE 100 or the Nikkei 225. When you own a FTSE 100 index-tracking fund, it's like owning a bit of every single company in that index, from AstraZeneca to Vodafone. As companies get bigger and smaller, new ones enter the FTSE 100 and old ones drop out. And so, the companies you own a bit of change, too.

Index funds mimic the performance of stock market indices. They do not try to beat the market.

Something new under the sun

In 1974, John (known affectionately as Jack) Bogle was fired from his position as chairman of fund management firm Wellington after approving a disastrous company merger.

In that same year the late Nobel prize-winning Massachusetts Institute of Technology (MIT) academic Paul Samuelson – seen by many as the most influential economist of the late 20th century[358] – published a paper in *The Journal of Portfolio Management* called "A Challenge to Judgment[359]".

In it, he challenged the performance of the active fund management business that had sprung up in the '50s and '60s and said: "At the least, some large foundation should set up an in-house portfolio that tracks the S&P 500 Index – if only for the purpose of setting up a naïve model against which their in-house gunslingers can measure their prowess."

Bogle, who was founding Vanguard at the time, read the paper and was inspired. And so, in 1976, the first index fund was born.

Bogle has turned on its head the received wisdom that active fund managers always beat the market. For many years, his fund – derided at first as "Bogle's Folly" – made him the laughing stock of the industry he'd worked in for 25 years since graduating from Princeton University in 1951. Now the 89-year-old is having the last laugh with that fund alone having $403bn[360] in assets and passive, index-tracking funds accounting for 29% of the entire US market[361].

In summary, a MIT professor's peer-reviewed research then a huge step into the unknown by one of the world's true visionaries sparked a passive investing snowball that has gathered momentum in the past five years.

What did Samuelson make of it all? Way before index investing took off, seven years before Mr. Money Mustache put finger to keyboard, and four years before his death in 2009, he had this to say: "I rank this Bogle invention along with the invention of the wheel, the alphabet, Gutenberg printing, and wine and cheese: a mutual fund that never made Bogle rich but elevated the long-term returns of the mutual-fund owners. Something new under the sun[362]."

Benefits

Nowadays every decent fund management firm offers index trackers. The choice is almost limitless. Bogle sparked a revolution, one that all midlife professionals can benefit from. Here's why you should be one of them:

- **Cost.** In contrast to their lauded cousins, the actively managed funds, index-tracking funds cost as little as 0.06% in the UK. Granted, some cost 0.5%, but that's when you're looking at specialist ones such as those tracking smaller companies. As we'll discover, you can build a globally diversified portfolio of index-tracking funds for a combined "ongoing charge" (OCF) of 0.08%. Compare that to the average 1.3–1.5% for actively managed funds and I know which I'd have in my portfolio.

- **Performance.** Study after study confirms that passive funds do better than actively managed ones. Eighty-two per cent of the time, according to Vanguard.
- **Time.** Once set, rebalance once a year. Compare that to the work involved in stock-picking, house-trading or generating rental income.
- **Rational?** As humans, we're irrational and not as smart as we think. Unless we're super-intelligent wise investment gods like Warren Buffett, we should keep well away from investment decisions. The market's not rational either, but it's a lot more rational than us[363].
- **Simplicity.** The type of indexing approach *RESET* is suggesting is set-and-forget. No dabbling. No peeking, and if you ever do catch a glimpse of the FTSE 100 or see it on the news, you'll know that that portion of your investment has gone up or down in line with the index. It also helps planning. All the financial calculations in **STEPS A-D** are based on *index* investing. If you choose the actively managed fund route, you could be one of the lucky 18% and beat the *index*, but, as we've discovered, there's a four in five chance you won't be.

Leading proponents

We're not talking a ragbag of back-bedroom bloggers. Proponents of index funds count among them some of the finest minds on the planet: Warren Buffett; Paul Samuelson; Eugene Fama; Jack Bogle; Pete Adeney; JL Collins; Harold Pollack; ex-star fund manager at Magellan, Peter Lynch; and Douglas Dial, ex-portfolio manager of the US's largest pension fund. Here's their two-penneth.

Buffett said, in his annual shareholder letter of 2013: "[When he dies] my advice to the trustee [of his estate, his wife] couldn't be simpler: Put 10% of the cash in short-term government bonds and 90% in a low-cost S&P 500 index fund. (I suggest Vanguard's.) I believe the trust's long-term results from this policy will be superior to those attained by most investors – whether pension funds, institutions or individuals – who employ high-fee managers[364]."

Renowned (actively managed) fund manager Peter Lynch[365] said: "Most individual investors would be better off in an index mutual fund[366]."

Douglas Dial, former portfolio manager of the CREF Stock Account Fund, the largest pension fund in America, said: "Indexing is a marvelous technique. I wasn't a true believer. I was simply an ignoramus. Now I am a convert. Indexing is an extraordinary sophisticated thing to do. If people want excitement, they should go to the racetrack or play the lottery[367]."

And let's leave the last word to celebrity news magazine *US Weekly*. President Trump's then press secretary Sean Spicer – remember him? – tweeted: "Getting government updates from @Washingtonian is like getting stock tips from @usweekly." Their response to the derisory message was as follows: "Thanks, Spicey! @usweekly does not recommend investing in individual stocks. Stick with a broad mix of low-cost index funds[368]."

Action

I rest my case. If you agree with me, and them, it's time to forget the theory and focus on practicalities. Concentrate your mind on putting all the hard work and learning into action by reading RESET's ten-point investing plan then taking responsibility for your future.

CHAPTER 32

Section 3: Investing (*RESET's* 10-Point Investing Plan)

AT THIS JUNCTURE, IT bears repeating that *RESET* is a book: I am not giving personalised financial advice to you, the reader, for a fee. Instead, you paid for the information in the book, you can do with it what you like, and I'm not responsible for the consequences. Onwards (with the ten points).

1. Pay off any debt

If you have any debts on which you're paying more than 5.5% a year interest, tackle them first. Depending on what year you read this, it's unlikely that will include student loans or your mortgage. Whether you choose to pay down the mortgage principal (money you owe as opposed to interest you're paying on the loan) is a personal decision. If you're paying anything under a 5.5% interest rate, I'd invest.

2. Your work pensions

Next up is your defined contribution work pension (if you have one). If you are salaried and in the UK, you will have one. (If you're lucky enough to have a defined benefit [final salary] scheme, we'll come to that right after we've finished this ten-point plan.)

Starting April 2018, UK employers must offer a workplace pension and pay in 2% of your salary while you need to pay in 3%. From April 2019, it's 3% and 5% respectively[369]. In practice, it's likely you and they are paying in more. Perhaps you are lucky enough to be contributing 6% of your salary while your employer is whacking in an extra 10%.

Most salaried midlife professionals go through life oblivious to their work pension. Their pension contribution is a mere footnote on their monthly payslip. Then, in their early fifties, comes the dawning realisation that they'd better read up on this thorny topic because that's what they're going to be living on for the rest of their lives.

The first thing you need to check – there's an argument for doing this before paying off your debt – is whether you are missing out on any free pension money from your employer.

Many people, when they're younger and more spendthrift, make a minimum pension contribution and don't take advantage of the employer match (the amount your employer contributes typically rises to a maximum in line with your contribution).

Because they don't understand pensions, they never up their own contribution as they rise through the ranks (particularly when the increased cost of kids comes along), losing out on tens of thousands of free employer pounds along the way.

Contact payroll

Contact your payroll department or your employer's defined contribution scheme provider to see if you're receiving the maximum employer contribution. Forget about the past, you can't change that; it's the future that matters.

If you're not receiving the maximum employer contribution, use however much you can of that, eg, monthly £800 you're saving to up *your* pension contribution, thereby unlocking the free money on offer from your employer. Contact payroll and make sure your contribution comes straight off your monthly pay packet before it's taxed. Check the effect this has on your take-home pay and work out what remains of that £800 to invest.

Rejig your investments

This is crucial for anyone who's worked for an organisation for a long time. If you're salaried, you're stuck with your employer's pension until you move on. That's because it makes no sense to transfer out/close your defined contribution pension if your employer is putting that free money into it. Why would you?

After you've maximised the employer match, you need to have a close look at how your money is invested (it's likely you ticked a box many moons ago and have forgotten about it).

Depending on your work pension, there'll be anything from little flexibility to lots, and charges will vary. But you know this because you've already done the telephone-call-legwork in **STEP C**.

I can say with 99% certainty that you won't have invested your work pension optimally. So here's what you need to do:

- Find out how it *is* invested.
- Find out the investment options within your work pension.
- Pick the least worst/best options closest to what *RESET* suggests in Point 7 below.
- Use common sense.
- If you ever leave your job, assuming no exit charges, transfer out into your Sipp, and invest the money how *you* want to.

For example, my wife is in the People's Pension through her work. She maximises the employer contribution. The overall charge is 0.5%. The People's Pension offers four investment options based on attitude to risk: adventurous, balanced, cautious and self-select. Everything bar the self-select option incorporates a 15-year glide path (decreasing your risk – and reducing your returns – gradually as you reach retirement).

We picked self-select (no glide path required thank you). Discounting cash, annuity, Shariah, ethical and pre-retirement, we were left with three global fund choices: up to 60% shares, up to 85% shares and up to 100% shares.

A bit of digging on fund-rating sites Trustnet[370] and Morningstar[371] revealed that although the actively managed 100% equity fund was more in tune with *RESET's* asset allocation and global diversification, the up to 85% shares actively managed fund had a much better long-term record and star rating, outperforming rather than underperforming its benchmark.

Yes, I'd much prefer to invest in a globally diversified passive 100% equity portfolio of my choosing, but if we have to put all my wife's eggs in one active fund basket, a well-rated 80% global equity/20% bond one with an all-in charge of 0.5% is an OK alternative.

3. Consolidate the mishmash

You've sorted your partner and you's work pensions. Great, that money's now working as hard as it can for you.

But what about those piles of other random investments and pensions, plastered with hundreds of Post-it notes, plonked in a huge pile on the spare bedroom floor? The fruit of those lengthy telephone conversations during those two long afternoons in **STEP C**?

Sorry, but it's time you wrestled that behemoth off the floor, tamed the beast and banished it to kingdom come, never to rear its ugly head again.

If you're anything like the average midlife professional, you'll have a bewildering array of random investments contained within pensions, Isas and elsewhere, including:

- Inheritances.
- Windfall shares.
- Building society windfalls.
- Privatisation shares.

- Shares bought at market peaks that seemed like a good idea at the time.
- With profits funds.
- Index trackers.
- Actively managed mutual funds.
- Random cheques sent to old addresses that you didn't know about (yes, really).
- Payment protection insurance (PPI) claim money.
- Money in funds you never invested in but were ported to another investment house when the fund closed down.
- Shares that are so bad they've lost you money. Who knew that was even possible?
- And – God forbid – cryptocurrencies.

And you know what you'll find when you go through **STEP C** and come out the other side?

- Most will be charging you too much for looking after your money.
- Yes, I did say *your* money.
- Many won't allow you to invest in the funds suggested by *RESET*.
- Having *your* money scattered across a bewildering array of different pots, with a bewildering array of different rules, and a bewildering array of online portals – when they exist – will make your head hurt.
- Most won't charge you a penny to withdraw your money or transfer it over to another provider.
- Even if it's not in a tax-advantaged account – unless you've either lucked out or invested a significant amount in the first place – you won't pay capital gains tax[372] if you cash in your individual shares. You won't pay *any* if you decide to keep the shares and stick them in an Isa[373].

So, what to do? It's simple, and you'll be kicking yourself for not realising this 20 years ago:

- You need to invest *your*, and your partner's, money in tax-advantaged accounts with one, or at most two, providers.
- You need to work out how much you both have in money you can't touch right now (pensions).
- You need to work out how much you have in money you can access instantly (usually Isas).
- You then need to work out how much you *need* access to quickly (usually Isas).

Unlike your current work pension where your choice is limited, you can invest this money wherever you want. Hell, even if it's in a pension, you can convert it to cash and stick it under the online mattress. You are not tied to any of these investments you've accumulated over the years. I'm not asking you to invest more of your mishmash in the stock market. Just get what already is there working harder.

It's *your* money. You're in control. It's time you took it.

4. Fidelity or Vanguard?

Whether you're in the US, UK or Timbuktu, Vanguard or Fidelity are your go-to money managers, if you're following the transformational process in *RESET*. Here's why:

- Both have easy-to-understand literature and low costs.
- Both have excellent websites.
- Both have excellent UK-based enthusiastic experts, based in Edinburgh and London, able to answer your queries by phone.
- Both have good fund choice for the suggested *RESET* portfolio. Fidelity shades it here with its access to funds from other providers whereas with Vanguard you can only buy Vanguard funds.
- Both have an excellent ethos. One is a co-operative[374], owned by its members (you), and set up by Jack Bogle; one a family firm that has embraced passive investing[375].

At time of going to press (late August 2018), if you're in the UK and using the *RESET* portfolio, choose Fidelity for your Sipps and Vanguard for your Isas. Here's why:

- Vanguard doesn't yet offer Sipps.
- Vanguard does offer Isas and is 0.16% cheaper – account fee + ongoing charge (OCF) – under the suggested *RESET* portfolio[376].
- If you want to go with one provider to **keep it simple**, choose Fidelity for now.

In 2019, Vanguard should have its Sipps up and running in the UK[377]. When this happens, move everything to Vanguard. Here's why:

- It's likely more of your money will be in pensions than Isas. You can only transfer out pensions to other pensions, in your case a Vanguard Sipp. A variance of 0.16% a year may be small beer when investing £10k in an Isa, but if we're talking ten or 20 or 30 times that amount in a Sipp, the difference in charges and lost compounding will soon add up.
- Vanguard is a co-operative. Owned by its members it has no incentive to, and cannot, turn a profit. Safe in that knowledge, you don't need to keep an eye on costs; you can set and forget.
- I feel I owe it to the mellifluous tones of Jack Bogle, founder of Vanguard, whose passive investing ethos runs through Vanguard like tree rings.

Action

As a UK investor, if you want a simple home for your money now, pick Fidelity[378]. Then port it over to Vanguard when Vanguard starts doing Sipps. It's easy to sign up to either provider, and transferring your existing investments is a mere online form, telephone conversation and two-to-three-week Fidelity-or-Vanguard-managed process away. For a little more hassle, pick Vanguard for Isas and Fidelity for Sipps, which gives you the bonus of assessing both companies and their excellent websites, and seeing which one you prefer.

5. Isas or Sipps?

Sorry again, US readers and those elsewhere, for all this talk of Isas and Sipps and the UK tax system. However, there's plenty of advice in books like JL Collins's *The Simple Path to Wealth* on, eg, how to maximise your Roth IRA contribution. I've spent the past few years trying to "put a kilt on[379]" the US financial independence movement and I've found its teachings are translatable to the UK market with the power of Google, so the reverse holds true if you're reading this ten-point investing plan in the States or wherever you are. Suffice it to say that Isas and Sipps are tax-advantaged accounts and have their US equivalents, which I won't do justice to in *RESET* when the likes of JL Collins have done this so comprehensively already.

Isas or Sipps then? That is the question. The right answer will depend on different factors, such as do you need access to the money, what tax-advantaged wrapper your existing stash is in already, how old you are, when you can get at the money and when's your target FIRE date.

However, for most midlife professionals planning to retire early (eg, before 60), the advice is simple. Place most of your money in a Sipp and receive the government's 20% top-up if you're a basic rate taxpayer (40% if you're a higher rate taxpayer, 45% if you're an additional rate taxpayer, and the rules are slightly different in Scotland[380]). Remember, depending on when you were born, you can start living off the interest of this money when you're 55 (or 57 from 2028 onwards). And what's more, you can withdraw 25% of it *tax-free.*

Remember also, most of your money will be in pensions anyway, so if you follow *RESET*, a Sipp is the only choice. What about the other stuff though? Those odd shares, mutual funds, windfalls from Uncle Gerry. If you don't need access to the money, cash them in, whack the money into a Sipp and invest *a la RESET*. If you do need access, do the same, but stick it in a stocks and shares Isa.

Your partner and you can **each** squirrel away £20k a tax year into an Isa, and £40k into a pension (unless you earn more than £100k). So unless you're Mr and Mrs Moneybags, you won't run out of tax-advantaged homes for your money any time soon.

6. Two types of asset allocation

Before we come to the big reveal – the *RESET* portfolio – a note on asset allocation[381]. There are two types of asset allocation: your stash asset allocation and your net worth asset allocation. Let me explain:

1. **Stash:** the suggested *RESET* portfolio is based on a **100% equity allocation**, invested in six index-tracking funds across six different geographies **(there is a super-easy option, too, which I'll come to in a minute).** No bonds (until we reach FIRE, when it moves to an 80% equities/20% bonds split), no cash. To some, this might seem risky. But as we've seen from the past 150 years, if you're investing over 10–15 years-plus, this approach is going to make *your* money work hardest for *you*. We're including here your current work pension – that you can't get out of, and wouldn't want to – that is invested as far as possible the *RESET* way.

2. **Net worth:** for most UK midlife professionals, their net worth asset allocation will break down as follows: stash, house equity and you/your partner's final salary pension (if you're lucky).

For example, let's say you *are* lucky and your net worth allocation is:

- Stash: **£150k.**
- House equity (house value minus money you still owe on the mortgage): **£150k.**
- Final salary pension transfer value (we'll come to that later): **£150k.**

Now do you feel better? Your asset allocation is now a conservative: **one-third equities, one-third home and one-third final salary.** So when that bear market inevitably comes, take heart that your net worth is diversified, even if your stash asset allocation is aggressive (100% equities during the wealth-amassing period).

7. The suggested *RESET* portfolio

When deciding how to invest, you have to know how you will deal with fear, factor in your health and consider your age. Only you can do that. Everyone is different.

That said, because *RESET*'s a book, it gives advice based on the average.

The average UK higher managerial woman will live until 89 (man to 87), according to the Office for National Statistics[382]. And life expectancy is increasing not decreasing. As a UK midlife professional aged 35 to 60, you have between 27 and 54 years of investing ahead of you. If you're in reasonable health (and can set, forget and handle the fear), why wouldn't you invest in a simple, globally diversified portfolio of index-tracking funds?

Here's the stash asset allocation *RESET* suggests. Whether you're investing through a Sipp or Isa, you can access exactly the same funds in either.

- UK: 25%.
- US: 45%.
- Europe Ex-UK: 13%.
- Japan: 7%.
- Emerging Markets: 7%.
- Pacific Ex-Japan: 3%.

Here are the funds. (If you follow the suggested *RESET* portfolio, make sure you pick the Acc – Accumulation – versions; they're the ones that reinvest dividends, leading to better compounding over time.)

Fidelity

- Fidelity Index US Fund P Accumulation.
- Fidelity Index UK Fund P Accumulation.
- Fidelity Index Europe Ex-UK P Accumulation.
- Fidelity Index Emerging Markets P Accumulation.
- Fidelity Index Japan P Accumulation.
- Fidelity Index Pacific Ex-Japan Fund P Accumulation Shares.

Vanguard

- US Equity Index Fund – Accumulation.
- FTSE UK All Share Index Unit Trust – Accumulation.
- FTSE Developed Europe Ex-UK Equity Index Fund – Accumulation.
- Emerging Markets Stock Index Fund – Accumulation.
- Japan Stock Index Fund – Accumulation.
- Pacific Ex-Japan Stock Index Fund – Accumulation.

Charges

Here's how the overall charges stack up under the suggested *RESET* portfolio. The calculations[383] assume your stash is under £250k, meaning an account service/fee charge from Fidelity of 0.35% and Vanguard of 0.15%.

- The charge for investing with Fidelity, choosing all Fidelity funds is **0.43%** (0.35% + 0.08% [combined OCF]).
- The charge for investing with Vanguard, choosing all Vanguard funds is **0.27%** (0.15% + 0.1225% [combined OCF]).

Remember. At time of going to press (August 2018), Vanguard doesn't offer retail investors Sipps, so you can either keep it simple and stick your stash in Fidelity. Or put your Isa money in Vanguard and your Sipp money in Fidelity. While you're using Fidelity as your fund manager, pick the Fidelity funds – they are cheaper than their Vanguard alternatives, and the performance won't differ much.

Last, **flick to the Glossary of Terms and check out "transaction costs" (TCs).** These are hidden charges built into the fund price. Invest a la *RESET* in the Fidelity funds and you'll pay a combined TC of **0.03%**; Vanguard **0.0575%**. This is caused by Vanguard's far-too-high 0.15% TC on its all share fund vs Fidelity's 0.04%. Switch (not recommended) from Vanguard's all share to its FTSE 100 Index Unit Trust Acc and your combined Vanguard TC drops to 0.02%.

Notes on fund choice and stash asset allocation

Fidelity and Vanguard offer passive and active funds. *RESET* is based on passive investing, hence the choice of low-cost index funds.

No active funds lurk in this portfolio, so no inefficient humans dabbling with your hard-earned money. The funds offer a simple, globally diversified portfolio, with a weighting to the home (UK) market, in line with Vanguard's approach[384]. From a UK investor's perspective, a diversified global portfolio is the way to go if you want to guard against underperformance of a particular index, maximise returns and minimise risk[385].

If you piece together a globally diversified portfolio of funds, it will cost you slightly less than, for instance, buying a one-world equity fund. It also offers more transparency to people with even a passing interest in investing: you can watch your portfolio as regions rise and fall, and track performance over time.

8. The *RESET* portfolio: other options

There you have it. Just go on to the Fidelity UK website, sign up for an account for you and your partner, then move all your different pots into Sipps and Isas.

Then arrange a monthly direct debit and invest your money as per the percentage asset allocation suggested in *RESET*. When

Vanguard starts offering Sipps, move both your Sipps and all your Isas from Fidelity, pick the equivalent Vanguard funds and save yourself a whopping 0.16% (0.1325% if you include TCs).

Pretty simple, eh?

But how about if you can't be bothered with six different funds, don't give a stuff about a few hundredth per cent saving on investment charges and have zero interest in how different regions of the world's economy are performing?

Even simpler

Fear not, because help is at hand. Here are a few one-stop options[386], in order of preference:

A. Vanguard LifeStrategy® 100% Equity Fund – Accumulation

- OCF: 0.22%. TC: 0.08%.
- MO: globally diversified portfolio, including emerging markets, mainly comprising Vanguard index trackers and Exchange-Traded Funds (ETFs). It also has a 25% UK weighting, which helps with currency risk[387], assuming you're going to spend most of your life spending pounds. This is a passive fund where rebalancing is taken care of by the fund manager. If you want ultimate simplicity or you're setting up a set-and-forget portfolio for someone else – who you know will never take the blindest bit of interest in it – choose this one. For someone who's never going to touch their investments again, I'd take the 0.1–0.14% hit on OCFs (compared to the suggested *RESET* portfolio) ahead of the deleterious effect of them never re-balancing their portfolio.

This is the super-easy option and you'll receive no argument from me if you decide to forget about the suggested *RESET* portfolio and follow this route. Put another way if you're after a really

easy life and don't mind the 0.1–0.14% OCF-drag on your stash returns versus the suggested *RESET* portfolio, invest your money here. When you retire, switch to the 80% equity fund of the same name. How simple is that!

B. A Vanguard two-fund option of FTSE Developed World Ex-UK Equity Index Fund – Accumulation (75%) and FTSE UK All Share Index Unit Trust – Accumulation (25%)

- Two-fund combined OCF: 0.1325% (compared to 0.08% for the suggested *RESET* portfolio using Fidelity funds and 0.1225% using Vanguard funds). Two-fund combined TC: 0.0375%.
- MO: Vanguard's Developed World Ex-UK passive fund tracks 2,030 large and mid-sized companies stocks around the world. The UK element is taken care of with Vanguard's UK All Share fund. A good, cost-effective two-fund solution, but you do sacrifice the exposure to emerging markets (including China and India) that Vanguard's one-stop LifeStrategy 100 fund gives you.

C. Vanguard FTSE All-World UCITS ETF (VWRL)

- OCF: 0.25%. TC: 0.01%.
- MO: a well-diversified (3,129 stocks) passive all-world fund, including emerging markets. If you're not bothered about currency risk (6.1% UK weighting) and want a diversified global fund (including emerging markets), look no further. Personally, the 0.25% charge and meagre UK exposure puts me off – I'd go for the LifeStrategy 100 every day of the week.

D. Vanguard Target Retirement [TRF] 2065 Fund – Accumulation

- OCF: 0.24%. TC: 0.09%.

- MO: Vanguard is famous for these every-five-year 2015–2065 TRFs, which become more conservative the lower the year. The way to achieve the maximum equity allocation is to pick the year farthest away. The 2065 TRF has an 80% equity, 20% bonds allocation and invests in a globally diversified portfolio comprising Vanguard index trackers and ETFs. Only consider this one if you simply must have bonds in your portfolio or it's the best option in your work pension.

E. Fidelity Index World Fund P Accumulation

- OCF: 0.12%. TC: 0.03%.
- MO: a low-cost passive fund that tracks the 23-country MSCI World Index[388]. But with only a 6.5% UK weighting; a too-heavy (for a UK investor) 63% North America weighting; and minimal (0.46%) exposure to emerging markets, I'd only suggest this fund if your work pension leaves you with no other choice.

Remember, whether you choose Fidelity or Vanguard as your fund manager, you can invest in all of these one-stop funds (except the last one – after you've switched to Vanguard – which is immaterial anyway: there's a reason it comes fifth).

Small-caps and Value

Now we're really getting into the weeds. All you need to know here is that over time small companies (small-caps) and value stocks outperform the market.

If you're in the US, you might have heard of Betterment, a firm that came to the attention of the financial independence community when Pete Adeney started using it to manage his money in preference to Vanguard[389]. Sadly, Betterment is not available in the UK and has no plans to set up shop this side of the Atlantic but, if you're using it in the US, you are benefiting from the fact that "Betterment's portfolio includes both value and small-cap tilts[390]."

Why? Here's Nobel prize-winning economist Eugene Fama again, who, along with fellow University of Chicago Booth School of Business professor Ken French, found that value and small-cap stocks outperform their growth and large-cap counterparts[391]. If the research is good enough for Betterment is it good enough for us?

Yes. And there's loads of other research and analysis backing up Fama and French's findings. *What to do?* This depends on how complex you want to make this investing business. For the moment, I'd stick to the suggested *RESET* portfolio. However, if you get into investing, and assuming you want to add another layer of complexity to your six-fund *RESET* portfolio: **reset your stash asset allocation as follows:**

- UK: 23%.
- US: 41%.
- Europe Ex-UK: 11%.
- Japan: 6%.
- Emerging Markets: 6%.
- Pacific Ex-Japan: 3%.

Leaving 5% for a world small-cap fund and 5% for a world value fund. I would invest 5% in:

i. Vanguard Global Small-Cap Index Fund – Accumulation

- OCF: 0.38%. TC: 0.11%.
- MO: a globally diversified (4,313 stocks) passive fund tracking the 23-country MSCI World Small-Cap Index[392].

And 5% in:

ii. Vanguard Global Value Factor UCITS ETF (VVAL)

- OCF: 0.22%. TC: 0.13%.

- MO: an actively managed fund, but it is a low-cost one and the "investment manager's quantitative model implements a rules-based active approach." I like rules, I trust Vanguard and, for an active fund, it's cheap as chips. It invests in 1,135 stocks: "primarily...[those] included in the FTSE Developed All Cap Index and Russell 3000 Index[393]."

There you have it, your own low-cost globally diversified set-and-forget eight-fund portfolio for the UK investor[394], complete with small-cap and value "tilt".

Action
If you choose this suggested RESET portfolio (with a tilty twist), all you need do now is set a yearly reminder in your online calendar to rebalance and Bob's your uncle.

9. More stash asset allocation options
I've presented *RESET's* suggested portfolio, shown you the "tilt" twist and mapped out even simpler options (**most notably Vanguard's LifeStrategy 100 fund**). Here are a few other approaches recommended by the experts. As always, do your own research and make up your own mind before investing.

A. JL Collins's one-fund approach
Jim recommends a 100% equities portfolio when stash-building and a 75/20/5% equities/bonds/cash split once you reach FI. During what he calls the "wealth accumulation stage", he recommends investing in one fund only: the Vanguard Total Stock Market Index fund (VTSAX), arguing because of the large number of worldwide companies that generate more than 50% of their profits from overseas in this fund, this provides all the global diversification you need[395]. Writing in 2011, Pete Adeney recommended a similar approach[396].

RESET View

A simple low-cost approach **aimed at US investors.** The equivalent UK fund is the Vanguard FTSE UK All Share – Acc, which offers similar international diversification. Nevertheless, placing all your eggs in one UK basket – however international the constituent members of the FTSE All Share index – is not recommended.

B. Goldberg five funds

Another one for the US investors among you: UK readers can find the Vanguard UK-equivalent funds easily enough. Using five Vanguard funds, Kiplinger contributor Steven Goldberg[397] suggests: 40% Vanguard Total Stock Market Index (VTSAX), 10% Small-Cap-Value Index (VSIAX), 20% FTSE All-World Ex-US Index (VFWAX), 5% Emerging Markets Stock Index (VEMAX) and 25% Inter-mediate-Term Corporate Bonds Index (VICSX). All five are passive funds; all five are low-cost. Goldberg suggests annual rebalancing and upping the bond quotient by 5% every five years from 15 years before your target retirement date.

RESET View

A diversified, 25%-bond, five-fund portfolio for the US investor.

C. *Monevator's* slow and steady portfolio

Set up in 2011 with £3,000, an extra £900 has been invested every quarter, complete with quarterly blog post and the numbers tracking progress. It's an all-index-funds, no-dealing-charges portfolio aimed at the UK investor. This passive portfolio uses threshold rebalancing[398]. In April 2018[399], it comprised:

- Vanguard FTSE UK All Share Index Trust: 5.79%.
- Vanguard FTSE Developed World Ex-UK Equity Index Fund: 35.45%.
- Vanguard Global Small-Cap Index Fund: 6.91%.

- iShares Emerging Markets Equity Index Fund D: 10.03%.
- iShares Global Property Securities Equity Index Fund D: 6.64%.
- Vanguard UK Government Bond Index: 29.02%.
- Vanguard UK Inflation-Linked Gilt Index Fund: 6.16%.

RESET View

Monevator is the UK FI index investing guru (actually two anonymous bloggers, The Investor and The Accumulator), who I first discovered through a recommendation on the *Mr. Money Mustache* forum[400]. I've since devoured as many *Monevator* blog posts as I have *Mustache* ones. This is a good portfolio with the research and heavy lifting done by *Monevator*. Follow it to the letter and you get a spot-on quarterly review (in the form of a blog post) of your investment performance. Even with a 35% bond weighting, this portfolio has produced an annualised return of 9.48% since its establishment in 2011. You can piece it together using Fidelity as your fund manager (Vanguard UK doesn't offer a property fund otherwise you could use it as well, swapping iShares Emerging Markets for the Vanguard-equivalent fund). Note the global property securities fund. If you do want to invest in property, a real estate fund (compared with buying property yourself) is a no-hassle risk-diversified way to invest in this asset class.

- **Pros:** low-cost, for such specialised funds; safer, because of bonds; globally diversified; targets asset classes that outperform the market historically, eg, small-caps; you can copy *Monevator.*
- **Cons:** UK weighting in line with MSCI World Index at 6%, not the 25% suggested in the *RESET* portfolio and baked in to Vanguard's LifeStrategy 100 fund. Bonds up at 35% decreases potential returns in the stash-building phase.

D. Bogleheads' three-fund portfolio

The Bogleheads are a vibrant, mainly online – but also physical, with 60 chapters worldwide[401] – community of individuals who love passive investing and Jack Bogle. The three funds recommended for US investors are[402]:

1. Vanguard Total Stock Market Index Fund (VTSMX).
2. Vanguard Total International Stock Index Fund (VGTSX).
3. Vanguard Total Bond Market Fund (VBMFX).

Opinions differ on the percentage allocation to each. Followers of this approach like its simplicity, low cost, international diversification and (depending on what percentage of your portfolio is in bonds) reduced risk.

RESET View

A good and popular approach, somewhere in the middle between a higher-cost LifeStrategy 100 one-fund approach and the six-fund – plus two, if you add in small-cap and value funds – suggested *RESET* portfolio.

E. Investing direct in individual shares

Never ever invest more than 5% of your stash in individual shares. If possible, avoid this practice and focus on passive funds. We've covered why already: remember that monkey and its dart board. Nevertheless, if you develop an interest in investing, and you must have a flutter – I know, you're only human – here's what to do:

1. Sign up for an online brokerage account (website) through which you can buy and sell shares.
2. Compare fees and ease-of-use first[403]. Make your decision on price.
3. Check you can buy US shares through the website.
4. If the cost isn't prohibitive, pick the fund manager you use to manage your money to buy and sell your shares. Fidelity now offers this expanding service to UK small investors (us) without having to go through an adviser.

5. Do your stocks research.
6. Favour stocks that pay dividends, but consider those that don't, too.
7. Adopt a long-term (five-year-plus) stock investment strategy, as Warren Buffett does.
8. Don't try to time the market; set and forget.
9. Let that globally diversified low-cost Stakhanovite bunch of index funds do 95%-plus of your portfolio's heavy lifting.
10. Keep an eye on the charges.

For example, towards the middle of 2017, we invested well under 5% of our stash in three companies: Apple (quarter), Microsoft (quarter) and Berkshire Hathaway B (half) after cashing in Standard Life windfall shares. I did my (extensive) research on all three firms, after discarding scores of alternatives. Fidelity didn't offer a share dealing service to direct customers without an adviser at the time so I picked online share portal IG[404] as my broker because it charged nothing for managing the funds (as long as one of them paid dividends). And at a tenner a pop to buy each stock, I thought it would appear rude not to take advantage. With wild fluctuations, the trend has nevertheless been upward and one year on we were sitting on (before-inflation) returns of 24% Apple, 53% Microsoft and 21% Berkshire Hathaway B. This against a **suggested-*RESET*-portfolio** return – I practise what I preach – during the same period of 8%. However, IG changed its charging structure, and starting July 2018, we would have *had* to pay a monthly management fee, dividends or no dividends. Aware of this, and having calculated the percentage fee-drag on the small amount invested, we sold the three stocks, closed our IG account and split the money between the two Vanguard small-cap and value funds suggested above.

RESET View

Don't invest in individual stocks. But if you must, never commit more than 5% of your stash. And be in it for the long-term (unless your fund broker changes its charging structure, that is).

10. Final practical advice on your stash

You've picked your fund manager, set up your Sipps and Isas, transferred over your existing stash-of-randomness to your chosen funds and set up your monthly pension/Isa direct debits. Fantastic, well done, bravo! Before we move on to the ever-so-exciting-yet-mercifully-short-and-practical topic of pensions state and final salary, a few quick stash-housekeeping points to finish.

- Set, forget, automate; don't dabble.
- Check your portfolio every month, not every day.
- If you ever have a lump sum – eg, when you gather your random pots of money into one big existing stash – invest it as a lump sum; don't split it into 12 and invest monthly. You're thinking *I can't do this anyway: if I move my pensions into a Sipp, I'll have to put it in as a lump sum.* Well, yes and no. You have to transfer out (and in) the entire amount, but you can have your life savings sitting in cash in your Sipp forever if you want. Remember the rule: don't try to time the market. If the period 1970 to 2013 is anything to go by, the chances of the market going up are 77%; down 23%[405]. Invest on statistics and keep your fear well out of it.
- Rebalance every year unless there's a market drop of more than 20% or you're whacking a huge chunk in (such as an inheritance). If either of these two events occurs, rebalance when they do.

Action

There's your RESET ten-point investing plan, complete with twist and options. Now for the boring but necessary bit. Read on, Macduff.

CHAPTER 33

Section 3: Investing (Final Salary and State Pensions)

IN THE UK, EVERYONE is entitled to a state pension, whereas latest figures from the UK Pension Regulator show that only 1,650,491 UK residents are members of defined benefit/final salary schemes[406].

Final salary schemes

These are pensions based on years of service and either your final salary before leaving your employer/when the scheme closed/when you retire or the average of your salary over a set time (eg, five years). They are commonly 1/60th or 1/80th affairs.

For example, say you worked for an employer for 30 years, they operated a 1/60th final salary scheme and your final salary was £40,000, you'd receive a before-tax pension of £20,000 a year until you popped your clogs. Typically, you either can't draw a final salary pension until 65 or the money you get every month reduces if you do.

A gold-plated Rolls-Royce?

Legend has it that final salary pensions are gold-plated. The Financial Conduct Authority (FCA) refers to them as "Rolls-Royces".

This is true as far as it goes, but like most things in life, dig deeper and it ain't as simple as all that.

On the one hand, final salary pensions are safe, they de-risk your overall net worth, they typically provide death benefits (like life insurance) to your spouse and if you die first, your partner will probably still receive 50% of your pension for the rest of their life.

Certainly, if you're a member of a final salary scheme with your current employer and you are still paying in, it's hard to make a case for leaving.

However, if you've left the employer, or your current employer's final salary scheme has been closed to new benefits building up (eg, it's still there, but you are no longer contributing and neither is your employer regarding new benefits), that's different. *Let's take a closer look.*

A closer look

While it's fair to say former chancellor of the exchequer George Osborne has his detractors, we midlifers should be grateful to the man for his 2015 pension reforms.

Bye-bye being forced to buy an annuity in retirement, hello freedom and choice.

In fact, I'd say George Osborne has done more to further financial independence for UK professionals of our generation than anyone.

But what he may not have envisaged is the little-known rush to cash in final salary schemes, which saw an estimated 120,000 final salary scheme members "transfer out" in 2017/18, up from 80,000 in 2016/17[407].

This is due to two factors:

1. Osborne's reforms, which mean you can convert your final salary scheme to a lump sum and transfer it into a Sipp.
2. The fact that the Cash Equivalent Transfer Value (CETV) of some final salary schemes has risen by as much as 40% in recent years as gilt yields have gone down.

Why should you consider transferring?

- You control how you invest *your* money.
- You can access this money from age 55/57.
- Depending on your age and when you want to retire – but assuming 60, and that you're aged between 35 and 60 now – you have up to 25 years to invest this money before you need to draw on it.
- CETVs are at record highs.
- You cannot leave your final salary pension to your kids. Once you and your partner are gone, so is it. Not so with a DC scheme or Sipp. If you're single and expect to die early, it's a no-brainer.
- You could knock *years* off your working life.

For instance, let's look at the Aggarwals one more time (age 50, £200k existing stash, saving and investing £2k a month). We've established earlier that with an SWR of 3.5% it will take our couple 13 years to hit their target stash of £855,000. They'll be **63.**

Remember, Sunil quit his job a couple of years back to go it alone. Previously, he'd worked for one employer for 20 years, finishing on a salary of £40k. It's a 1/80th scheme, so Sunil's due £10k a year from 65. Sunil's had more time since setting up on his own to read. He's heard about the final salary reforms and contacted his previous employer with a transfer value request (you can submit one request a year free – it's the law).

He's received a fair valuation of **£142,571**[408].

Let's run the numbers. Say that after IFA costs, Sunil receives £140,000, how will that affect Patricia and Sunil's retirement plans? Age 50, target stash £855,000, existing stash £340,000 (£200k plus £140k), saving and investing £2k a month. They're now looking at eight years and 11 months until they reach £855,000. They'll be **58.** They *could* find themselves able to retire five years earlier than planned.

What to do?

If you have a final salary pension from a previous employer or you're a member of a scheme with your current employer to which you and they are no longer contributing with respect to new benefits, follow these steps:

1. Submit a transfer value request.
2. Once you receive the valuation, you have three months to decide whether to take it.
3. Do your research. Is this a poor, fair, good or very good valuation? Online calculators[409] will help you find out.
4. Watch the scheme doesn't have a built-in clause ("Paragraph 2 of Schedule 1A of the Occupational Pension Scheme [Transfer Values] Regulations 1996") that protects the scheme members (including you), but reduces the value of your transfer by a percentage agreed by the scheme trustees. If this has been applied, because your scheme's in deficit, do not transfer. The percentage is not set in stone and may change next year if you submit another transfer value request. If you're thinking *can they do this? Seems a little arbitrary;* you're not the only one.
5. Do your maths. The Aggarwals' example illustrates a key point. The longer you invest, the better the chance your planned stock market returns will be realised. If you're planning to retire at 60, a 15-year investment time horizon is preferable to just eight. Google it until you're satisfied, speak to friends, then make your mind up.
6. Only when you have a good idea of what *you* want to do, contact a financial adviser. Current legislation dictates that for any final salary transfer value above £30,000 you must receive advice from an Independent Financial Adviser (IFA). Expect to pay between 1% and 3% of the CETV to the IFA for this advice.
7. When contacting an IFA, ask: "do you support insistent clients?" An "insistent client" (or "pain in the arse" in IFA-lingo) is one who listens to the expert's advice then does their own thing anyway. The IFA may be right to advise against transferring;

you're paying for their advice so listen up. But it may be that you disagree, in which case (even if they have to tape you or receive a signed letter), will they support your transfer? You must establish this before spending a £k or few on your chosen IFA.

8. Call some IFAs for costs. Choose based on their "insistent client" policy, any friend/family recommendation and price.

9. If you do wish to go ahead with the transfer, the money will be converted into a lump sum. All you need to do then is whack it into your Fidelity/Vanguard Sipp (it must go into a pension) and decide which funds to invest in (I hope you invest the *RESET* way).

10. Remember that if you do transfer out, the risk is *all* on you. The market could fall by 50% in the next year, and you would lose your guaranteed retirement income and that death benefit.

11. If, having done your research, you decide that now is *not* the time to transfer out, set a recurring online calendar reminder for next year.

12. Then submit the free yearly transfer value request to which you're entitled.

13. You can transfer out of private sector final salary schemes and you can transfer out of "funded" public sector schemes, such as a local council pension. You can't transfer out of "unfunded" public sector pensions, such as the NHS scheme.

14. Last, if you're working for an employer where you're a member of a final salary scheme that's closed (to new benefits building up), call the administrator. Most paid-up schemes calculate your pension on your final salary/career average *when* they closed. But some retain the salary link until you *leave* your employer. In this case, if you ever see yourself being promoted, wait until you reach your peak salary before considering transferring out.

The state pension

This one's easy. Did you know that the full new state pension stands at **£8,546.20** a year or **£17,092.40** a couple[410]? With an ageing population and the government increasing what employers must pay in to workplace pensions, I know fine well that by the time my wife and I can draw the state pension when we're 67/68[411], it won't be £17,092 in 2040 prices, and they might have pushed the qualifying age back a year or two. Hell, it might even have become means-tested.

There probably won't be a double-lock, never mind a triple-lock[412]; in fact the door might be wide open. But I'm damn certain there'll be something, and it will not be sniffed at in the Sawyer household.

And I'm also damn sure that in two other Sawyer households no sniffing will be heard by our boys' families after my wife and I are able to cut our stash withdrawals by more than half every month. If everything goes to plan – and bear in mind, *RESET* is based on conservative estimates – our two boys will be millionaires even in today's terms after we die. At an age when they'll be old and wise enough to appreciate it.

Action

(Yes, there is one.)

Sit down. Whip out your laptop and google "Check Your State Pension[413]". Have your passport number handy. If it's your first time on GOV.UK, you'll need to sort the verification malarkey, and have your mobile with you for verification codes. Still sitting down? See how many years you and your partner need to make National Insurance contributions before you qualify for the full state pension.

Please note, qualifying for the full state pension is different from getting at it. However, it does tell you, crucially, what age you both need to work until to maximise this additional (and huge) source of retirement income. This will depend on various factors: the government redid the state pension a year or two ago. It's complicated[414]. All you need to do right now is go online and check.

CHAPTER 34

Section 3: Investing (Legacy – After You've Gone)

THAT'S IT. THE **FIRE Triumvirate** of budgeting, efficiency/frugality and investing in one comprehensive actionable plan. Follow this plan and you'll be a lot happier, knock years off your working life and, along with the other parts of *RESET*, live a more meaningful existence.

But what happens when you die? When either you or your partner departs this mortal coil and exits stage left? Answer: who knows, but you need to plan for this, too. Here are a few things to consider when providing for your remaining immediate family after you die.

Big money admin

First, after effecting the huge consolidation of your financial assets mentioned above, contact the remaining firms you've charged with your money and make sure your partner is the 100% beneficiary if you die. This includes any final salary pension scheme you may or may not have. Simple. You can specify what you want to happen with most of your stash by going online/telephoning/filling in the odd form with the fund manager/scheme provider.

Life insurance

Arrange an adequate level of cover for your partner and you: joint policies tend to be cheaper than two singles.

If you have a final salary scheme, work out what the death benefit is to your partner and see whether that's enough to forgo a life insurance policy for them (you don't want to double up).

Research different life insurance providers. Not one pays if your partner kills themselves, and records of paying out for other causes of death differ from company to company. *RESET* suggests making your decision on two factors: which provider is most likely to pay in full, and which has highest probability of paying in full while causing the least hassle for those you leave behind. In the UK, Beagle Street[415] has a good reputation, and is *RESET's* top pick.

Next, set your level of cover. There are two types of life insurance, decreasing term and lump sum. What cover you go for depends on a host of factors including how will your partner cope if you die tomorrow, how good is your partner at managing investments, how flexible is your partner, how healthy is your partner, how are your partner's genes (life expectancy). *RESET* favours decreasing term life insurance based on your mortgage value at time of purchasing. This way, if you die, your partner has no mortgage debt to worry about and their (and your kids') home is secure. Lump sum life insurance (where the payout is usually more than even the highest payout under decreasing term) gives more comfort, but costs more a month, and is insuring for something you may not need.

Last, make sure you place your life insurance in a trust: many companies such as Beagle Street offer this service for nothing. This is because *in trust* your life insurance doesn't form part of your estate. This means it cannot be subject to inheritance tax. Plus, those you've left behind receive the payout much quicker if your life insurance policy is in a trust.

Action

Look at your life insurance and work out your current and future needs.

It's likely that any life insurance you're paying (life insurance is not mandatory by law) is out of date for the payout required. For instance, did you update your life insurance every time you moved house or do you have a decreasing term life insurance based on your first home, which will in no way cover the costs of your astronomical existing mortgage loan if you die tomorrow? Your policy in and of itself is worthless. All those 15 or 30 pounds you pay in over the years only benefit your partner if you die; it's just like any other insurance. Once you achieve FIRE, consider cancelling your life insurance – unless you still have a huge home loan (very unlikely), you don't need it anymore.

Wills

Next, sort your wills. If you don't, you're storing up a whole load of heartache for your loved ones after you snuff it.

Wills are not only about your money: much of that you'll have sorted with your "big money admin" above. They also cover things like your house, funeral plans and (if you're a business owner) what happens to your business. In addition, most importantly, who takes care of your children after you've gone. If nothing else, if you fall into the category of the two-thirds of UK citizens aged 35 to 54[416] who haven't written a will, do it for your children.

Options abound, from do it yourself to free solicitor-drafted wills in March and October in Scotland, England and Wales (if you're 55 or over[417]). Life insurance companies like Beagle Street even throw in will-writing support from a solicitor as part of the sign-up benefits.

At the most, it'll cost you a few hundred quid, which might be the best few hundred quid you ever spend. Because if you don't have a will, you risk the government grabbing lots of your money when you die, instead of it going to your kids, loved ones or favourite charities (there is more protection for those who die without a will in Scotland than others parts of the UK[418]).

For anything like wills, my go-to sources of advice in the UK are always *Money Saving Expert* and *Which?* Both are comprehensive, and *Which?* offers a will-writing service.

Penultimately, it's rare that both partners are interested in investing. If, for instance, you have the suggested *RESET* portfolio with a "tilty" twist, yet your partner doesn't understand investments and wouldn't know an annual rebalancing from an elbow, make sure your stash is invested in a true set-and-forget style after you've gone. Given the fact you'll – with any luck – die in retirement and be in the withdrawal not the wealth-amassing period of your financial lives, *RESET* suggests specifying that your stash is switched to the **Vanguard LifeStrategy 80**[419] globally diversified fund, which is invested up to 80% in equities and 20% in bonds. Vanguard takes care of the rebalancing forever, and your surviving partner and children (and you) can rest easy. **A steal at 0.22%**[420].

Final point. Wills are about what happens after you die. But what about when you're alive and, for some reason or another (for example, dementia), you become unable to make decisions? Consider setting up a Lasting Power of Attorney[421] for your property and financial affairs; and health and welfare. Pick the person you trust to act in your best interests (usually your partner).

Inheritance tax

You've sorted your wills and made a power of attorney. But what *happens* to your money when you die? How do you make sure *as much as possible goes to your loved ones, not the government?* This is how it works.

Let's say you're a married couple with kids. In most cases, when one of you dies, you can leave your assets to your partner without the government taking a penny. Assets include cars, house, investments, your business and any life insurance payout. (If you've taken the sensible and often free precaution of placing it in trust, the life insurance payout is not counted as part of your estate and won't affect your inheritance allowance.)

If you die and leave your assets to your spouse, they get *your* inheritance allowance as well. Which means when you, the last woman or man standing, die (assuming that happens in the

2020/2021 tax year onwards), after deducting expenses and debts, you can leave up to **£1m** to your now 61-year-old kids[422]. Without paying *any* inheritance tax (assuming part of that inheritance is your one main home[423]). On anything above a million, you pay 40% tax to the government.

Let me repeat that. **You can leave £1m, in 2018 money, tax-free, to whoever you want when you die.** (If you think you're in any danger of having over £1m, do more research or consult an expert for advice.)

Now think of the *RESET* investing plan, think of that stash that has a statistical probability (at 3.5% SWR) of being worth more than when you started drawing on it if you live into your eighties. Think of the life you want to live when you're financially independent, and the good and meaningful life you're going to lead on your journey there. Then think of your legacy, and the financially secure future your children will have in *their* retirement. *Do you see how powerful this all is, when you see it in the round, when you understand how it fits together?*

Before we finish...

Nearly there now. In Part IV, we've covered the principles of financial independence and the practicalities. You've learned how to: budget, build efficiency into your everyday life, save as much as you can, and follow a simple set-and-forget approach to building your assets that lets you get on with what's important in life.

Before we move on to Part V (where we distil everything we've discussed in Parts I to IV into a set of 11 principles to live your life by), here are a few nuggets of advice that may help you in all three sections of the **FIRE Triumvirate**.

- Use one email address and a bombproof password extension. Don't try to use one email address for one task and one for another. Simplicity is key.
- Read biographies and listen to podcasts[424] of successful investors/people like you.

- Read the best FIRE books[425]. In this order: *Your Money or Your Life, Early Retirement Extreme, The Simple Path to Wealth, The Millionaire Next Door, Rich Dad Poor Dad* and *Secrets of the Millionaire Mind.* All of them are American. All of them are excellent. Translate the non-applicable US-specific advice through reading UK blogs.
- Read these six blogs: *Monevator* (amazing, all the UK translation you'll need), *Mr. Money Mustache, Mad Fientist, Budgets are Sexy*[426], *Millennial Revolution*[427] and *Physician on FIRE*[428].
- You're only as good as your partner. Marry the right person and involve them every step of the way. Compromise, focus on the vision and make sure you build in regular treats and date nights.
- Invest for your kids and teach them good habits. Our children (aged eight and ten) have junior Isa investment accounts with Vanguard, with asset allocation as per the suggested *RESET* portfolio. Fifty per cent of their pocket money is invested, 50% they can do what they want with. Any cash windfalls they receive, they can spend, save (they both have regular savings accounts) or invest – up to £200 a year. When they're 18, the money is theirs. This teaches them good lessons and they can track the magic of compound interest through their online accounts over the next ten years.
- In order to enjoy that long and happy financial independence, reaping the benefits of *RESET*, it helps if everything is working properly – never take your health for granted.

CHAPTER 35

Part IV Index Card

- Don't forget the **FIRE Triumvirate**: budgeting; efficiency and frugality; and investing.
- Reject consumerism.
- Build efficiency into every nook and cranny of your life. Make it a game.
- Do your stash maths.
- One pot to simplify your budgeting and stash-tracking.
- Automate your monthly investment, set, forget, rebalance annually...and don't peek.
- Maximise your work pension; consolidate the rest.
- Invest in a global portfolio of index trackers through Fidelity or Vanguard. If in doubt, go for the **LifeStrategy 100** one-fund option (switch to the **80** version when you achieve FIRE).
- Treat your state pension as a bonus: don't rely on it.
- Leave a legacy.
- Remember The LAHs.

And finally...

Walter Isaacson[429] is a wise American journalist (ex-editor of *Time* magazine and *CNN*). He's also written acclaimed biographies of some of the most talented people who have ever lived, including

Benjamin Franklin, Leonardo da Vinci, Steve Jobs and Albert Einstein. Every human being, he contends, is trying to find "where they fit in": all "searching" for meaning in life and our place in it[430]. It took me more than 40 years to find mine. Running – we'll touch on that in Part V – gave me hope, but there's no higher purpose; digital PR gave me pride and is something I excel in, but it's a means to an end; decluttering made me see clearly again, got my brain firing and opened up a host of possibilities. Discovering financial independence was different though. A holistic, practical community dedicated to one thing: striving to live a good and meaningful life. Now I had a framework, a purpose and a measurable goal, which would take years to accomplish and make my family's journey through life happier. Finally, after leaving the comfortable numbness of corporate life, and years of searching, I'd found my way home.

PART V

11 Core Principles to Guide You in Work and Life

I shall be telling this with a sigh
Somewhere ages and ages hence:
Two roads diverged in a wood, and I –
I took the one less traveled by,
And that has made all the difference[431].
Robert Frost, *The Road Not Taken*

I'VE BEEN WORKING SOLIDLY on *RESET* for nine months. It's based on 45 years' experience, including an unconventional six-year journey of discovery that's seen me embark on more adventures, meet more people and read more books than many people do in a lifetime. Until now, *RESET* has focussed on practical, step-by-step advice while taking care to explain the theory, the why. Part V is different. Yes, there's tactical advice by the bucketload, but view what follows as the *paving stones* of the *RESET* way. If you look hard, you'll notice these 11 principles guide everything that's gone before in this book. Ways of approaching life that will, little by little, day by day, month by month, then year by year, help you live a good, meaningful and happier existence. I've picked them for their universality. There's no order to them: they just are. Enjoy applying these principles, don't focus on the results and be grateful for every step you take on your journey. After reading *RESET*, you'll be at a fork in *your* life. Follow these principles and everything'll be fine, whether you turn right *or* left (or go straight on).

CHAPTER 36

RESET's 11 Core Principles

1. Be Different

> *Conformity is the jailer of freedom and the enemy of growth*[432].
> **John F. Kennedy**

Aviemore. October 2nd 2004. On top of Cairn Gorm, in the Ptarmigan restaurant. My brother stands up. The audience falls silent. Ian begins his speech.

> *Everyone in this room knows Dave, some better than others.*
> *But I think there's one thing we can all agree on...let's face*
> *it...he's a bit weird.*

He brought the house down with that one. What ensued was an affectionate romp through my different approach to life, one that I've replayed on video more times than I care to remember.

But it's this difference, not caring what others think about me – or at least not letting it get in the way of what I want to do – to which I attribute my greatest successes. Whether in your business, personal or hobby life, don't be afraid to be different. In a sea of conformity, different is good. Don't follow what everyone else is doing, double down on your strengths. Take a leaf out of Warren Buffett's book and measure yourself by your own inner scorecard, not others'.

Never give a monkey's chuff what people think. Be authentic, don't worry if folks don't like you – we're not living in tribes anymore – focus on those who do.

Remember, you're never alone in this online world. Whatever your interests and dreams, whatever your immediate community thinks about you, there's always an alternative community that celebrates that difference. However weird.

Switching to the world of business, in *Different: Escaping the Competitive Herd*, Youngme Moon said: "What if working like crazy to beat the competition did exactly the opposite – made you mediocre and more like the competition? Rethink your business strategy, stop conforming and start deviating, stop emulating and start innovating. Because to stand out you must become the exception, not the rule[433]."

She cites, among others, IKEA, JetBlue, Cirque du Soleil, *The Simpsons*, Swatch, Birkenstock, Red Bull, Mini, Apple, Benetton, Dove, Harley-Davidson and Marmite as examples of different brands that disrupted their industry and created a niche of their own. I'd add Innocent, Skoda, Freeagent, Lidl and Aldi to the list. If you'd rather be a Marmite than a malleable lump of clay, here are a few suggestions:

- Set your own goals.
- To think outside the box it helps if you've been in the box first[434].
- Don't be the average person who watches four hours-plus of TV every day[435]. Don't play computer games or devote much time to social media.
- Learn. Ignorance breeds conformity, knowledge gives you the courage of your convictions, whatever anyone else thinks.
- Don't spend time in echo chambers or you'll start thinking like everyone else.

- Fight fear and take action in line with your values.
- Don't feel the need to justify yourself.
- Work out what you stand for and against. Follow the for.

Remember Bronnie Ware's research from Part I? That the number one regret of the dying is not having the courage to live the life they wanted to live, but instead living the life others expected of them.

In summary, take risks and stop worrying what the Joneses think. As Mark Manson writes: "You can't be an important and life-changing presence for some people without being a joke and embarrassment to others[436]."

2. Put one foot in front of the other

I run because long after my footprints fade away, maybe I will have inspired a few to reject the easy path, hit the trails, put one foot in front of the other, and come to the same conclusion I did: I run because it always takes me where I want to go[437].
Dean Karnazes

We'll cover this in more detail in Principle 11, but if you believe that running is a metaphor for life, like Oprah[438] and me, this quote from US ultramarathoner Dean Karnazes reveals one of its fundamental truths.

Action always beats inaction. Without it you get nowhere. In *The Compound Effect*, author Darren Hardy talks of the power of small actions repeated daily which, over time – you guessed – compound. Until one day "Big Mo" turns up and hey presto, you've made your own luck. Ask 1980s basketball legend Larry Bird[439], the Williams sisters or Ronaldo what made them world-beating athletes, and I bet they'd tell you about the 500 free-throws they practised every morning as a kid, or those early morning drills with their dad, or that staying late at training after their teammates had left.

Little Prince author Antoine de Saint-Exupéry said: "What saves a man is to take a step. Then another step[440]."

No one's going to say well done, no one's going to notice. No one cares. But if you can teach yourself to act without motivation, despite not being in the mood, in the face of fear. If you can run even when it's pouring with rain and blowing a gale, eventually you'll receive your reward. Yes, feeling good can lead to action, but action can often lead to feeling good.

There'll never be a time when the stars are aligned, and it's the perfect night to do something.

Don't wait for divine inspiration to strike, take small actions daily, and *luck* will come to you.

3. Routines and habits: be boring

We are what we repeatedly do. Excellence, then, is not an act, but a habit[441].
Will Durant

One of the keys to achieving and getting things done is adopting and adapting routines to suit your aims and circumstances.

Mason Currey's *Daily Rituals* book unpicks how the greatest creatives of the modern era, from Beethoven to Hemingway, went about their business. Some preferred mornings, some worked through the night. Maya Angelou wrote her books in motel rooms, Thomas Wolfe at a makeshift standing desk (the top of his fridge). Anthony Trollope fitted in writing around his job as a post office civil servant. Marx frequented the British Museum Reading Room between 9am and 7pm; Jung built a two-storey tower and worked there. Margaret Mead rose at 5am, Proust wrote in bed. And author John Cheever worked from the basement of his apartment block – in his boxer shorts.

Routines make sure you continue to put one foot in front of another, whatever. For example, it took me seven weeks to first-draft this book. I set myself an ambitious word count of 2,000 words during the week and 1,000 at weekends. Every evening I loaded my bag with reference material, laid out my clothes and went to bed by 21:30. Every morning I got up at 05:06, had a shower, coffee and was at my health club by 06:00, ready to work. During those seven weeks, many things happened in our lives, but every day I followed my routines, showed up, and did my work. Forty-two days later, I'd completed an 87,000-word first draft. Because everything was automated, all I needed to do was arrive at the same place at the same time every day and hit my word count. And, channelling my inner Charlie Spedding, because I did, every day was perfect.

I forgive the outside observer, watching me sit at the same desk every day for seven weeks, for thinking my life was regimented.

Counterintuitively, mundanity can lead to great creativity. In fact, the most interesting people I know live lives that at first glance look a tad monotonous.

Embrace monotony. If you do the same thing every day for a few weeks, it soon becomes a habit. One that's embedded. You can then build another habit on top of it. Soon that group of habits becomes a routine. The more good routines you adopt, the more your mind can focus on what matters, as the everyday takes care of itself.

Currey quotes V.S. Pritchett, in 1941, writing about historian writer Edward Gibbon, in observing: "Sooner or later the great men turn out to be all alike. They never stop working. They never lose a minute. It is very depressing[442]."

As midlife professionals, our aspirations are perhaps less lofty than tracking the fluctuating fortunes of the Roman Empire[443]. Nevertheless, if we want to live good and meaningful lives, we need to allocate time.

The key to doing this is a combination of an uncluttered mind, solid routines and our fourth principle, hard work.

A note on tracking

Routines and habits help you achieve. The only way to see if you're achieving is to monitor your performance. Here's what I track:

- **Money.** Money in, money out, investment performance. Track every pound you earn.
- **Deep work.** The time every day I spend working undistracted.
- **Routines.** These range from running, to social media use, to reading books to the kids. Track anything you consider important. I use a self-drawn table in a notebook. Others use online tools such as Exist.io[444] to track and tweak their habits[445].
- **Thoughts.** These go on index cards and find their way into my blog posts and weekly *Zude's Top 4* newsletter. You can use an app like Evernote, but having tried many ways to organise my thoughts, you can't beat the index card for its versatility.
- **Time-based commitments.** These go in my online diary.
- **Someday/Maybe.** For important things that I need to do but don't know when, I have a "Someday/Maybe list[446]".
- **Journal.** Sometimes I journal. Remember Morning Pages.
- **Big focus trackers.** If you're trying to achieve something big, you need a bespoke tracker. If I'm training for a marathon PB or writing a book, I use a paper running log or computer spreadsheet. You wouldn't go to work and *not* track your performance against set goals. Why should your life be any different? Which is more important?

4. Persistence, perseverance and hard work

Stickability is 95 per cent of ability[447].
David Schwartz, PhD

Routines help. However, there's no denying the fact that no matter how automated your life, the secret to getting the compounding effect of small actions repeated daily is sheer hard work. To work hard, persist and persevere:

1. You need desire (motivated by a compelling vision).
2. You need a purpose.

3. You need a stubborn streak that never knows when to give up.
4. You need a plan.
5. You need conviction.
6. You need focus and determination.

Here the upwards of one-third of the general population who are introverts have the advantage. As *Quiet* author, Susan Cain, said: "Persistence isn't very glamorous. If genius is one percent inspiration and 99% perspiration, then as a culture we tend to lionize the one per cent. We love its flash and dazzle. But great power lies in the other ninety-nine percent[448]."

Remember Colonel Sanders? He never gave up, putting one foot in front of the other day after day in an effort to sell his secret recipe. And day after day, he returned to his car empty-handed.

Remember Charlie Spedding, the guy who finished last in the 100 metres at his school sports day in Durham? He never gave up: twenty years and tens of thousands of miles later, he was standing on the podium at the Olympic Games in Los Angeles. Every successful person I know toiled away for years before achieving anything. Life isn't *The X Factor*[449] and the world's not full of reality TV stars. In the final reckoning, you get out what you put in and nowt beats hard graft. Apart, perhaps, from distraction-free hard graft.

5. The importance of deep work

> *You will never reach your destination if you stop and throw stones at every dog that barks[450].*
> **Winston Churchill**

Cal Newport, PhD is assistant professor of computer science at Georgetown University. His book, *Deep Work,* has had a profound effect on how I approach achieving my goals.

Here's the why, what and how on this fundamental *RESET* principle.

The problem

We live in a fast-changing world, full of distractions. A world of open-plan offices, a world where work has encroached on home life and we're expected to be contactable 24/7. A world of multiple meetings, social media, instant-reply emails, a world of multi-tasking. A world where appearing busy is more important than producing quality work, a world where the office politician always beats the conscientious objector. This leads to distracted, cluttered minds, unused to concentrating, unable to learn, with no time to do anything bar shuffle paper and emails from one place to another.

All this in a world where technological change means that geography is no barrier. As we discovered in Status Quo, we're now competing for jobs, respect and promotion not only against people in our local area but also with people across the globe. The same technological change that is increasing our mental distractedness is leading to these changes in the job market, which mean we'll need to learn more efficiently if we are to compete. But our inability to focus stops us doing this and leaves us clinging on to jobs we don't like for a retirement unplanned. No wonder we're unhappy.

The solution

The solution is deep work, which Newport describes as: "The ability to focus without distraction on a cognitively demanding task. It's a skill that allows you to quickly master complicated information and produce better results in less time... Deep work is like a super power in our increasingly competitive twenty-first century economy[451]." You can apply this super power to every part of your life, not just work. Embed this principle and you'll achieve more. Where once you were Swamp Thing now you'll be Superman, more efficient than a speeding bullet.

The prescription

We all have the ability to do focussed work. Here's the *RESET* way:

- **Learn how to say no.** This is an easy one. Work out what is the most important facet of your life/work right now and focus on that. Say no to anything else that hinders you achieving that goal. There are many things you *could* be doing, but what matters is what you *should* be doing. Speaking engagement? No. Meeting to talk about X? No. Going round to a mate's for dinner? No. And say no quickly. Don't keep opening and marking unopened that email asking you to do something in a few weeks' time. Say no now. Nicely, obviously. Word to the wise: these no's can be great ways to share what you're working on with the person you're saying no to. An honest reason goes a long way and builds trust.
- **Out of office**. If you're working on something, or know that you work best between X and Y times every day, stick an out of office on saying you'll be checking your emails at set times once or twice a day. Then if they want you, they can ring you on your mobile (*they* never do). This way you can focus on your work without the mental distraction caused by other people's I-expect-an-immediate-reply expectations.
- **Develop a system to deal with things.** Here, I've found nothing better, as a framework, than David Allen's *GTD* system[452]. My adapted version is as follows:

1. My email inbox is my in-tray, which I always empty twice a day. Aside from that, I don't look at them.
2. If I can deal with items in my email in-tray in two minutes, I do so. If not, I move them to somewhere else.
3. I have physical alphabetised foolscap folders for reference material, replicated on the cloud for electronic documents.
4. Anything time-based goes in my Google Calendar.
5. I have a "Someday/Maybe list" for what I *may* do in the future.
6. I have a to-do list, scrapped and started again daily.
7. Every week I look at my calendar for the month ahead and my "Someday/Maybe list". I plan. And start again.
8. This system helps free my mind to focus on the vital tasks that are important to me.

- **Become hard to reach.** Try working somewhere without a phone signal. Disable your notifications. If people expect you to be in your office, go somewhere else. It'll take them a while to get used to, but constant interruptions do nothing for your ability to do proper work. You end up doing thoughtful writing in the evening, eating into your family time, making you resent work even more.

- **Avoid meetings.** There's no bigger drag on the midlife careerist's work time than meetings. No one prepares, there's always some idiot who likes the sound of their own voice, they lead to groupthink and there are invariably too many people to make a decision. If you can avoid a meeting, do so. If you need ideas from a group, send individual emails. You'll be surprised at the uptick in quality compared to a group brainstorm where emotions and one-upmanship trump considered thought.

- **Don't work in an open-plan office.** If you're one of the 70%[453] of us who do, make sure you spend as little time in it as possible. The constant distractions of the open-plan workplace are not conducive to deep work. A mountain of research backs this up. As Susan Cain writes: "Open-plan offices have been found to re-duce productivity and impair memory. They're associated with high staff turnover. They make people sick, hostile, unmotivated and insecure[454]." To do deep work, you need time to think, which you ain't going to get if one ear is on Bill's latest ail-ments, while your mouth is having to advise how to deal with something else.

- **But coffee shops are fine.** Just ask J.K. Rowling. Maybe it's the social interaction without the obligation. Maybe it's the need to be around humans. David Burkus nails it in his October 2017 *Harvard Business Review* article in saying: "In our offices, we can't stop ourselves from getting drawn into others' con-versations or from being interrupted while we're trying to focus. Indeed, the EEG [electroencephalographic] researchers found that face-to-face interactions, conversations and other dis-ruptions negatively affect the creative process. By contrast, a co-working space or a coffee shop provides a certain level of ambient noise while also providing freedom from interruptions. Taken together, the lesson here is that the ideal space for focused work is not about freedom from noise, but about freedom from interruption[455]."

- **Add 50% to your time estimates.** If you follow this version of Hofstadter's Law[456], you'll spend less time chasing your tail and beating yourself up for being unproductive, leaving more energy to focus on work that matters.

- **Sleep well.** We need deep sleep. Bill Clinton said every big mistake he had made in life was due to lack of sleep[457] (I'd pay good money to see that list). Get seven hours a day, preferably eight.

- **Obsession.** You won't find many people following the advice above: there's always a good reason not to do something. *My boss won't like it, that'll never work in our company, I like working in an open-plan office with my colleagues; it helps germinate ideas.* The fact few other people make time for deep work is no reason to body-swerve it. The fact people will talk about your weird working practices is no good reason to rule it out. To achieve and make your life better you have to develop an obsessional streak, a focus. Given time, that's where the treasure is buried. Warren Buffett has an obsessional streak; he researches a market, invests in a good-value company and holds it for the long-term. He was once asked: "Warren, you're the most successful investor. Why don't people copy you and get rich?" His answer was: "Because people don't want to get rich slowly[458]."

Deep work is not the easy option, it'll badge you as different. But your obsession is your life and developing your deep work super power will pay superhuman dividends in the long run.

6. Hardest thing first

Procrastination is opportunity's natural assassin[459].
Victor Kiam

How do you decide what's most important, what to pour your heart and soul into, what to focus your deep-working on? What do you do when you need to decide what to do first? You procrastinate, of course. And there's nothing worse.

Psychology Today describes us thus: "Procrastinators chronically avoid difficult tasks and deliberately look for distractions. Procrastination in large part reflects our perennial struggle with self-control as well as our inability to accurately predict how we'll feel tomorrow, or the next day[460]." To cure procrastination and propel me in the direction of deep work, I adopt a simple principle: **do the hardest thing first**. Here's the method I use:

1. Ask yourself, what are you most scared of? What's eating away at you the most? What do you dream of? Whose achievements do you envy? What is the itch you need to scratch? You will find the bigger the fear, the more you want the prize.
2. Having identified your hardest thing, do your research, rough out a plan and start working, putting one foot in front of another, modifying said plan as you go along.
3. Set targets, and an end goal. How will you know when you get there?

Here are the things that would have helped me overcome my procrastination if I'd known them during the first 40 years of my life:

- **Imposter syndrome**[461]. Everyone suffers from it, no matter how brilliant they are. Don't let the fact that others have got a head start distract you from your goal.
- **Fear is good**, and you'll always have it. It's not about conquering your fear; it's about learning to act despite it.
- **Doubt is good, too**. Always beware the over-confident. Real experts spend most of their time scared they've got it wrong.
- **Master your instant gratification monkey.** *Wait But Why's* Tim Urban is an arch-procrastinator, whose TED talk on the topic

has 11m views. Interviewed on the *Art of Charm*[462] podcast, he talks about the limbic brain being the instant gratification monkey, which always dominates the rational decision-maker in all of us, until the "panic monster" roars into the room with minutes to go, leading the rational decision-maker to wrest control. But what this means is most of the time the arch-procrastinator is not doing what's important. Instead, they're trapped in a dark playground of guilt, not spending time with their kids like they ought to be. Don't be an arch-procrastinator. Lock that monkey back in its box.

7. Inspiration and enthusiasm

Strike while the iron is hot.
Anon

In *ReWork*, visionary business people Jason Fried and David Heinemeier Hansson offer this life-altering advice: "Inspiration is perishable... If you want to do something, you've got to do it now[463]."

Inspiration comes from everywhere, especially from people you know.

A few Christmases ago, a friend who never writes on Facebook revealed in a casual post that she'd read 89 books over the past year. Her enthusiasm inspired me to act: making reading part of my daily routine has benefitted my life.

Follow your passion; go off at obsessional tangents. Just do it. Harness that enthusiasm now, while you have the bit between your teeth, or you may live to regret it.

Brutus expresses it best in Act IV, Scene III of Shakespeare's *Julius Caesar*: "There is a tide in the affairs of men, which, taken at the flood, leads on to fortune; omitted, all the voyage of their life is bound in shallows and in miseries. On such a full sea are we now afloat. And we must take the current when it serves, or lose our ventures[464]."

8. Belief

The mind is its own place, and in it self
Can make a Heav'n of Hell, a Hell of Heav'n[465].
John Milton, *Paradise Lost*

Belief is different from confidence. No one's expecting you to be larger-than-life motivational speaker Tony Robbins. But to *RESET* your life and maintain its principles you have to have an enduring belief in your ability to do so.

That your worldview matters. That your instincts hold true. That if you apply yourself, you'll get out of life what you put in.

Knowledge helps, good friends and relationships help, but it's actions repeated over time, hard work, that cements this belief. Action gives you something to base your sincere and honest belief that you can succeed at anything if you apply your mind.

Don't let any *thing* or *person* limit you, never give up, manage your mind and let your actions speak louder than your words.

Believe in yourself and the world, and all that's in it, is yours.

9. Using negative motivation

Nothing gets me more worked up than someone who doesn't
believe in me[466].
Gary Vaynerchuk

What happens if people or events try to limit you? What happens if life deals you poor cards? What happens if someone has it in for you and there's nowt you can do about it? The first thing to remember is bad things happen; it's how we react to them, how we analyse and learn from them, that defines us. Looking back, some of the most painful and life-altering experiences make us who we are.

The second thing to remember is that if you float through life on a high cloud, you ain't going to learn much.

It's our failures that make us. As Michael Jordan said: "I've missed more than 9,000 shots in my career. I've lost almost 300 games. Twenty-six times I've been trusted to take the game winning shot...and missed. I've failed over and over and over again in my life. That is why I succeed." Einstein didn't speak until he was four years old and couldn't read until he was seven. Henry Ford failed and went broke five times before he succeeded. Two-time Oscar-winner Michael Caine's headteacher told him he'd be a labourer[467]. Never give up, don't be afraid to fail and when you do, get back on your feet, start walking and fail again.

The third thing to remember is that anger, even hate, well-channelled, can be a powerful force. The urge to prove your doubters wrong is a great starting point that can propel you on to great achievements. Get angry. That teacher at school who upbraided you in front of the class for poor spelling, that colleague who used to undermine you for being no good in court, that group of mums who make your daily pickups a misery, bank it and use it. And don't be worried that you're using a negative experience to motivate you. As Darren Hardy explains in *The Compound Effect*: "It's within our ability to cause everything to change. Rather than letting past hurtful experiences sap our energy and sabotage our success, we can use them to fuel positive, constructive change[468]."

The fourth and final thing to remember is this. Use negative motivation as much as you want, but don't let it define you. Don't let it become your purpose in life. Never ever measure yourself by others' yardsticks: choose your own. Because if you pick the wrong battle, no amount of money or success is going to make you happy.

Last year, I read *The Subtle Art of Not Giving a F*ck*[469]. Author Mark Manson recounts a story (widely known[470], but not by me), which struck a chord. When I was growing up, heavy metal passed me by as a musical genre, but I'd heard of the likes of *Megadeth* and *Metallica*. Household names both. What I didn't know was the story of Dave Mustaine. In 1983, the guitarist was given his marching orders from *Metallica*, then unknowns ready to record their first album. He resolved that day to start his own band, and that the new group would be more successful than his old. He'd show them.

Mustaine formed *Megadeth*, who would go on to sell 25m albums. The problem was that *Metallica* sold 180m, and (in a tearful interview in 2003) Dave admitted that because of this, despite the millions, he still considered himself a failure. Mustaine was amazingly successful, but by the yardstick he chose, "One-up *Metallica*", he failed.

The lesson here is, by all means use a negative "get it right up them" as one means of motivation...but don't let it be your driving force. Comparing yourself to others is a road paved with dog turds.

10. Be a jack of all trades: a Renaissance man

> *A Renaissance man[471] is a person who is competent in a wide range of fields, covering intellectual areas as well as the arts, physical fitness, and social accomplishments. This contrasts with the more modern, specialist approach, where a person is encouraged to build skills in a single vocation and use the income from that to pay for everything else[472].*
> **Jacob Lund Fisker**

Be a generalist, not a specialist. Be curious. See the value in learning. Sponge it up. Your job in this world is to develop your own frame of reference, your own worldview, your own philosophy of life. Work out what you think, and plough your own family's furrow, regardless of others.

The more you learn, the more actions you take, the more you'll be able to make connections between often disparate, previously compartmentalised, parts of your life – for the benefit of the new non-compartmentalised you. Your mission is to master a few subjects and be competent in a whole range of others, not to place all your eggs in one job basket and watch the industry you love crumble around you like cheshire cheese. *Your* mission is to know a little about a lot.

Greek philosopher Heraclitus said: "Character is destiny[473]." In a working world where specialisation is valued above all else, you might be forgiven for thinking that doubling down on your work specialisation is the best way of advancing your career. However, long-term, developing your character through educating yourself is what will pay dividends.

Charlie Munger, one half of the most successful investing partnership ever, gave a talk to USC Business School in 1994[474]. His premise: to pick stocks – or do anything – exceptionally, you have to understand the world; be wise. To do this, it's not enough just to learn facts. You need what Munger calls a "latticework" on which to attach, and make sense of, these facts. You need to learn "models". You need to understand and have studied the basic principles of mathematics, accounting, engineering, psychology, micro-economics. You have to understand the why, not the what.

In *Mastery*, Robert Greene examines the lives of great historical figures and contemporary leaders and distils the traits and universal ingredients that made them masters. He writes: "The future belongs to those who learn more skills and combine them in creative ways[475]."

It was ever thus. In 1899, that Renaissance man extraordinaire Jack London[476] said: "The only way of gaining [a life] philosophy is by seeking it, by drawing the materials which go to compose it from the knowledge and culture of the world... You must have your hand on the inner pulse of things. And the sum of all this will give you your working philosophy, by which, in turn, you will measure, weigh, and balance, and interpret to the world. It is this stamp of personality, of individual view, which is known as individuality."

No one embodies this more than Winston Churchill, a talented writer, farmer, orator (who mastered a speech impediment), painter, racehorse breeder, scriptwriter, parrot owner and qualified bricklayer[477]. A contrarian who came back from the political wilderness to lead his country through its darkest, and finest, hour. Someone whose curiosity and thirst for knowledge – and whisky, by all accounts – knew no bounds[478].

Now more than ever, with the internet making available every morsel of knowledge on the planet to a worldwide audience, it's those who use its enabling technology to learn and thrive that will lead happy and prosperous lives, while it's those who use it un-wisely that won't.

So put your back into it, commit to lifelong learning, read, ask five whys until you get to the bottom of whatever it is you're curious about, piece it together and see the world and all it has to offer open up for you.

It doesn't have to be the way it was.

You are the master of *your* fate.

You, and no one else, are the captain of your soul.

11. Run: an experiment

Our values are our hypotheses: this behavior is good and important; that other behavior is not. Our actions are the experiments; the resulting emotions and thought patterns are our data[479].
Mark Manson

I have a theory. People don't commit themselves to lifelong learn-ing for two reasons:

1. The misplaced belief that learning stops at school or university.
2. They have nowhere to experiment.

We discovered earlier in *RESET* that (1.) is bunkum. But (2.)? Do you need to test things out? Surely, you can develop your own worldview from books and reading accounts of others' experiments.

No. We all learn through experience and everyone needs a place to experiment. To answer questions, like:

- What will happen if I make a plan instead of making it up as I go along?
- Is it better to do things with other people or on my own?
- How does what I eat and how I sleep affect my performance?

- That latest scientific research, does it stand up to scrutiny?
- Can I use negative motivation to improve my performance?
- Are there certain fundamental principles I need to follow to succeed?
- Are there different ways of achieving the same objective?
- What happens if I adopt these values instead of those?

Over the past six years, I've been doing hundreds of experiments in my twin laboratories: *my owner-managed business and the crucible of running. RESET* assumes you're a salaried employee, so let's leave the benefits of running a small business to one side for a minute and focus on the latter.

Like an estimated two million people across the UK[480], I run. I suggest you do as well. Or find your own research lab and start testing. Here's what running has taught me:

- **Running breeds confidence.** My journey began six years ago when I started to run. I soon realised the potential of this magical life-giving pursuit. All I had to do was be effective; if I worked hard, the results would come.
- **Running is fair.** You know why? Because the rules are simple and progress is measurable: you can't cheat the clock.
- Running gives you time to think. **Reflect, recharge.**
- **Running adds three years on to your life.** If you're a midlife professional and run four hours a week, you'll add three years on to that early retirement[481].
- **Runners need fuel.** Like in your other activities, what you eat and drink affects your performance.
- **Running makes friends and communities.** Sharing a common interest with people in your local area brings you friends and increases mental well-being.
- **Fewer goals more success.** I've learned over the years that chasing multiple running goals leads to disappointment. Better to focus on one or two concrete objectives and plan your training around them.

- **You never regret a run.** It's unheard of to return home in a worse mood than when you left.
- **Running rewards knowledge.** The more you learn about running, the more you run, the more you read, the more you chat to other runners, the faster you'll become.
- **Running rewards experimentation.** Training for a marathon, do you run lots of slow miles or fewer fast miles? I've tried both and know what works for my mind and body.
- **The successful are not exceptional, they're obsessed with improvement.** Take Charlie Spedding, for example. Not an exceptional talent, but he squeezed every last drop of potential out of his 5ft 8in frame and, on a few memorable occasions, trans-formed a self-styled caterpillar into a beautiful butterfly. He wanted it, made sacrifices, aimed for the stars and grabbed them.
- **Plan and adapt.** I agree with Mike Tyson. You can have the best, most detailed plan in the world, but when fate (in the form of injury) makes an appearance, you have to adapt.
- **Mind games.** Marathoning, my passion, is 50% physical and 50% in the mind. You can run your times through any marathon time predictor you want, but when you pass that 20-mile marker, it's you, the tarmac and the clock. The body may be willing, but the mind had better be, too.
- **Suffering.** Perhaps the reason many midlife professionals take up running, and particularly endurance running, is because their lives are too comfortable. As Brad Stulberg said: "In a world where comfort is king, arduous physical activity provides a rare opportunity to practice suffering[482]."
- **Age shall not wither us.** "When I run, I never try to beat anyone in my age group, I try to beat everybody. I think I am just a 25-year-old wolf." These were the words of 54-year-old American Doug Fernandez on winning the Harrisburg Marathon in 2:40:22 on Sunday November 9th 2014. He added: "The key is not to put age barriers in your mind, and you'll do so much better. People get old, prematurely, in their minds. You've always got to think that you're young[483]."

- **You'll find a mentor.** Mine's my coach at Giffnock North A.C. running club, Bernie Campbell. Having someone who cares about your running is kinda cool.
- **A virtuous circle.** Running improves every aspect of your life.
- **Persistence.** Running, and particularly marathoning, is all about the struggle, the striving as John Coltrane says. Hitting a stretch target through persistence, overcoming setbacks, coming back stronger when others have written you off. That's a good feeling.

Author Charles Duhigg, in his 2012 best-seller *The Power of Habit*[484], calls exercise a "keystone habit", or a change in one area of life that has positive effects in other areas. Duhigg says keystone habits are powerful because: "they change our sense of self and our sense of what is possible[485]."

Like many before me, running has changed my life. I have found that there is no substitute for hard, consistent, well-directed effort, day after day after day. Good thoughts lead to good habits lead to good outcomes. Since starting running, I've surpassed what I thought was my potential. Actually, surpassed is not the right word. Smashed. I had no interest in athletics at school and came towards the back of the 100 metres. I started running aged 39 and three-quarters to get fit. Then realised I liked it. Then that I was OK at it. I worked harder. I read books, joined a running club, watched films about it, and watched what I ate. For two years, I improved, markedly, and in 2014 was the first, adopted, Scot home at the Berlin marathon.

Running has shown me what I can achieve if I focus. It's the laboratory in which I've developed and tested my worldview against the timing clock that never lies. And I've applied what I've learned to all aspects of my life ever since.

CHAPTER 37

Part V Index Card

- Be different.
- Take small actions every day.
- Turn habits into routines.
- Work hard, say no, and focus.
- Follow your fear.
- Act on enthusiasm while it lasts.
- Believe.
- Show 'em what you're made of.
- Be a generalist, not a specialist.
- Experiment and run.

And finally...

That's – almost – all folks. But before we wrap up, here's a short part comprising the nuggets I've gleaned over the past six years of *searching*, which I can't find a home for elsewhere in the book. Think of what follows as *RESET*'s *parting shots.*

PART VI

12 Do's and 12 Don'ts

CHAPTER 38

12 Do's

1. Play

As a kid what excited you? Rediscover it.

2. Be grateful

Count your blessings. Keep a gratitude journal. I wrote one for my wife every day for four months – she couldn't read my writing. Here's an entry from 2015: "Beautiful, kind and thoughtful wife, two amazing children, lots of interests, lots of friends including big safe circle, health – me and family, willpower and drive, a hobby I love, reinvigorated work life, nice local community and home, love of the outdoors."

We all have lots to be thankful for, and we should shout our gratitude from the rooftops.

Everyone craves praise if it's sincere. Don't *just* write it down, tell people.

Keep a gratitude journal for your partner; send a letter of thanks to a family member; compliment one of your friends when they've done something thoughtful for you. It's these out-of-the-ordinary interactions with loved ones that contribute to their (and your) happiness[486].

Your relationships matter.

3. Laugh

Have a sense of humour. Watch your favourite comedian. Ring your funny mate. If all else fails, force a smile, it works[487]. Life's tough. Laugh and the world laughs with you...don't worry, be happy.

4. Some stress is good

A life without stress is a life without challenge. To avoid the rest: keep in touch with family and friends, seek new local networks, do things you're avoiding, don't smoke or drink excessively, limit your coffees to two a day before 15:30. Try new hobbies, read every day and keep a worry pad rating the chances of those worries happening from one to ten.

5. Don't live in London

Belgian graphic designer Sara De Bondt, writing in *How to be a Graphic Designer, Without Losing Your Soul*, said: "The risk of working in a capital city like London is that you begin to believe yourself at the centre of the world, to lose that excitement of being on the periphery and feeling that you are not there yet, that you still have to learn[488]."

It's easier to be striving, struggling–and–always–learning, when you're on the periphery not in the centre. The best original thought often comes from those without too much face to lose, those who've not *yet* "made it".

6. Seek adventures

There's no better word in the English language than adventure: "an exciting experience that is typically a bold, sometimes risky, undertaking[489]." In Britain, and throughout the world, we love our Captain Scotts, our Ernest Shackletons, our David Attenboroughs.

Adventures feed the soul. When I'm in the wilderness, in the mountains, climbing, I'm in the moment – nothing else matters.

I'm in control, worries recede, life is simpler and sometimes I get those Polaroid moments that stick, providing sustenance. I recall one unusual day on the Black Cuillin with my brother-in-law in the late 1990s. Fifteen hours after leaving Glen Brittle, 22:00 saw us wet-through and bivvied-down, under an overhanging rock by a hut on the shore of Loch Coruisk. At dawn, we set off and stopped in our tracks as a deer and her three fawns crossed the confluence exiting the loch to the sea.

Nowadays, we must plan these trips months ahead, but building weekly adventures – whatever form they take – into your family's lives is the best investment you'll ever make.

7. Let's get physical

Stand up and work, use marker pens for to-do lists, pin things on walls and look for patterns, use whiteboards, static sheets, Post-it notes, index cards.

There's a magic in the physical act of writing and moving that the time-efficient sedentary act of computing will never match.

Move around, who cares if you receive funny looks. If you're not working well in one area of the room, go somewhere else. If the creative juices aren't flowing, do ten press-ups, stroll for five minutes, swim 20 lengths.

Walk faster. Speak in social situations. If you're going to an event, be a front-rower and make sure you always ask a question. When you meet someone, stand tall, make strong eye contact and apply a firm handshake.

All of this physicality matters. And it'll make you a little happier and more productive, too.

8. Make a movie

We used to have a movie camera growing up, with rolling film. Thirty years on at a family get-together, I remember watching in awe as grainy footage, of my brother and me clambering over the Peak District's gritstone, flickered on to the wallpaper. Now we use

1 Second Everyday app[490] to take a second of video each day on my smartphone. I can't wait to see what it makes of our year. One day our children will, in the words of US writer Joyce Carol Oates, become like us: "ghosts haunting the lost landscapes of our childhood[491]." And they'll thank us for mementoes like these.

9. Ticking tomato anyone?

The Pomodoro [productivity] Technique[492] involves setting a preferably ticking kitchen timer – often shaped like a tomato – for 25 minutes. When the timer finishes, you take a five-minute break, then repeat thrice. Then take a longer break. You should try it. It works.

10. Small to-do lists

Keep your daily to-do lists small. Plonk the most important task at the top. You can only have one priority.

11. The importance of chit-chat

The strongest predictor of how long you'll live is your daily interactions with strangers. Not the quality of your close relationships (albeit that's a close second), not whether you smoke, booze, exercise or are fat or thin. In a meta-analysis of 300,000-plus people[493], researchers at Brigham Young University found that the key to living a long life is social integration.

Those chats with your neighbours, people at the school gate, the bloke serving you coffee at Starbucks, the guard on the train; it's those daily interactions on which we place no emphasis that make a long life. How much, and with what positivity, you interact with people who don't mean a great deal to you as you move through your day.

Watch Susan Pinker's TED talk[494], and the next time the old lady passes your house with her doddery dog, ask her how she's doing. She'd like that.

12. Go it alone

Self-employment is not for the faint-hearted. Eight out of ten entrepreneurs who start businesses fail within the first 18 months, according to *Bloomberg*[495]. But if you can make it through those first few years (I'm on my fifth), there's much to be said for joining the ranks of the one in 25 UK workers who work for themselves[496].

Let's be clear. *RESET* is written for you: the salaried midlife professional, searching for a more meaningful life. Nowhere does it say jack in your job and go it alone. But if you ever do get the chance, don't reject it out of hand. Here's a quick rundown of why:

- **Fulfilment:** you can work on what you want, when you want.
- **Control:** it's all down to you and no one else. *You are the captain of your ship.*
- **Non-compartmentalised life:** a typical afternoon could comprise working on a client report, going online to pay for your kid's school trip, checking your cloud budgeting software, then a swim. You design your lifestyle to suit your family and you. You'll soon get used to it.
- **No mind tension:** work on projects that fit your values.
- **It's your wagon now:** and it's not hitched to anyone else's.
- **Bye-bye office politics:** hello people you *want* to spend time with.
- **Time:** you'll have more time to breathe, more time to learn. Leaving aside the self-actualisation process in this book, you'll need to master new skills if you're going to run a successful business, however small. Websites, accounting, tax, billing, proposals, client management and marketing: the list is endless. And the more you learn, the more you'll *want* to learn.
- **Pride:** "Small is not just a stepping-stone. Small is a great destination in itself... Anyone who runs a business that is sustainable and profitable, whether it's big or small, should be proud[497]." Couldn't agree with you more, *ReWork* dudes.
- **Money:** here's what they don't tell you as a salaried employee. Yes, setting up on your own is risky, yes you might look a

complete idiot and have to come crawling back to your old network like a skulking dog. But if your business succeeds and prospers that risk will be rewarded by paying far less tax than your safe-as-houses ex-colleagues do. Although it's not as tax-efficient as it was a few years ago, running a limited company is still a good way of earning a living. If you want to learn more, my favourite drink is a latte (as long as you're buying it).

- **Millionaires next door:** dig through Danko and Stanley's *The Millionaire Next Door* and you'll find oodles of huge-sample-size research showing that self-employment is the best way of accumulating wealth. "In America, fewer than one in five households, or about 18 percent, is headed by a self-employed business owner or professional. But these self-employed people are four times more likely to be millionaires than those who work for others." And: "if you're frugal and a conscientious investor and you own a business that is profitable...you're likely to become wealthy[498]."
- **FIRE transition:** I love my job, and love working, so when our stash grows big enough that we can live on it, I'll be on the financial independence side of the FIRE fence, not the early retirement one. Already owning my consulting business will make life easier to take on work that interests me. I imagine if I'd worked for employers all my life, the post-FIRE switch to self-employment would be that daunting I wouldn't bother.

Last, if you do set up on your own, never drop your hourly rate. If anything increase it because of the time and effort you're investing in learning, which benefits your clients. Charge your value. You're worth it.

CHAPTER 39

12 Don'ts

1. Don't abandon news

I have sympathy with the rubbish-in-rubbish-out school of thought regarding news. Bad news sells. Why would you want to fill your brain with negativity? Focus on you and yours – that's what matters. k an obvious interest here. My job dictates I must stay on top of what's happening outside my immediate sphere. But even if this weren't the case, I'd still passionately argue that knowing what is going on in the world is important, particularly the bad bits. I've been listening to *Today* and reading newspapers since I was a kid. What I've heard and learned helps me make sense of what's happening now; they give me context and have shaped my worldview.

Complement with learning and self-improvement. Meet new people, join new organisations, try new hobbies, but read, watch and listen to grownup news from trusted sources. You owe it to yourself and the world to be informed about what's going on in it.

2. Never blame other people

Blame yourself. When you take the blame, you inspire others with your honesty. Then reflect and learn. Taking the blame is not a sign of weakness: covering up your mistakes is.

3. Don't be terrified of taking risks

A former mentor of mine once took me aside and said: "What are you afraid of, Dave? There's no mess you can create that can't be fixed. And we'll be there for you when that time comes."

4. Don't say "not bad"

Change your vocabulary. English is a rich and diverse language. Use it. Most days I pick my eight-year-old son up from school. "How was your day, Jude?" I say. "Good," he replies. Be Jude.

5. Keep it real

Don't change your mates or the way you look based on the oft-repeated mantras that you're judged by the company you keep and your appearance. Be real. Form genuine friendships with people you like, not people you think will advance your wealth or career. Your associations will define you and genuine connections will enrich your life in more ways than you can imagine. However, your disassociations will define you just as much. Don't hang on to relationships that have run their course or turned sour. If some-one's not a positive influence anymore, drop them. Life's too short.

6. Don't always be taking

As a midlife professional, your biggest problem is time. Find a charitable cause that matters to you. If you can't give time, give money. But give something. It helps the world and it'll make you a little happier, too.

7. Don't be a workaholic

Remember, looking back at your life, you're never going to regret *not* working harder, but you will wish you'd spent more time with your family, doing what mattered to you.

8. Never think you know it all

We have a saying in the UK: "No one likes a smart arse." Gathering wisdom, forming your own worldview, is all about listening and little about shoving your knowledge down people's throats.

Don't be the person who answers questions meant for other people. Don't interrupt others when they're explaining a point. Don't assume people are going to be interested in what you say just because *you're* saying it. Do be humble and listen. Who knows: you might learn something.

9. Don't trust your gut for small decisions

Be rational. But for big decisions, go for your life.

According to *Help!* author Oliver Burkeman's extensive research, big decisions involve: "so many factors that rational analysis will make things worse: you'll fail to take account of some potential considerations, or assign too much or too little importance to others[499]."

What I do is work out which way my gut is going after researching whatever it is I need to decide on. But the clincher is finding someone online that can show me the way. When I committed to financial independence that person was Mr. Money Mustache. I sincerely hope that for you *that person* can be me.

10. Don't be perfect

In *Bird by Bird*, Anne Lamott writes: "Perfectionism is the voice of the oppressor, the enemy of the people. It will keep you cramped and insane your whole life...[500]" By all means strive, but don't go for perfection. Focus on one task at a time, do the best that you can, then move on to the next. This is not a recipe for low standards. Always try to exceed expectations: yours and others. But the key is to take action, put your best foot forward and make sure the other follows it quick sharp.

Nobody's perfect – who wants to be nobody?

11. No whingeing

Nothing's worse than a whinger, a drain. I'm not saying you have to be happy all the time, far from it. It's only when we're dissatisfied with life that we're receptive to transformative change. But don't whinge about it. Do your research, make a plan and seize the day.

12. Nobody cares about you...

Apart from your close friends and family. Everyone else cares only what they can get out of you, how you can benefit them[501]. What are you doing that adds something to the world? What use are you? It's not what's inside of you that matters, it's what you do with it.

What footprint are you going to leave when you die? You'd better start working on that or life will pass you by. If you need further motivation to take action, google "Alec Baldwin Speech *Glengarry Glen Ross*[502]". Don't stand there. Just do it. Now.

CHAPTER 40

Part VI Index Card

- Do adventures.
- Do get physical.
- Don't be perfect.
- Don't just stand there.
- It's not what's inside that counts, it's what you do with it.
- Listen.
- Be informed.
- Be Jude.

And finally...

You're at the end of the *RESET* road less travelled by. Let's say you've followed the plan; what did the journey look like? You started at your status quo, mastered your fears, found your purpose, future-proofed your career, decluttered, implemented the **FIRE Triumvirate** and re-discovered 11 foundational principles to lead a good life. You defeated the ugly troll, crossed the humpback bridge and are lying in the green fields marvelling at how fresh the mountain air smells. You have FIRE peak in your sights and you can even spot the path to the top. You've reached Nirvana. *How does that feel?*

NIRVANA

YOU DON'T KNOW HOW it feels is the simple answer. You've read a book: it's what you do now that counts.

I can give you a glimpse though. If Status Quo was your life unlived. What will your lived one be like? When your soul is released, what will the difference be? I'd love to give you a rallying call now. But that would be dishonest. If you spend the next year doing a reset, yes, your life will be transformed.

1. Yes, you'll be in control.
2. Your pride will be restored.
3. You won't worry about money as much.
4. Your career will be back on the right trajectory.
5. You'll have reconnected with your values.
6. You'll have renewed purpose, a clear vision and a plan of how to get there.

In a year's time life, your life, will be a whole lot better. But will everything in your garden be rosy? Is Nirvana achievable for the midlife professional? No.

I have sympathy with polymath, the late Christopher Hitchens's pessimistic view that: "The search for Nirvana, like the search for Utopia or the end of history or the classless society, is ultimately a futile and dangerous one. It involves, if it does not necessitate, the sleep of reason. There is no escape from anxiety and struggle[503]."

RESET is not about achieving "A transcendent state in which there is neither suffering, desire, nor sense of self...[504]" – life will still be a challenge. You will still have to dodge the slings and arrows of outrageous misfortune. You'll still shout at the kids occasionally and swear at annoying drivers.

Life's a struggle. Twas ever thus. But instead of a hopeless ever-shifting battle, it'll be a cause worth fighting, striving for. So once you've done your own reset, inhale, breathe in that mountain air. Then thrust back your shoulders, don your steel helmet, and get back to work. By reading *RESET*, you've just given yourself the chance of a fresh start: make sure you seize it with both hands.

And finally...

And I mean it this time, we reach the end, dear reader. Let's say goodbye to *Nirvana* – I never liked them anyway, even their late stuff – struggle free of the mosh pack, through the fire exit, past the smokers, and sit still for a minute. In the conclusion, I'll tell you what *I* think.

CONCLUSION

LIKE ANY GOOD SELF-HELP book, *RESET* is sprinkled with statistics, studies and quotes from a cast of inspirational characters. I hope you've enjoyed their company as much as I have this past six years. However, with the curtain about to come down on our time together and those characters melting away into the darkness, all that remains is you and me.

Come over here. Closer. I have **three things to share.**

First, life might be a bit meh for you right now. If so, don't worry, keep putting one foot in front of the other, and work at it.

RESET is not a one-off event. It sounds like pressing a button. But the key is to reset every day, every time two roads diverge, every choice in life – reset on to your right path. Soon this will come naturally because it comes from within – this regular reprogramming of our behaviour leads to a more lasting reset of our lives. We all have our own strengths, weaknesses and interests: all made from a different kit of parts. My genuine ambition is you apply some of what's resonated with you in this book and bag a better future. It's never too late. Who knows where you could be in a year's time?

Second thing. We began *RESET* sitting in a light blue Vauxhall Chevette, and I'm ending it there by answering the question: *was Mum right?*

Is life about being happy or *is it* not as simple as all that?

Here's what the intervening 35 years have taught me as I've striven to make sense of my time on Earth.

Life centres on the elusive pursuit of happiness, but (paradoxically) the more we chase it the more elusive it becomes. Sometimes we attain elation. Sometimes we deserve it – the runner's high after achieving a marathon PB, or the moment we win a prestigious award. More often we don't – an afternoon with Sky Sports *Super Sunday*, or winning £10 on the lottery. Either way, such feelings of elation are unsustainable: soon we're back in our car en route to the office with only our minds to console us. True, lasting, happiness comes from purpose, fulfilment and meaning. Living a life we're proud of, being the best we can. Hard work, good choices, strong convictions, values that mean something to *us*.

Doing the right thing, the hard thing, isn't easy. But if there's one *thing* you'll remember from this book, it's that taking small deliberate actions day after day is what leads to contentment.

Do, don't watch. Treat failures as opportunities. Invest in yourself and always be searching. Be nice to people without expectation. Choose experiences over possessions – every time. Work hard at your career, make money, build your net worth and get *it* working hard for you. But listen – for your own sake and your family's – to Bronnie Ware[505].

Do this and you'll be happier, in the true, *RESET*, sense of the word.

Third, what of love? I'm not a big fan of musicals, but I watched *Moulin Rouge*, on the recommendation of my cousin, Paul. In the opening sequence[506], David Bowie sings Nat King Cole's haunting "Nature Boy" with its famous denouement: "The greatest thing you'll ever learn is just to love and be loved in return[507]."

Love can be the most painful emotion in the world but also the most fulfilling. Picking the right partner to share your life with is critical to happiness. I'm lucky to be married to a remarkable, kind woman I've spent a quarter of a century with, whose views on what matters mesh with my own. Like many others, we've been our happiest since having kids. They've made sense of our lives and given us a core purpose, which'll be there until the day we die.

"Life's about being happy, *and* it's not as simple as all that." *See, Mum? We were both right.*

AFTERWORD

IN SEPTEMBER 1940, THE RAF stood on its last legs. Hitler's Blitz terror campaign rained down on English cities. Germany was making plans to invade and Britain stared into the jaws of defeat.

Carrying the hopes of the nation under his top hat, one Renaissance man[508] refused to give in, making an extraordinary effort to rally a country on its knees.

One year later, returning to London after signing a joint declaration with President Franklin D. Roosevelt, Winston Churchill gave this speech to a packed House of Commons on September 9th 1941:

> *Thus far then have we travelled along the terrible road we chose at the call of duty. The mood of Britain is wisely and rightly averse from every form of shallow or premature exultation. This is no time for boasts or glowing prophecies, but there is this: A year ago our position looked forlorn, and well-nigh desperate to all eyes but our own. To-day we may say aloud before an awe-struck world: 'We are still masters of our fate. We are still captain of our souls[509].'*

ACKNOWLEDGEMENTS

OK WINSTON, BACK IN your box now. At this point, why do I want to say: "I would like to thank...", as if I'm on stage at the Oscars?

Ahem *clears throat*, *here goes...*

My wife, Rachel, has not read a word of my book: I hope she likes its contents. If I'd been her, I would have been resentful going out to work every day for nine months while I gave birth to a childhood dream. To the best of my knowledge, she wasn't. All I received was encouragement and belief. Love you, Rach.

Zak is quite taken by the fact he can tell his friends in the playground that his dad's an author. Jude wishes this book had been finished three months ago as it's taken Daddy away from him. Thanks kids, this is my view on life halfway through. I hope you read it when you're older (excuse the swear words) and don't think your dad put his old age ahead of your right to MilkyWays. (And no, Zak, you still can't sign up to my email list. It's for over-18s only.)

My folks made me who I am today: I thank you dearly for all the bits I like; I forgive you for the few bits I don't (only joking, they're down to me). I am so glad you hearted *RESET* when I mustered the courage to show it you. Love you, Mum and Dad: you're an inspiration.

I couldn't have written this book (yes, I know, those Oscars again) without the support of some unconventional individuals straight out of my favourite film, *The Big Lebowski* (why that movie didn't win an Academy Award, I'll never know). I could say they're too numerous to mention, but, if I'd reached the Acknowledgements, having helped a friend – and spent hours and days listening to his incessant self-indulgent obsessing – I'd be a bit miffed if my name didn't appear in lights.

Let's invite them up to take a bow.

First up, influencer marketing expert Scott (Guthrie). I've met Scott only once, yet his friendship has come to mean a great deal to me. We've both worked in the PR industry for more years than we care to remember. And we both "went digital" at pretty much the same time, starting in 2013; him in Sydney, me in Glasgow. Over the last two years, we've skyped (often glass in hand) every month. Scott has been invaluable in helping loosen tight knots in *RESET*'s structure, and listening. Love you mate.

Second, the rest of my alpha readers (people who read your shitty first draft out of kindness and obligation). What a stellar band they've formed. There's Cousin Paul (Thompson) on meaning, purpose and so much more; Jane (Cumming) the PR guru on grammar; big third sector cheese Ian (Williams) on intro-cutting and gentle persuasion; Neal (Gibson) the ultramarathoner on inadvertent sexism (mine not his); Kenny (Barr) the top newsman on meeting me to say how fantastic he thought it was; Rob (Sykes) the accountant on intro-hatred and questioning the maths; Peter (Donelan) the Tanzanian shoulder-dwelling devil, who made me think in a writerly fashion about such elevated topics as the narrator's voice; Steve (Murray) on monthly trips to the best front-room-bar in the world ("Matthew's"), and well-meant but offensive casual remarks (again, mine, not his); and sister-in-law Robyn (Maguire) who demanded I remove that bizarre comment about cats. Adoration to you all.

Third, the beta readers (they scan the final, polished draft, along, in my case, with many of the alphas – so grateful). Thanks to: Matty (Sanders), a friend with more flash cars and "time tokens" than I've had hot dinners, and a photographic memory of our childhood; Chris (Black), Brendan (Moriarty) and Hamish (Barbour) – the runners; Paul (Sutton), the social media expert; northern soul-mate JP (McCormick); the most talented writer I know – Japan Tim (Maughan); and Stuart (Macdonald), the cerebral businessman with more brainpower than the Count of Monte Cristo had doubloons[510]. Mwaah.

Fourth, those who commented on my first book proposal, way back when. Including: Stephen (Waddington), Dan (Slee), Campbell (Docherty) and Nick (Sharpe) – all eminent digital PR people; Andy (Lee) the management consultant and ex-PR; and Christie (Barlow) – who's gone on to become a superstar author. Their feedback made me scrap the original concept and produce something I would want to read. Heart emoji, people.

Fifth, to my running hero, Charlie Spedding who – though we only have a tenuous connection through JP, Durham and marathoning – consented to read my book and pen a perfect foreword. A pint of Eureka to you, Charlie.

Sixth, it's customary to thank your agent, publisher, designer, typesetter, indexer, marketer, etc. A big round of applause here for David (Sawyer).

Now for the meandering paragraph. To everyone who's shown an interest in what I've been doing this past six years, particularly during the book-producing process – cheers, it is much appreciated. You know who you are and how much I value your opinion. Thanks to my former employers for giving me the opportunity to earn my spurs (or chops, if you're in the US). Love to my family (particularly Ian, my brother) and friends for such a wonderful childhood growing up in Cheshire and then Durham. My clients, you deserve a medal: I couldn't have written this book without what you've taught me; and Andy (McFarlan), big thanks for your perseverance. Also, I am indebted to those I've referenced, quoted and mentioned in RESET. Without your unknowing tutelage over the past six years, this book would be a shadow of itself. Big love to the giants on whose shoulders I am standing.

The encore

Everyone's left the Oscars and my Jools Holland-esque[511] rhythm and blues band have repaired to the pub (hopefully chatting about what a great guy I am). Even my family have left the building. I walk to the middle of the stage (it's like Northwich Odeon only ten times bigger, and not an ice-cream seller in sight). The spotlight's on me. I don't want to leave, reader: you can tell, can't you. I'm desperate to find out if you do the hard work outlined in *RESET*. Nevertheless, I know, we must now go our separate ways.

But before you *badoing* that front-row seat you've been perching on throughout this book, my final acknowledgement is this. I wrote *RESET* primarily for me. But it's become – during nine months spent largely in my head – for you.

I've been trying to imagine what you're like, who you are, what you dream about when you fall asleep. Where you'll be reading this, whether you're taking notes in the margins, is it sunny or cold? Without the knowledge that you would one day hold this book in your hands, I couldn't have written it. Love you, too. (Oh, and if you were to leave a review on Amazon, I would be most grateful.)

P.S. In the spirit of the Oscars, finally, I'd like to pay tribute to my hairdresser, Michael Dooey (and his erstwhile nextdoor neighbour, Matthew Casserly), who gets more of my money for less work the older I get.
P.P.S. Spotlight down. Over to you...

GLOSSARY OF TERMS

- **Asset allocation:** an investment strategy that aims to balance risk and reward by apportioning a portfolio's assets according to an individual's goals, risk tolerance and investment horizon.
- **Bonds:** loans made to large organisations. These include corporations, cities and national governments. A bond is a piece of a big loan.
- **Careerist:** a professional person who has fallen into the habit of putting their career before their life.
- **CETV:** stands for Cash Equivalent Transfer Value, the monetary value of your final salary pension.
- **Defined Contribution (DC) and Defined Benefit (DB):** the former refers to work pensions run by your employers where *they* contribute a set percentage every month, and you do, too. DB normally refers to final salary pensions in the UK.
- **Early retirement:** in *RESET*, this means retiring before the age of 60 (well before, ideally). Early retirement means never working again, which might be your thing. However, *RESET* suggests aiming for financial independence: never having to work again if you don't want to.
- **Final salary scheme:** a company pension scheme in which employees' pension payments are calculated according to their length of service and their salary at time of retirement.
- **Financial Independence (FI):** having enough money that you can live off the income from your assets and never *have* to work again.

- **FIRE:** stands for Financial Independence Retire Early.
- **F.U. Money:** having enough assets that you never have to do anything you don't want to for money ever again. With F.U. Money you have the options to either politely decline, or say: "Fuck you".
- **IFA:** stands for Independent Financial Adviser.
- **Index investing:** otherwise known as passive investing, where you invest in low-cost funds that track stock market indexes, such as the S&P 500.
- **Isa:** stands for individual savings account, a tax-free way to save or invest in the UK.
- **Midlifer:** someone aged between 35 and 60.
- **Mutual funds:** baskets of stocks. They give more diversification than individual stocks. Humans can manage them (active funds) or they can be set to track an index (passive funds), such as the FTSE 100 in the UK.
- **Net worth:** for the typical midlifer this will comprise: value of all investments (including pensions), cash savings and house equity (value of house minus money owed on mortgage).
- **One pot:** the principle of getting all your money viewable in one place, as far as you possibly can. This increases transparency and motivation when building your stash.
- **PB:** running term that stands for Personal Best (known as PR or Personal Record in the US).
- **Public Relations (PR):** looks after reputation, with the aim of earning understanding and support and influencing opinion and behaviour.
- **Rebalancing:** realigning the proportions of assets in a portfolio as needed. Say you decided you wanted to invest 50% of your money in an S&P 500 index tracker and 50% in a FTSE 100 tracker. But over the course of one year, one did well and one did terribly. By the end of the year, your portfolio could be 40% UK/60% US. To maintain your desired weighting (eg, 50/50) you would sell US units and buy UK ones. Rebalancing is commonly done once every six months or a year or when you come into money.

- **Retail investor:** an individual who buys shares for his or her own personal account rather than for an organisation. Retail investors typically trade in much smaller amounts than institutional investors such as mutual funds, pensions, or university endowments.
- **Safe Withdrawal Rate (SWR):** an extremely important retirement planning figure used to estimate how much you can withdraw from your stash each year without running out of money before you die.
- **SEO:** stands for search engine optimisation: the art of improving your website's search engine rankings (appearing as high as possible when you type/speak a phrase into, eg, Google's search engine).
- **Shares:** the stock of a company is sold in units called shares. A share is a unit of ownership, or equity, in a company or a corporation.
- **Sipp:** stands for self-invested personal pension, a UK pension plan that enables you to choose and manage your investments.
- **Stash:** your net worth minus your house equity and final salary pension (if you're lucky enough to have one) transfer value. *Stash* is a term popularised by Mr. Money Mustache.
- **Stock:** a type of security that signifies ownership in a corporation and represents a claim on part of the corporation's assets and earnings.
- **Tilt:** a portfolio "tilt" is industry slang for an investment strategy that overweighs a particular investment style, eg, small-cap or value stocks.
- **Transaction cost (TC):** let me tell you a story. Until January 2018, anyone investing in index funds in the UK paid hidden charges, on top of their account/service fee, on top of their **ongoing charge figure (OCF)**, covering such things as "broker commissions, entry and exit charges, spreads, stamp duty, transactions tax and foreign exchange costs". And few of us knew it. From the turn of this year (2018), European legislation called MiFID II forced hands, and now you can spot these "transaction costs" on investment firms' – such as Fidelity and

Vanguard – websites (if you look hard enough). And still, few of us know it. To this observer, it strikes me as a scenario akin to the airline industry pre-consolidation of consumer pricing, and one that cannot continue. To locate Vanguard's transaction costs (such as the 0.15% TC it charges for its 0.08%-OCF UK all share fund) you have to navigate to toreset.me/vantcs – I can't even find it searching now, it's so buried. Fidelity is slightly better (transaction costs are listed on its individual fund pages, under the OCFs). But both still give the impression on their main fees pages that there are no hidden charges (maybe not hidden, but certainly buried on their websites). I have sympathy for these firms. OCFs have historically been *the* way investors compare fund costs. However, eight months after the legislation came in, isn't it time for real transparency? To be clear, transaction costs are ongoing charges, not to be confused with you transacting funds, whether lump sum or monthly. And not to be confused with the ongoing charges figure itself, which covers "charges for investment management, custody, fund accounting, audit, compliance, transfer agency, trustee and tax reporting". Confused? I don't blame you. Until this situation changes, all you need to do for now is tot up the combined portfolio transaction cost (TC), the ongoing charge figure (OCF) and **account/service fee** to establish the overall percentage cost of investing. And it's that number you should base the investment-costs element of your investing decision on. Vanguard's pdf does a brilliant job of breaking down the charges to allow you to do this. It's just a pity (and not in keeping with the firm's excellent/open ethos) that it's to be found in its website's nether regions.

BIBLIOGRAPHY

EVERY BOOK CITED IN the Notes section of *RESET* is included here in the Bibliography. I have read and can recommend them all. Non-affiliate Amazon links to each book can be found in the Notes, should you wish to buy. (The book page numbers in the Notes refer to the book editions in the Bibliography, not those in the Amazon links, albeit in most cases they will be one and the same.)

Allen, David. *Getting Things Done: The Art of Stress-Free Productivity.* Little Brown Book Group, 2015.

Arana, Marie. *The Writing Life: Writers on How They Think and Work: A Collection from the Washington Post Book World.* Public Affairs, 2003.

Burkeman, Oliver. *Help!: How to Become Slightly Happier and Get a Bit More Done.* Faber and Faber, 2011.

Cain, Susan. *Quiet: The Power of Introverts in a World That Can't Stop Talking.* Penguin, 2013.

Cameron, Julia, and Emma Lively. *The Artist's Way for Parents: Raising Creative Children.* Jeremy P. Tarcher/Penguin, a Member of Penguin Group (USA), 2014.

Causton, Richard. *The Buddha in Daily Life: An Introduction to the Buddhism of Nichiren Daishonin.* Rider, 1995.

Cialdini, Robert B. *Influence: The Psychology of Persuasion.* Collins, 2007.

Clason, George S. *The Richest Man in Babylon.* Signet/New American Library, 2008.

Collins, JL. *The Simple Path to Wealth: Your Road Map to Financial*

Independence and a Rich, Free Life. CreateSpace, 2016.

Covey, Stephen R. *The 7 Habits of Highly Effective People.* Simon & Schuster, 2004.

Currey, Mason. *Daily Rituals: How Great Minds Make Time, Find Inspiration, and Get to Work.* Picador, 2014.

Dahl, Roald, and Quentin Blake. *Boy: Tales of Childhood.* Puffin Books, 2013.

Duhigg, Charles. *The Power of Habit: Why We Do What We Do in Life and Business.* Random House Trade Paperbacks, 2014.

Economist, The. *The Economist Style Guide.* Profile Books, 2001.

Eker, T. Harv. *Secrets of the Millionaire Mind: Think Rich to Get Rich.* Piatkus, 2005.

Fisker, Jacob Lund. *Early Retirement Extreme: A Philosophical and Practical Guide to Financial Independence.* ERE, 2010.

Frankl, Viktor Emil. *Man's Search for Meaning: The Classic Tribute to Hope from the Holocaust.* Rider, 2004.

Fried, Jason, and David Heinemeier Hansson. *ReWork.* Vermilion, 2010.

Gladwell, Malcolm. *Outliers.* Penguin, 2009.

Greene, Robert. *Mastery.* Profile, 2012.

Handley, Ann. *Everybody Writes: Your Go-To Guide to Creating Ridiculously Good Content.* John Wiley & Sons, 2014.

Hardy, Darren. *The Compound Effect: Jumpstart Your Income, Your Life, Your Success.* Da Capo Press, 2013.

Harris, Russ. *The Happiness Trap: How to Stop Struggling and Start Living.* Trumpeter, 2008.

Hicks, Wynford. *English for Journalists.* Routledge, 1995.

Hill, Napoleon. *Think and Grow Rich!* Wilder, 2007.

Holiday, Ryan. *The Obstacle Is the Way: The Ancient Art of Turning Adversity to Advantage.* Profile Books, 2015.

Holiday, Ryan. *Perennial Seller.* Profile Books, 2017.

James, Oliver. *Affluenza.* Vermilion, 2008.

Johnson, Spencer. *Who Moved My Cheese?* Random House, 1999.

Karnazes, Dean. *Ultramarathon Man: Confessions of an All-Night Runner.* J.P. Tarcher/Penguin, 2006.

King, Stephen. *On Writing: A Memoir of the Craft.* Hodder, 2012.

Kiyosaki, Robert T. *Rich Dad Poor Dad.* Plata, 2017.

Kleon, Austin. *Show Your Work!: 10 Things Nobody Told You about Getting Discovered.* Workman, 2014.

Kondo, Marie, and Cathy Hirano. *The Life-Changing Magic of Tidying.* Vermilion, 2014.

Lamott, Anne. *Bird by Bird: Some Instructions on Writing and Life.* Anchor Books, 1995.

Manson, Mark. *The Subtle Art of Not Giving a F*ck: A Counterintuitive Approach to Living a Good Life.* HarperOne, 2016.

McKeown, Greg. *Essentialism: The Disciplined Pursuit of Less.* Virgin Books, 2014.

McPhee, John A. *Draft No. 4: On the Writing Process.* Farrar, Straus and Giroux, 2017.

Moon, Youngme. *Different: Escaping the Competitive Herd.* Crown, 2011.

Newport, Cal. *Deep Work: Rules for Focused Success in a Distracted World.* Piatkus, 2016.

Peters, Steve. *The Chimp Paradox: The Mind Management Programme for Confidence, Success and Happiness.* Ebury Press, 2012.

Pressfield, Steven. *The War of Art: Break through the Blocks and Win Your Inner Creative Battles.* Black Irish Entertainment, 2012.

Priestley, Daniel, and Andrew Priestley. *Oversubscribed: How to Get People Lining up to Do Business with You.* J. Wiley and Sons, 2017.

Robin, Vicki, et al. *Your Money or Your Life: 9 Steps to Transforming Your Relationship with Money and Achieving Financial Independence.* New York, 2008.

Salazar, Alberto. *14 Minutes: A Running Legend's Life and Death and Life.* Rodale, 2013.

Schwartz, David J. *The Magic of Thinking Big.* Ebury Publishing, 2016.

Seuss,... *I Can Read with My Eyes Shut!* Beginner Books, a Division of Random House, 2017.

Shaughnessy, Adrian. *How to Be a Graphic Designer, Without Losing Your Soul.* Laurence King, 2010.

Spedding, Charlie. *From Last to First: A Long-Distance Runner's Journey from Failure to Success.* Aurum, 2014.

Stanley, Thomas J., and William D. Danko. *The Millionaire Next Door: The Surprising Secrets of America's Wealthy.* Taylor Trade Pub., 2010.

Strunk, William, and E.B. White. *The Elements of Style.* Pearson, 2000.

Syed, Matthew. *Bounce: The Myth of Talent and the Power of Practice.* HarperCollins, 2011.

Taggart, Caroline, and J.A. Wines. *My Grammar and I (or Should That Be 'Me'?): Old-School Ways to Sharpen Your English.* Michael O'Mara, 2011.

Truss, Lynne. *Eats, Shoots & Leaves: The Zero Tolerance Approach to Punctuation.* Fourth Estate, 2009.

Vaynerchuk, Gary. *#AskGaryVee: One Entrepreneur's Take on Leadership, Social Media & Self-Awareness.* Harper Business, 2016.

Ware, Bronnie. *The Top Five Regrets of the Dying: A Life Transformed by the Dearly Departing.* Hay House, 2012.

Waterhouse, Keith. *Waterhouse on Newspaper Style.* Penguin, 1993.

Welsh, Tom, et al. *McNae's Essential Law for Journalists.* Butterworths, 1995.

Zinsser, William. *On Writing Well: 30th Anniversary Edition.* Collins, 2006.

ABOUT THE AUTHOR

DAVID SAWYER IS A 45-year-old professional who, six years ago, decided to change his life. The result, *RESET*, could change yours. He lives in Glasgow, Scotland, with his wife, Rachel, and primary-age kids – Zak and Jude.

- When the mood takes him, he can be found on Twitter @zudepr and LinkedIn at uk.linkedin.com/in/davejsawyer.
- You can learn more about *RESET* at zudepr.co.uk/reset.

If you like this book, it would please David immensely if you were to do two things:

- Leave a one-paragraph *RESET* book review on Amazon.
- Sign up to his free newsletter (never salesy, just sharing what he knows) at zudepr.co.uk/zudes-top-4.

Thanks for listening. (Talking about listening, the *RESET* audiobook is now available on Audible, too.)

.

NOTES

[1] *"I am the captain of my soul"*: "Invictus by William Ernest Henley | Poetry Foundation." toreset.me/1.

Disclaimer

[2] **millions of middle-aged midlifers:** "Middle age begins at 35 and ends at 58 – Telegraph." 16 Mar. 2010, toreset.me/2. The age range differs from country to country, as this article shows. In *RESET*, all references to middle age and midlife refer to the period 35 to 60, albeit under-35s and over-60s can benefit from many aspects of the step-by-step process in this book.

Introduction

[3] **six in ten are "not engaged" at work:** "85% of People Hate Their Jobs, Gallup Poll Says – Return to Now." 22 Sep. 2017, toreset.me/3.

[4] **just to help out your Chimp**: "The Chimp Paradox: The Mind Management Programme to Help You…" toreset.me/4.

[5] **Paul Cézanne held his first art exhibition at 56:** "Cezanne the Prophet, the Inventor – The Washington Post." 23 Oct. 1977, toreset.me/5.

[6] **he published** *On the Origin of Species* **in 1859, aged 50:** "People Who Became Successful After Age 40 – Business Insider." 9 Sep. 2014, toreset.me/6.

[7] **pressure cookers, flour and spice blends:** "How KFC founder Colonel Sanders achieved success in his 60s…" 25 Jun. 2015, toreset.me/7.

[8] **turned down 1,009 times:** "Rich Dad Poor Dad: What The Rich Teach Their Kids… – Amazon UK." toreset.me/8, p. 261.

[9] **British sprinter Charles Eugster**: "Incredible 95-year-old man sets world record in 200-meter dash | For…" 10 Mar. 2015, toreset.me/9.

[10] **"well beyond the age of fifty"**: "Think and Grow Rich!: The Original Version, Restored and Revised…" toreset.me/10, p. 146.

[11] **J.K. Rowling was "as poor…country":** "J.K. Rowling: 'I was as poor as it's possible to be' | Daily Mail Online." 26 Oct. 2013, toreset.me/11.

[12] **stretch to the cost of photocopying:** "9 Famous People Who Will Inspire You to

Never Give Up – The Muse." toreset.me/12.

[13] **tennis stars Venus and Serena Williams:** "16 People Who Worked Incredibly Hard To Succeed – Business Insider." 5 Sep. 2012, toreset.me/13a and toreset.me/13b.

[14] ***The 7 Habits of Highly Effective People:*** "The 7 Habits of Highly Effective People: Powerful... – Amazon UK." toreset.me/14.

[15] **Malcolm Gladwell's *Outliers*:** "Outliers: The Story of Success: Amazon.co.uk: Malcolm Gladwell..." toreset.me/15.

[16] **Matthew Syed in *Bounce*:** "Bounce: The Myth of Talent and the Power of Practice: Amazon.co.uk..." toreset.me/16.

[17] **It's how you direct that time that counts:** "The '10,000-hour rule' about being an expert is... – Business Insider." 27 Aug. 2017, toreset.me/17.

[18] **"not to have conquered but to have fought well":** "The Olympic Creed – Janecky." toreset.me/18.

Status Quo

[19] ***"Latin for 'the mess we're in'":*** "Status quo, you know, is Latin for 'the mess we... – Goodreads." toreset.me/19.

[20] **well in the top quintile:** "How rich are you? Work out where your income... – This is Money UK." 12 Jan. 2017, toreset.me/20.

[21] **Bren's £48,616:** "The Salary Calculator – Take-Home tax..." toreset.me/21.

[22] **top 0.17% of income earners in the world:** "Global Rich List | UK." toreset.me/22.

[23] **"[We] never had it so good":** "BBC ON THIS DAY | 20 | 1957: Britons 'have never had it... – BBC News." toreset.me/23.

[24] **greater democracy and life expectancy:** "9 ways the world got a lot better in 2017 – Vox." 7 Jan. 2018, toreset.me/24.

[25] **hierarchy of needs theory:** "Abraham Maslow's hierarchy of needs – Wikipedia." toreset.me/25.

[26] **0.004% of Earth's history:** "History of life on Earth – BBC." toreset.me/26.

[27] **4000 and 2000BC:** "The First Cities and States (4000 – 2000BC), A History of the... – BBC." 19 Mar. 2010, toreset.me/27.

[28] **"The very notion...only began with the Industrial Revolution:** "Your Money or Your Life – Amazon UK." toreset.me/28, p. 198.

[29] **with a third clocking more than 50:** "More than 80pc of white-collar workers clocking up 40-hour weeks..." 21 May. 2013, toreset.me/29.

[30] **"(...febrile moods or confused identity)":** "Affluenza: Amazon.co.uk: Oliver James: 8601300061856: Books." toreset.me/30, p. vii.

[31] **"constructing a radically more complex world":** "Influence: The Psychology of Persuasion: Amazon.co.uk: Robert B..." toreset.me/31, p. 277.

[32] **"single, usually reliable feature of it":** Ibid., pp. 277–8.

[33] **by 2030 everyone will be:** "6 Essential PR Predictions for 2018 | Ketchum." toreset.me/33.

[34] **"yet it will never be this slow again":** "Trudeau: 'The pace of change has never

been this fast' – YouTube." 23 Jan. 2018, toreset.me/34.

35 **telephone to reach 50 million users:** "50 million users: How long does it take tech to... – Interactive Schools." 8 Feb. 2018, toreset.me/35.

36 **Fortnite phenomenon:** "How Fortnite Captured Teens' Hearts and Minds | The New Yorker." 21 May. 2018, toreset.me/36.

37 **management consulting firm McKinsey:** "Skill shift: Automation and the future of the workforce | McKinsey..." toreset.me/37.

38 **automation and robotics:** "50% of low-skilled jobs will be replaced by AI and automation, report..." 21 Jul. 2017, toreset.me/38.

39 **"in terms of both quality and speed":** "Deep Work: Rules for Focused Success in a Distracted World – Cal..." 5 Jan. 2016, toreset.me/39, p. 29.

40 **one of those lucky 13%:** "Only 13 per cent of people worldwide actually like going to work – The..." 10 Oct. 2013, toreset.me/40.

41 **We should all be working four-day weeks:** "Forbes misses the point of the 4-day work week – Signal v. Noise." 20 Aug. 2008, toreset.me/41.

42 **"Which do you prefer?":** "Early Retirement Extreme: A Philosophical and Practical Guide to..." toreset.me/42, (Kindle version) Location 329.

43 *Status Quo:* "Status Quo – The Official Site." toreset.me/43.

1. Happiness

44 ***"With more than my share of happiness":*** "Ken Dodd – Happiness Lyrics | Genius Lyrics." toreset.me/44.

45 **20 others attempting to kill themselves:** "'Depression: let's talk' says WHO, as depression tops list of causes of..." 30 Mar. 2017, toreset.me/45a and "WHO | Suicide data." toreset.me/45b.

46 **"we all are seeking something better in life":** "Quote by Dalai Lama: 'I believe that the very purpose of our life is...'" toreset.me/46.

2. Fears

47 **"we're all cowards":** "Standing On The Starting Line, We Are All Cowards – Your World Within." toreset.me/47.

48 **"dread-free artist":** "The War of Art: Break Through the Blocks and Win Your... – Amazon UK." toreset.me/48, p. 79.

49 **"hardest battle which any human being can fight":** "The Courage to Be Yourself: E.E. Cummings on Art... – Brain Pickings." 25 Sep. 2017, toreset.me/49.

50 **"doing the eulogy":** "Amazing Leaders Who Once Had Stage Fright – Visme Blog." 30 Jul. 2015, toreset.me/50.

51 **Julia Roberts**: "Famous People with Fear of Public Speaking – High Performance U." toreset.me/51.

52 **Princess Di:** "The Eloquent Woman: Five famous speeches by women who feared..." 24 May. 2013, toreset.me/52.

53 **"become the person we sense in our hearts we really are":** "The War of Art: Break

Through the Blocks and Win Your... – Amazon UK." toreset.me/53, p. 143.

[54] **"not in the mood to act"**: "Secrets Of The Millionaire Mind: Think rich to get rich: Amazon.co.uk: T..." toreset.me/54, p. 168.

3. Life's a Struggle

[55] **23:59:59**: Earth is 4.5bn years old, *Homo sapiens* arrived 200,000 years ago (0.004%), the Industrial Revolution started 250 years ago (0.0000055%) and there are 86,400 seconds in a day.

[56] **"more happiness in a modern life"**: "What is Stoicism and How Can it Turn your Life to Solid Gold?." 2 Oct. 2011, toreset.me/56.

[57] ***Man's Search for Meaning***: "Man's Search For Meaning: The classic tribute to hope... – Amazon UK." toreset.me/57.

[58] **"striving, man, it's that I want"**: "Top 20 John Coltrane Quotes – uDiscover Music." 23 Sep. 2016, toreset.me/58.

[59] **"striving and struggling for a worthwhile goal"**: "Man's Search For Meaning: The classic tribute to hope... – Amazon UK." toreset.me/59, p. 110.

[60] **"without the display of feelings and without complaint"**: "stoicism | Definition of stoicism in English by Oxford Dictionaries." toreset.me/60.

[61] **"problem or weakness or issue"**: "The Obstacle is the Way: The Ancient Art of Turning Adversity to..." toreset.me/61, p 177.

[62] **"problems you enjoy having and enjoy solving"**: "The Subtle Art of Not Giving a F*ck: A Counterintuitive... – Amazon UK." toreset.me/62, p. 31.

[63] ***Boy:*** "Boy: Tales of Childhood – Roald Dahl – Roald Dahl Website." toreset.me/63.

[64] **"'strike you as the most beautiful'"**: "The Subtle Art of Not Giving a F*ck: A Counterintuitive... – Amazon UK." toreset.me/64, p. 85.

4. Finding Meaning

[65] ***The Hitchhiker's Guide to the Galaxy***: "The Hitchhiker's Guide to the Galaxy (novel) – Wikipedia." toreset.me/65.

[66] **Adeney:** "How to Give Money (and Get Happiness) More Easily." 4 Dec. 2017, toreset.me/66.

[67] **Frankl:** "Man's Search For Meaning: The classic tribute to hope... – Amazon UK." toreset.me/67, pp. 146–147.

[68] **"little stuff falls into place"**: "Get the Big Things Right | The Happy Philosopher." 11 Dec. 2017, toreset.me/68.

[69] ***"liberation in life"***: "Arthur Schopenhauer On death and life as dying — DOP." toreset.me/69.

[70] ***TEDxGlasgow***: "TEDxGlasgow: Exploring Ideas & Stimulating Change." toreset.me/70.

[71] **David Eustace:** "Journal — David Eustace." 30 Oct. 2017, toreset.me/71.

[72] **happiness was, in fact, a choice:** "Regrets of the Dying – Bronnie Ware." toreset.me/72.

[73] **"verge of death?"**: "Man's Search For Meaning: The classic tribute to hope... – Amazon UK." toreset.me/73, p. 145.

[74] **"meet the person you could have become"**: "10 Remarkable Quotes That Will Inspire You To Take... – Zero to Skill." toreset.me/74.

[75] **"trade winds in your sails"**: "Twenty Years From Now You Will Be More Disappointed By The..." 29 Sep. 2011, toreset.me/75.

5. On Purpose

[76] **"meaning to life"**: "Man's Search For Meaning: The classic tribute to hope... – Amazon UK." toreset.me/76, p. 105.

[77] **"almost any how"**: "Quote by Friedrich Nietzsche: "He who has a why to live for can bear..." toreset.me/77.

[78] **"mundane, and laborious"**: "The Compound Effect: Amazon.co.uk: Perseus: 9781593157241: Books." toreset.me/78, p. 63.

[79] **"to choose one's own way"**: "Man's Search For Meaning: The classic tribute to hope... – Amazon UK." toreset.me/79, p. 75.

[80] **"loadsamoney!"**: "Loadsamoney – Wikipedia." toreset.me/80. Loadsamoney was a character created my English comedian Harry Enfield. I remember him on Ben Elton's *Friday Night Live* show. The idea was that Loadsamoney had loads of money, and wasn't shy telling you about it. Enfield's alter ego came to symbolise the excesses of 1980s Britain.

[81] **"small daily increments"**: "Daily Rituals: How Great Minds Make Time, Find Inspiration, and Get..." toreset.me/81, p. xvi.

[82] *What Matters to You:* "What Matters to Me" – a new vital sign | Jason Leitch... – YouTube." 29 Jun. 2016, toreset.me/82.

[83] **he had an epiphany:** "From Last to First: A long-distance runner's journey from... – Amazon UK." toreset.me/83, pp. 73–86.

[84] **"I felt absolutely fantastic"**: Ibid., p. 204.

[85] **"When will we know when it's done?"**: "If I Read One More Platitude-Filled Mission Statement, I'll Scream." 4 Oct. 2012, toreset.me/85.

[86] **"what does it take to satisfy me?"**: "The Magic Of Thinking Big: Amazon.co.uk: David J. Schwartz..." toreset.me/86, pp. 302–304.

[87] **five-year plans:** "Five-year plans of China – Wikipedia." toreset.me/87.

[88] **"busy working on his career"**: "Rich Dad Poor Dad: What The Rich Teach Their Kids... – Amazon UK." toreset.me/88, p. 281.

6. Values and Your Worldview

[89] **"congruent with our values"**: "The Compound Effect – Darren Hardy." toreset.me/89, pp. 65–66.

7. Plan and Goals

[90] **"punched in the mouth"**: "Mike Tyson explains one of his most famous quotes –

tribunedigital..." 9 Nov. 2012, toreset.me/90.

8. Part I Index Card

[91] **"why we are here"**: "Bird by Bird: Some Instructions on Writing and Life: Amazon.co.uk: Anne..." toreset.me/91, p. 32.

Part II: Going Digital – How to Future-Proof Your Career

[92] **"support traditional methods"**: "Digital transformation – Wikipedia." toreset.me/92.

9. Trapped in "Digital or Die" Land

[93] **90.1% in the US:** "Wage and salaried workers, total (% of total... – World Bank Data." toreset.me/93. Figures are based on November 2017 data.

[94] **Zero Moments of Truth:** "Oversubscribed – How to Get People Lining Up to Do Business with..." toreset.me/94, p. 134. "Google...calls it Zero Moments of Truth (ZMOT), which is another name for various data points that a person might find about you as they are making a purchasing decision. Their research indicates that it takes an average of 11 'ZMOTs' or touches to build up trust with someone. They also advocate that a lot of these touch points can be found online as digital content."

10. PR: a Case Study

[95] **"press release for their bedtime story"**: "The bedtime test of content marketing and PR – SHIFT Communications." 20 Oct. 2014, toreset.me/95.

[96] **future father-in-law for the first time:** "Days of Wine and Roses (1962) - Jack Lemmon explains PR - YouTube." 8 Feb. 2016, toreset.me/96.

[97] **1.66m:** "List of newspapers in the United Kingdom by circulation – Wikipedia." toreset.me/97.

[98] **71,000:** "The Scotsman circulation in the UK 2003–2016 | Statistic – Statista." toreset.me/98.

[99] **15,870:** "Regional ABCs: Circulation growth for Scotsman and Irish News but..." 24 Aug. 2017, toreset.me/99.

[100] **giveaways to airline travellers:** "Roy Greenslade: What are bulk sales? Here's a simple guide | Media..." 9 Apr. 2009, toreset.me/100.

[101] **12% of PR practitioners...confident in their social and digital skills:** "Senior PR practitioners lack digital and social media management skills." 24 Feb. 2015, toreset.me/101.

[102] **Terry Pratchett:** "Terry Pratchett Biography | Terry Pratchett Books." toreset.me/102. Pratchett worked for seven years as a nuclear industry press officer.

[103] **80,000 PR people work in the UK:** "Survey finds that PRs outnumber journalists by large margin | Media..." 10 Jun. 2016, toreset.me/103.

[104] **"building a modern production company"**: "#AskGaryVee: One Entrepreneur's Take on Leadership, Social Media..." toreset.me/104, p. 261.

[105] **"world's most stressful jobs":** "8. Public Relations Executive – The Most Stressful Jobs In 2017 – Forbes." toreset.me/105.

[106] **December 6th 2017:** "[Glasgow event recap] Putting a value to comms not a vanity metric…" 8 Dec. 2017, toreset.me/106. I attended this event in Glasgow on December 6th 2017 to glean an insight into the challenges facing UK public sector communicators. The Glasgow City Council statistics in *RESET* comes from my notes taken at the conference. Others can be found in the blog post above.

11. How to Master Your Digital Fear: a 25-Point Plan

[107] *"the more places you'll go":* "I Can Read with My Eyes Shut!: Green Back Book (Dr. Seuss – Green…" toreset.me/107.

[108] **Neil Patel:** "Neil Patel." toreset.me/108.

[109] **Jeff Bullas:** "Jeffbullas's Blog." toreset.me/109.

[110] **Brian Dean:** "The Backlinko SEO Blog by Brian Dean." toreset.me/110.

[111] **(he's a popular guy):** "Paul Sutton: Social Media Consultant & Digital Media Trainer." toreset.me/111.

[112] **Ryan Holiday, whose blog posts:** "How To Read More — A Lot More | RyanHoliday.net." 15 Oct. 2013, toreset.me/112.

[113] **Amazon's Save for Later:** "Amazon.co.uk Help: About the Shopping Basket." toreset.me/113.

[114] **the Feynman Technique:** "Learn Anything In Four Steps With The Feynman Technique – Curiosity." 14 Dec. 2016, toreset.me/114.

[115] **I have plastic boxes:** "Advantus Corporation 13-1/4-Inch-by-12-3/4-Inch-by-6-Inch Cropper." toreset.me/115.

[116] **Ryan Holiday:** "Ryan Holiday – Wikipedia." toreset.me/116.

[117] **Anne Lamott:** "Anne Lamott – Wikipedia." toreset.me/117.

[118] **Robert Greene:** "Robert Greene (American author) – Wikipedia." toreset.me/118.

[119] **Oliver Burkeman:** "Oliver Burkeman | The Guardian." toreset.me/119.

[120] **Vladimir Nabokov:** "Vladimir Nabokov – Wikipedia." toreset.me/120.

[121] **Ludwig Wittgenstein:** "Ludwig Wittgenstein – Wikipedia." toreset.me/121.

[122] **Audible:** "Audible UK – Audiobooks | Start Your Free 30-Day Trial | Audible.co.uk." toreset.me/122.

[123] **LibriVox:** "LibriVox." toreset.me/123.

[124] **Seth Godin:** "Seth Godin – Wikipedia." toreset.me/124.

[125] *The Tim Ferriss Show:* "The Tim Ferriss Show | Listen via Stitcher Radio On Demand." toreset.me/125.

[126] *Freakonomics:* "Freakonomics – Wikipedia." toreset.me/126.

[127] **"worrying about embarrassing yourself":** "ReWork: Change the Way You Work Forever: Amazon.co.uk: David…" toreset.me/127, pp. 167–8.

[128] **"whole game in your favor":** "#AskGaryVee: One Entrepreneur's Take on Leadership, Social Media…" toreset.me/128, p. 289.

[129] **"overabundant information"**: "Curation – Brain Pickings." 16 Mar. 2012, toreset.me/129.

[130] **leaving "a bread-crumb trail"**: "Show Your Work!: 10 Things Nobody Told You About Getting..." toreset.me/130, p. 85.

[131] ***The Economist Style Guide***: "The Economist Style Guide: Amazon.co.uk: The Economist..." toreset.me/131.

[132] ***English for Journalists:*** "English for Journalists (Media Skills): Amazon.co.uk: Wynford Hicks..." toreset.me/132.

[133] ***Waterhouse on Newspaper Style:*** "Waterhouse on Newspaper Style: Amazon.co.uk: Keith Waterhouse..." toreset.me/133.

[134] ***Eats, Shoots & Leaves***: "Eats, Shoots and Leaves: Amazon.co.uk: Lynne Truss..." toreset.me/134.

[135] ***My Grammar and I***: "My Grammar and I (Or Should That Be 'Me'?): Old... – Amazon UK." toreset.me/135.

[136] ***On Writing***: "On Writing: A Memoir of the Craft: Amazon.co.uk: Stephen King..." toreset.me/136.

[137] ***Perennial Seller***: "Perennial Seller: The Art of Making and Marketing Work... – Amazon UK." toreset.me/137.

[138] ***Essential Law for Journalists***: "McNae's Essential Law for Journalists: Amazon.co.uk: Mark Hanna..." toreset.me/138.

[139] ***Bird by Bird***: "Bird by Bird: Some Instructions on Writing and Life: Amazon.co.uk: Anne..." toreset.me/139.

[140] ***The Elements of Style***: "The Elements of Style: Amazon.co.uk: William Strunk Jr., E.B. White..." toreset.me/140.

[141] ***On Writing Well***: "On Writing Well: The Classic Guide to Writing Nonfiction – Amazon.com." toreset.me/141.

[142] ***Draft No. 4:*** "Draft No. 4: Amazon.co.uk: John McPhee: 9780374142742: Books." toreset.me/142.

[143] ***The Writing Life:*** "The Writing Life: Writers On How They Think And Work... – Amazon UK." toreset.me/143.

[144] **"art is begun"**: "Why Writing Is So Important." toreset.me/144.

[145] **"Twenty-seven per cent...built with this software"**: "WordPress "quietly" powers 27% of the web – TechRepublic." 6 Feb. 2017, toreset.me/145.

[146] **using a website:** "Advanced Marketing Institute – Headline Analyzer." toreset.me/146.

[147] **free-to-use:** "Unsplash." toreset.me/147.

[148] **OK-if-you-credit:** "Foter." toreset.me/148.

[149] **"the thing that made them known"**: "#AskGaryVee: One Entrepreneur's Take on Leadership, Social Media..." toreset.me/149, p. 142.

[150] **consider making money from it:** "Most Frequently Asked Questions About How to Make Money From..." 7 Jan. 2018, toreset.me/150.

[151] **without touching their capital, by following this route:** "Don't Listen to Us // Blogs Don't Tell the Full FI Story | Our Next Life." 27 Mar. 2017, toreset.me/151.

NOTES

152 **Tim Urban:** "Tim Urban: How He Turned His Blog Into A Global Movement – Forbes." 17 Jan. 2017, toreset.me/152.

153 **MailChimp:** "MailChimp." toreset.me/153.

154 **join my list:** "Zude's Top 4: A Curated Newsletter Delivered to Email Inboxes…" toreset.me/154.

155 **"they send an email":** "Show Your Work!: 10 Things Nobody Told You About Getting…" toreset.me/155, p. 170.

156 **the law of reciprocity:** "Dr. Robert Cialdini on the Principle of Reciprocity – Influence at Work." toreset.me/156.

157 **(GDPR):** "General Data Protection Regulation FAQs – MailChimp KB." 25 May. 2018, toreset.me/157.

158 **Ryan had 80,000 subscribers to his list, including me**: "Perennial Seller: The Art of Making and Marketing Work… – Amazon UK." toreset.me/158, p. 189.

159 **90,000:** "22 Rules for Creating Work That Stands the Test of Time – Medium." 28 May. 2018, toreset.me/159.

160 **"internalise their accomplishments":** "Impostor syndrome – Wikipedia." toreset.me/160.

161 **"believing mirrors":** "The Artist's Way for Parents: Raising Creative Children: Amazon.co.uk…" toreset.me/161, p. 256.

162 **Here are a few of mine:** All contributed to a blog post I wrote in 2015. You can find brief biographies here: toreset.me/162.

163 **"knuckleballers":** "Show Your Work!: 10 Things Nobody Told You About Getting…" toreset.me/163, p. 139.

164 **Studies consistently show:** "Over nearly 80 years, Harvard study has been showing how to live a…" 11 Apr. 2017, toreset.me/164.

165 **Western Front on Christmas Day 1914:** "The truth about the Christmas Day football match – Telegraph." 24 Dec. 2014, toreset.me/165.

166 ***Birdsong:*** "Birdsong (novel) – Wikipedia." toreset.me/166.

167 **reciprocity:** "Dr. Robert Cialdini on the Principle of Reciprocity – Influence at Work." toreset.me/167.

168 **"we compare notes":** "Bird by Bird: Some Instructions on Writing and Life: Amazon.co.uk: Anne…" toreset.me/168, p. 198.

169 **sabbaticals in war zones:** "BBC Radio 4 – Desert Island Discs, David Nott." 5 Jun. 2016, toreset.me/169.

170 **"Selling you Bullshit":** "The Success Bloggers Are Selling You Bullshit. – THE WESTENBERG…" 30 Aug. 2017, toreset.me/170.

Part III: Declutter Your Life

171 **life-changing magic in tidying:** "The Life-Changing Magic of Tidying: A simple, effective way to banish…" toreset.me/171.

172 **most-saved long-form articles:** "Pocket: Best of 2017." toreset.me/172.

13. Digital Declutter

[173] **Pocket:** "Pocket." toreset.me/173 is an app that helps people save interesting articles, videos and more from the web for later enjoyment.

[174] **"Destroyed a Generation?":** "Have Smartphones Destroyed a Generation? – The Atlantic." toreset.me/174.

[175] **2,617 times a day:** "We touch our phones 2,617 times a day, says study | Network World." 7 Jul. 2016, toreset.me/175.

[176] **In a 2016 blog post:** "How Technology is Hijacking Your Mind — from a Former... – Medium." 18 May. 2016, toreset.me/176.

[177] **kids' screen time:** "Bill Gates and Steve Jobs limited screen time for... – Business Insider." 10 Jan. 2018, toreset.me/177.

[178] **Cook:** "Tim Cook – Wikipedia." toreset.me/178. The Apple CEO.

[179] **Horvath:** "Michael Horvath | LinkedIn." toreset.me/179. The Strava co-founder.

[180] **RescueTime:** "RescueTime." toreset.me/180.

[181] **Unroll.Me:** "Unroll.Me." toreset.me/181.

[182] **(3% of people)?:** "Sleep with your smartphone in hand? You're not alone – CNET." 30 Jun. 2015, toreset.me/182.

[183] **admiration for the two-thirds of adults who aren't active Facebook users**: "31 Facebook Statistics Marketers Need to Know – Hootsuite Blog." 14 Jan. 2018, toreset.me/183.

14. Mental Declutter

[184] **"all obstacles in my way...":** "Jimmy Cliff – I Can See Clearly Now With Lyrics – YouTube." 8 Apr. 2012, toreset.me/184.

[185] **Morning Pages in Oliver Burkeman's column:** "This column will change your life: Morning Pages | Life and style | The..." 3 Oct. 2014, toreset.me/185.

[186] *The Artist's Way for Parents*: "The Artist's Way for Parents: Raising Creative Children: Amazon.co.uk..." toreset.me/186.

[187] **"telegram to the Universe":** Ibid., p. 8.

[188] **"used as a therapeutic technique":** "mindfulness | Definition of mindfulness in English by Oxford Dictionaries." toreset.me/188.

[189] *The Happiness Trap*: "The Happiness Trap (Based on ACT: A revolutionary mindfulness..." toreset.me/189.

[190] **northern soul:** To find out what northern soul is about, which I suggest you do, watch journalist and broadcaster Paul Mason's 2014 *BBC Four* documentary *Living for the Weekend*: toreset.me/190a or read his article: "My life as a northern soul boy | Paul Mason | Music | The Guardian." 11 Oct. 2014, toreset.me/190b.

[191] *New Order's* **"Love Vigilantes":** "New Order Love Vigilantes Video – YouTube." 30 Nov. 2012, toreset.me/191.

[192] **it's to do with evolution:** "The Happiness Trap (Based on ACT: A revolutionary mindfulness..." toreset.me/192, p. 43.

[193] **Chicken Littles:** "Chicken Little Syndrome – Riskology." toreset.me/193.

[194] *The Buddha in Daily Life:* "The Buddha In Daily Life: An Introduction to the... – Amazon UK." toreset.me/194.

[195] **"clogged artery of your soul":** "The Ultimate Cheat Sheet To Writing Your First Book – Altucher..." toreset.me/195.

15. Physical Declutter

[196] **store their belongings?:** "21 Surprising Statistics That Reveal How Much Stuff We Actually Own." toreset.me/196.

[197] **I doubt things have improved:** "The Stats, Facts, & Inspiring Quotes — BoneClutter." toreset.me/197.

[198] **enough clutter to fill a whole room:** "How we are a nation of hoarders: One in five of us admits to having..." 19 Sep. 2013, toreset.me/198.

[199] **our lives looking for lost items:** "The Statistics of Clutter – Becoming Minimalist." toreset.me/199.

[200] **closet than after sex:** "The Stats, Facts, & Inspiring Quotes — BoneClutter." toreset.me/200.

[201] **"what you should and shouldn't do":** "The Life-Changing Magic of Tidying: A simple, effective way to banish..." toreset.me/201, p. 4.

[202] **Writing in the *Washington Post*:** "I was getting buried in clutter. Here's how I finally got free. – The..." 17 Jan. 2018, toreset.me/202.

[203] **article in *The Atlantic*:** "An Economist's Guide to Tidying Your Apartment – The Atlantic." 13 May. 2015, toreset.me/203.

[204] **sunk cost fallacy:** "Sunk cost fallacy – Behavioraleconomics.com | The BE Hub." toreset.me/204.

[205] **status quo bias:** "Status quo bias – Behavioraleconomics.com | The BE Hub." toreset.me/205.

[206] **changed their life:** "Customer Review – Amazon.com." toreset.me/206.

[207] **(discard lots and organise what's left):** "The Life-Changing Magic of Tidying: A simple, effective way to banish..." toreset.me/207. No page number; it's the premise of the book.

[208] **"Unfinished projects sap you of vitality":** "Your Money or Your Life – Amazon UK." toreset.me/208, p. 27.

[209] **"(get rid of it!!)":** "Early Retirement Extreme: A Philosophical and Practical... – Amazon UK." toreset.me/209, (Kindle version) Location 2,495.

[210] **"process your past":** "The Life-Changing Magic of Tidying: A simple, effective way to banish..." toreset.me/210, p. 136.

[211] **"ultimately defeat him":** "The goal of all inanimate objects is to resist man and... – Brainy Quote." toreset.me/211.

[212] **"sentimental items and keepsakes":** "The Life-Changing Magic of Tidying: A simple, effective way to banish..." toreset.me/212, p. 53.

[213] **(*That's not my lion*..., anyone?):** "That's Not My Lion: Amazon.co.uk: Fiona Watt, Rachel Wells..." toreset.me/213.

[214] **"without exception dramatically altered":** "The Life-Changing Magic of Tidying:

A simple, effective way to banish…" toreset.me/214, p. 206.

[215] ***Minimalism: A Documentary About the Important Things***: "Minimalism: A Documentary About the Important Things." toreset.me/215.

[216] **"elements of a fulfilling existence"**: "Your Money or Your Life – Amazon UK." toreset.me/216, p. xxiii.

[217] **his grey t-shirts**: "This photo of Mark Zuckerberg's closet is literally the least surprising…" 26 Jan. 2016, toreset.me/217.

[218] **versatile holdall**: "Osprey Porter 65 Travel Duffel – YouTube." 23 Jul. 2015, toreset.me/218.

[219] **Tim Ferriss's *5-Bullet Friday***: "Welcome to 5-Bullet Friday | The Blog of Author Tim Ferriss." toreset.me/219.

[220] **Pakt One venture**: "Pakt." toreset.me/220.

17. Halftime Downer Interval

[221] **Strawberry Mivvi**: "Mivvi Ice Creams – Do You Remember?." toreset.me/221. The best ice lolly ever made, in my humble opinion.

19. You're Not Alone – Money is the Commonest Problem

[222] **£23,679.68 after-tax**: "The Salary Calculator – Take-Home tax…" toreset.me/222. Based on 2018/2019 tax year figures.

[223] **0.6%**: "Global Rich List." toreset.me/223.

[224] **"only 12% have more than £100,000"**: "One in three UK retirees will have to rely solely on state pension…" 21 Oct. 2017, toreset.me/224.

[225] **$84,542 for those aged 45 to 54**: "Here's the average net worth of Americans at every age – Business…" 5 Jun. 2017, toreset.me/225.

[226] **primary cause of most relationship breakups is money**: "Secrets Of The Millionaire Mind: Think rich to get rich: Amazon.co.uk: T…" toreset.me/226, p. 38.

[227] **than reveal what salary they're on**: "Talking about money is Britain's last taboo | The Independent." 19 Sep. 2015, toreset.me/227.

[228] **distinct from being an entrepreneur**: "The Cult of Early Retirement Meets (Or Strangely, Doesn't Meet) The…" 28 Mar. 2017, toreset.me/228.

[229] **approximately £230,000**: "Cost of raising children in UK higher than ever | Life and style | The…" 15 Feb. 2016, toreset.me/229.

[230] **(if you're a doctor, reduce to two)**: "Financial Independence With Kids: How… – Physician on FIRE." toreset.me/230.

[231] **45,057,474 to one**: "UK Lotto Draw – Odds of winning the UK National Lottery…" toreset.me/231.

20. What Do Rich People Look Like?

[232] **legal professions**: "8 Secrets to Achieving Financial Independence – The Balance." 24 Dec. 2017, toreset.me/232.

[233] **(£56,000)**: "The Millionaire Next Door: Amazon.co.uk: Thomas J. Stanley,

William..." toreset.me/233, p. 56.

[234] **first-generation rich:** Ibid., p. 3.

[235] **"chose the right occupation":** Ibid., p. 3.

[236] **school teacher:** Ibid., p. 150.

[237] **Most are frugal:** Ibid., p. 29 and p. 34.

[238] **watching what they spend:** Ibid., p. 40 and p. 38.

[239] **"discipline, sacrifice, and hard work":** Ibid., p. 5.

21. Financial Independence and F.U. Money

[240] **yang and yin:** "Yin and yang | Define Yin and yang at Dictionary.com." toreset.me/240.

[241] **FI gospel:** "Rockstar Finance Directory: Bloggers." toreset.me/241.

[242] **website in April 2017 alone:** "The History of FIRE / Financial Independence, Retire Early." 8 May. 2017, toreset.me/242. A brilliant blog post explaining in detail the history of the FIRE movement.

[243] *Which?:* "Which? – Wikipedia." toreset.me/243.

[244] *Money Saving Expert* **Martin Lewis:** "Martin Lewis (financial journalist) – Wikipedia." toreset.me/244.

[245] **SpaceX:** "SpaceX." toreset.me/245.

[246] **Elon Musk:** "Elon Musk – Wikipedia." toreset.me/246.

[247] **"deep pits":** "An International Portfolio from The Escape Artist – jlcollinsnh." 12 Jan. 2018, toreset.me/247. JL Collins is one of my FI heroes, author of *The Simple Path to Wealth* and the person who introduced me to the liberating idea of F.U. Money.

[248] **Build your assets:** "Rich Dad Poor Dad: What The Rich Teach Their Kids... – Amazon UK." toreset.me/248, p. 85. "An asset is something that puts money in my pocket whether I work or not. A liability is something that takes money out of my pocket."

23. #1: Stash Maths

[249] **familiar with the word *stash:*** "A Brief History of the 'Stash: How we Saved from Zero to Retirement in..." 15 Sep. 2011, toreset.me/249.

[250] *Which?* **published...the results:** "How much will you need to retire? – Which.uk." toreset.me/250. Latest figures in *RESET* are based on the responses of 6,000 retired and semi-retired couples (and *Which?* members) in February 2018 (the May 2017 survey results were based on 2,700 responses). Although the figures-breakdown differed slightly in May 2017 v February 2018, the overall £26k and £39k figures remained the same.

[251] **Our figure is £28,740:** In 2018/19 the personal allowance (the amount of income each individual is entitled to receive tax-free each year) is £11,850. As a couple, our combined personal allowance is £23,700, leaving £6,300 on which to pay 20% income tax (£1,260). £30,000 minus £1,260 is £28,740.

[252] **x 28.5:** "Safe withdrawal rate UK / early retirement – MoneySavingExpert.com..."

19 Jul. 2017, toreset.me/252. *RESET* is based on a conservative Safe Withdrawal Rate (SWR) of 3.5% (more on that later). The 28.5 figure is arrived at by dividing 100 by 3.5. The £855k figure is in 2018 money. Make sure you update it yearly for inflation.

[253] (...**defined benefit scheme**): "The pensions landscape – Defined benefit pensions 2016." 1 Nov. 2016, toreset.me/253. In 2016, there were 1,650,491 people alive in the UK who were active members of defined benefit (more commonly known as final salary schemes in the UK), down a third from 2,421,255 in 2010.

[254] **Investment Calculator:** "Candid Money: Investment How Long Calculator." toreset.me/254.

[255] (**Other retirement calculators exist...**): "Early Retirement Calculator – Networthify.com." toreset.me/255a. Or toreset.me/255b. Or even toreset.me/255c.

[256] **Tap in 9 for C, 3 for D and 0.5 for E:** The C, D and E figures are based on the following conservative assumptions: **1. 9 for C:** You are investing long-term (10–15 years and over) from the UK in a 100% equity globally diversified fund/portfolio of funds. We are predicting after-inflation dividends-reinvested investment returns of 6% not 7.2% like Nutmeg: toreset.me/256. Nutmeg's 7.2% also factors in its fund and management charges, which *RESET* does not. **2. 3 for D:** Contrary to the low inflation rate of the past ten years, inflation rates in the UK average 3% in the long run. **3. 0.5 for E:** This plan is predicated on investing in low-cost index funds. If you follow this plan, and invest in a Sipp or Isa, what you pay (in combined OCF, and account fee) to invest your money should be no more than 0.12% eventually (eg, once Vanguard offers Sipps to UK retail investors and your stash is worth more than £250,000, more on that later). However, most people's main stash will be in their employer's defined contribution scheme. With the advent of auto-enrolment and workplace pensions, it is unlikely you will be paying more than 0.5% a year for the privilege of other people looking after the work pension tied to your current employer. For that reason, going with the experience of most midlife professionals, we'll run the numbers on a conservative annual charge of 0.5% not 0.12%.

[257] **"cFIREsim" and "FIRECalc":** "cFIREsim." toreset.me/257a and "FIRECalc: A different kind of retirement calculator." 28 May. 2017, toreset.me/257b.

25. #3: One Pot

[258] (**open banking reforms**): "Open Banking." toreset.me/258a and toreset.me/258b.

[259] **Personal Capital:** "Personal Capital." toreset.me/259.

[260] **Money Dashboard:** "Money Dashboard: Your personal financial assistant. View your past..." toreset.me/260.

[261] **Yahoo Finance:** "Yahoo Finance." toreset.me/261. I find Yahoo Finance an imperfect solution for one-pot portfolio monitoring and long for the day (which will not come) when Google resurrects its discontinued finance portfolio or Personal Capital sets up in the UK. The US-centric nature of Yahoo Finance often forces me to fall back on Vanguard (excellent) and Fidelity's UK retail investor websites (Fidelity's site only shows performance of Isas, not Sipps). At time of going to press (late August 2018) the UK is crying out for a Personal Capital-type website.

[262] **Morningstar Portfolio Manager:** "Folio Manager | Morningstar." toreset.me/262.

26. #4: 2015 UK Pension Reforms

[263] **(if you were born after 1972, it's 57):** "Pension age to increase from 55 to 57 by 2028 – Citywire." 21 Jul. 2014, toreset.me/263. For anyone born after 1972, it's now 57.

[264] **£150k...it's complicated:** "Earn £100,000 or more? You may fall foul of the complex pension..." 3 Jan. 2018, toreset.me/264.

28. Section 1: Budgeting

[265] **"without direction":** "The Millionaire Next Door: Amazon.co.uk: Thomas J. Stanley, William..." toreset.me/265, p. 78.

[266] **Life energy:** "Your Money Or Your Life: 9 Steps to Transforming Your... – Amazon UK." toreset.me/266, pp. 56–66.

[267] **"national living wage":** "National Minimum Wage and National Living Wage rates – GOV.UK." toreset.me/267.

[268] **Money Dashboard:** "Money Dashboard: Your personal financial assistant. View your past..." toreset.me/268.

[269] **Mint:** "Mint: Money Manager, Bills, Credit Score & Budgeting." toreset.me/269.

[270] **(YNAB):** "You Need a Budget." toreset.me/270.

29. Section 2: Efficiency/Frugality

[271] **Siouxsie and the Banshees:** "Siouxsie and the Banshees – Wikipedia." toreset.me/271.

[272] **The La's:** "The La's – Wikipedia." toreset.me/272. (the apostrophe hides a "d").

[273] **Asda:** "Asda.com – Online Food Shopping, George..." toreset.me/273.

[274] **Sainsbury's Local:** "Sainsbury's Local – Wikipedia." toreset.me/274.

[275] **Majestic:** "Majestic Wine." toreset.me/275.

[276] **Costco:** "Costco – Wikipedia." toreset.me/276.

[277] **Booker:** "Booker Group – Wikipedia." toreset.me/277.

[278] **Lidl:** "Lidl UK." toreset.me/278.

[279] **Aldi:** "ALDI UK." toreset.me/279.

[280] **Home Bargains:** "Home Bargains." toreset.me/280.

[281] **at 330:** "Sunday interview: Lidl's UK boss Ronny Gottschlich – Telegraph." 30 Nov. 2013, toreset.me/281.

[282] **in the UK:** "ALDI France – Page d'accueil." toreset.me/282. In France, specifically Provence, Lidls are like those in the UK; the French Aldis I've been to remind me of an early 1990s Sheffield Netto.

[283] **Quick Draw McGraw:** "Quick Draw McGraw – Wikipedia." toreset.me/283.

[284] **many award-winners:** "A red wine from Lidl has been crowned one of the best in the world..." 1 Dec. 2017, toreset.me/284.

[285] **In the US:** "Aldi and Lidl Take Supermarket Battle to the U.S. – Bloomberg." 11 Jun. 2017, toreset.me/285.

[286] **Lidls:** "About Lidl Supermarket – Lidl UK." toreset.me/286.

[287] **800 Aldis:** "Aldi opens 700th UK store and targets 1,000 by 2022 – The Grocer." 28 Feb. 2017, toreset.me/287.

[288] **commitments laid out on their respective websites:** "Supply Chain Information – ALDI UK." toreset.me/288a and "Our commitments – Lidl UK." toreset.me/288b.

[289] **B&M Bargains:** "B&M." toreset.me/289.

[290] **switched-on middle-class midlifer:** "How Aldi became the magnet for the middle-classes – The Telegraph." 6 Aug. 2016, toreset.me/290.

[291] *The One Pound [per person] Meals:* "One Pound Meals: Delicious Food for Less: Amazon.co.uk: Miguel..." toreset.me/291.

[292] **coffee habit over 20 years is $51,833.79?:** "The Compound Effect: Amazon.co.uk: Perseus: 9781593157241: Books." toreset.me/292, p. 41.

[293] *"love, and joy":* toreset.me/293a as quoted in: "Your Money Or Your Life: 9 Steps to Transforming Your... – Amazon UK." toreset.me/293b, p. 177.

[294] *The Good Life:* "The Good Life (1975 TV series) – Wikipedia." toreset.me/294.

[295] **"Keep the faith":** "Northern soul – Wikipedia." toreset.me/295.

[296] **"A millionaire is made ten bucks at a time":** "A Millionaire is Made Ten Bucks at a Time – Mr. Money Mustache." 1 Aug. 2011, toreset.me/296.

[297] **Beware status cocaine:** "Happy Ambition: Success, Status Cocaine, and Happiness." toreset.me/297.

[298] **JL Collins, 50%:** "The Simple Path to Wealth: Your road map to financial... – Amazon UK." toreset.me/298, p11.

[299] **Shangri-La:** "Shangri-La – Wikipedia." toreset.me/299.

[300] **Master your Chimp:** "The Chimp Paradox: The Mind Management Programme to Help You..." toreset.me/300.

[301] **"upsides of (say) a bigger house":** "HELP!: How to Become Slightly Happier and Get a Bit More Done..." toreset.me/301, p. 171.

[302] **£7,500 a year tax-free:** "Rent a Room scheme – how it works and tax rules – Money Advice..." toreset.me/302.

[303] **"own two or more vehicles":** "Your Money or Your Life, 9 Steps to Transforming Your Relationship..." toreset.me/303, p. 12.

[304] **Buy two- to three-year-old cars from a trusted dealer:** "The Millionaire Next Door: Amazon.co.uk: Thomas J. Stanley, William..." toreset.me/304, p. 123.

[305] **Norman Tebbit:** "Norman Tebbit's on your bike speech – YouTube." 27 Oct. 2013, toreset.me/305.

[306] **most efficient form of transport:** "What Do You Mean "You Don't Have a Bike"?! – Mr. Money Mustache." 7 May. 2012, toreset.me/306.

[307] **Skodas:** "Skoda UK." toreset.me/307.

[308] **Decathlon:** "Decathlon." toreset.me/308.

30. Section 3: Investing (Options, Interest and the SWR)

[309] **rate of inflation of 3%:** "Inflation in Great Britain – current and historic British

consumer price..." toreset.me/309a, you can find the historical rate of inflation here. Three per cent is a conservative estimate for retirement planning: toreset.me/309b.

[310] **purchasing power as it does now:** "4 Dangerous Assumptions That Could Hurt Your... – Morningstar." toreset.me/310.

[311] **average 2.25% return on their investment:** "Interest Rates on UK Savings Accounts since 1960." toreset.me/311.

[312] **dropped by 0.79% year-on-year:** If savings rates ever top 9% again in your lifetime you have my permission to reconsider this advice.

[313] **return on investment on property is 3% a year:** "Early Retirement Extreme: — a combination of simple living..." 24 Jun. 2010, toreset.me/313, (Kindle version) Location 4,075: "In the long run, real estate always goes up...at the rate of inflation! Despite ups and downs and bubbles and crashes, the rate of inflation is the long-term trend."

[314] **in the future:** Everyone's situation differs, but if your mortgage rate ever tops 6% you have my permission to consider diverting your monthly savings towards paying off your mortgage.

[315] **mortgage rate hovered at about 2%:** "Average mortgage interest rates in the UK 2014 and 2017 | Statistic." toreset.me/315.

[316] **(let's say 9% to be on the safe side):** "What's The Really Long-Term Return On Stocks? | Seeking Alpha." 2 Feb. 2017, toreset.me/316. This conservative 9% figure is for the sorts of companies that comprise the main stock market indices such as the FTSE 100 and Dow Jones. It assumes dividends are reinvested and does not allow for inflation.

[317] **(let's say 6% to be on the safe side):** "Average Stock Market Return: Where Does 7% Come From? – The..." 27 Mar. 2016, toreset.me/317, a 6–7% return assumes dividends reinvested, which is the default option you will take if you follow the investment advice in *RESET*. The figure is based on historical stock market returns over the longest time possible. (Different countries/regions go back different amounts of years. Always look at the longest period you can and plan accordingly.)

[318] **not to be sniffed at:** "Compound interest calculator – Monevator." toreset.me/318. All figures are courtesy of *Monevator's* online tool. Figures assume £12k invested once a year. Figures do not account for inflation. Assumes interest added yearly.

[319] **(including the government pension top-up):** "Tax on your private pension contributions: Tax relief – GOV.UK." toreset.me/319.

[320] **0.3% after you've reached FIRE**: "Fidelity International." toreset.me/320. At time of going to press (August 2018), on a £855,000 portfolio, you would pay a 0.2% service/account fee on a Fidelity Sipp and a 0.08% OCF on the internationally diversified portfolio of funds suggested in *RESET*. Total: 0.28% (let's say 0.3% to keep it simple). Vanguard UK is planning its own entry to the Sipp market, which will likely mirror its Isa charges. If you had the same £855,000 invested in an almost identical basket of internationally diversified index funds, but this time using all Vanguard funds, the charge would be £375 annually plus a 0.1225% OCF (let's say 0.12% for ease). In each case, once contributions to your employers' defined contribution scheme end after retirement (or you move jobs), *RESET* suggests switching the entire pot into either a Vanguard or Fidelity Sipp for reduced charges

and better choice/performance (remember to check out the TCs, too). If Fidelity and Vanguard charged the same, I would pick Vanguard, because of the company's co-operative, not-for-profit, ethos. When Vanguard charges less, the choice is simple.

[321] **28.5:** "Safe withdrawal rate UK / early retirement – MoneySavingExpert.com…" 19 Jul. 2017, toreset.me/321. *RESET* is based on a conservative Safe Withdrawal Rate (SWR) of 3.5% (more on that imminently).

[322] **reduces your SWR by 0.12%:** "The Impact of Investment Costs on Safe Withdrawal Rates – Kitces.com." 21 Jun. 2012, toreset.me/322.

[323] ***"pretty easily carries you to the end":*** "Michael Kitces – The 4% Rule and Financial Planning… – Mad Fientist." toreset.me/323.

[324] **"Determining Withdrawal Rates Using Historical Data":** "DETERMINING WITHDRAWAL RATES USING… – Retail Investor.org." toreset.me/324.

[325] **famous 1998 Trinity Study:** "Journal Portfolio Success Rates: Where to Draw the Line – OneFPA." toreset.me/325.

[326] **"The Trinity Study And Portfolio Success Rates (Updated To 2018)":** "The Trinity Study And Portfolio Success Rates (Updated To 2018)." 16 Jan. 2018, toreset.me/326.

[327] **"make it to the good returns":** "Michael Kitces – The 4% Rule and Financial Planning … - Mad Fientist." toreset.me/327.

[328] **stash last you the full 30 years:** "The Trinity Study And Portfolio Success Rates (Updated To … - Forbes." 16 Jan. 2018, toreset.me/328. The 100% figure is based on a 50%/50% equity/bond asset allocation and the performance of the S&P 500 and intermediate-term government bonds. For a 75% equity/25% bond split, the SWR figure drops to 98%.

[329] **4% initial withdrawal rate:** "Ratcheting The Safe Withdrawal Rate For Income Upside – Kitces.com." 3 Jun. 2015, toreset.me/329. Based on US index data between 1871 and 1985 and a 60%/40% equity/bond split.

[330] **as the years go by:** "Safe Withdrawal Rates With Decreasing Retirement Spending." 22 Feb. 2017, toreset.me/330.

[331] **"Does The 4% Rule Work Around The World?":** "Does The 4% Rule Work Around The World? | Retirement Researcher." 30 Jun. 2016, toreset.me/331.

[332] **ideal SWR allocation:** Ibid. Wade's research found that with an 80/20 equity/bond split, UK investors investing solely in the UK market over a 30-year period would have a 100% success rate of dying before their stash ran out, with an SWR of 3.77%. Even at 90/10 stocks/bonds, you're looking at a similar percentage of (from my reading of the graph) 3.73%. At 100% equities, it drops to 3.64%.

[333] **50/50 bond/equity portfolio:** Figures for an 80% equity/20% bonds portfolio are not available, but it is highly likely the percentage would increase above 0.21% because of the increased returns versus a 50/50 equity/bond portfolio split.

[334] **increase their SWR by 0.21%:** "Retirement Investing Today: Further Exploration of Safe Withdrawal…" 26 May. 2014, toreset.me/334a. The article also finds that for UK investors between 1900 and 2012 a globally diversified portfolio performed better in 78.6% of the cases versus 21.4% for domestic portfolios. For further reading consult: toreset.me/334b.

[335] **down at 3.86%:** "The Impact of Investment Costs on Safe Withdrawal Rates –

Kitces.com." 21 Jun. 2012, toreset.me/335.

[336] **SWR stays broadly the same:** Here is Kitces's summary toreset.me/336a. Remember, the 3.5% SWR for 40 years is based on US data. And here is some superb research that covers the topic in more detail: "The Ultimate Guide to Safe Withdrawal Rates – Part 1: Introduction..." 7 Dec. 2016, toreset.me/336b. See also Mad Fientist's assertion that a 3.5% SWR can be "considered the floor, no matter how long the retirement time horizon." "Safe Withdrawal Rate for Early Retirees | Mad Fientist." toreset.me/336c.

[337] **a good place to start:** "The Ultimate Guide to Safe Withdrawal Rates – Part 14: Sequence of..." 17 May. 2017, toreset.me/337.

[338] **"sequence of return risk":** Ibid.

31. Section 3: Investing (Wise Words & the Case for Indexing)

[339] **"Why do you want to get into that?":** "Everything You Always Wanted to Know About Money... – Freakonomics." 2 Aug. 2017, toreset.me/339.

[340] **inactive or dead:** "Fidelity's Best Investors Are Dead | The Conservative Income Investor." 26 May. 2015, toreset.me/340.

[341] **do not listen to stock market analysts:** "Don't listen to analysts if you want to make money on the stock market..." 10 Jan. 2018, toreset.me/341.

[342] **"while some rational person talks about long-term investing":** "The Simple Path to Wealth: Your road map to financial... – Amazon UK." toreset.me/342, p. 78.

[343] **"completely worthless":** "A Dozen Lessons on Investing from Ed Thorp – 25iq." 22 Jul. 2017, toreset.me/343.

[344] **"the magic of compound interest":** "Tony Robbins on stock market corrections: Get used to them..." 8 Feb. 2018, toreset.me/344a. And if you want to buy Tony Robbins's handy book *MONEY Master the Game: 7 Simple Steps to Financial Freedom* you can find it here: toreset.me/344b.

[345] **"very difficult way to make money":** "Everything You Always Wanted to Know About Money... – Freakonomics." 2 Aug. 2017, toreset.me/345.

[346] **"impulses waiting to run amok":** "The index investing road map – Monevator." 23 Jun. 2015, toreset.me/346.

[347] **"rather than deny your true nature":** "The Nobel Prize-Winning Investing Research Behind Betterment." 7 Nov. 2013, toreset.me/347.

[348] **(gains of 2,411% and 1,836%):** "FTSE All Share Index Performance 1800–2007: from Finfacts Ireland." toreset.me/348a. The FTSE All Share closed 1972 at 218.18. The Dow Jones broke 1,000 for the first time on November 14th 1972: "Dow Jones Finishes Above 1000 – The New York Times." toreset.me/348b. Both end figures are correct on July 19th 2018. Bonus article on the "freak case" of Japan: toreset.me/348c

[349] **"I don't care":** "A Dozen Lessons on Investing from Ed Thorp – 25iq." 22 Jul. 2017, toreset.me/349.

[350] **"people don't like them anymore":** "On My Radar: Buffett Burgers and The Hallelujah Chorus – CMG." toreset.me/350.

[351] **1.3% and 1.5%:** "Mutual Funds: The Costs – Investopedia." toreset.me/351.

[352] **Still, a whopping 71%:** "Index funds to surpass active fund assets in U.S. by 2024: Moody's." 2 Feb. 2017, toreset.me/352.

[353] **82% didn't:** "The Simple Path to Wealth: Your road map to financial… – Amazon UK." toreset.me/353, p. 75.

[354] **"finding the best coin flipper":** "Review: More investors are viewing active funds as a rip-off…" toreset.me/354.

[355] **"bad-mouth astrologers":** "Failure Of Active Management – Blackstone Wealth Management." toreset.me/355.

[356] **"they charge you a lot more than a monkey would":** "Everything You Always Wanted to Know About Money… – Freakonomics." 2 Aug. 2017, toreset.me/356.

[357] **Exchange-Traded Funds:** "ETFs vs index funds – Monevator." 3 Feb. 2015, toreset.me/357. Here's a full explanation by the brainy Monevator. Simply put, ETFs are often slightly cheaper than equivalent OEICs, cover more obscure indexes (eg, global small-cap and value), and sometimes come with small initial charges – watch for them in the small print – as well as the ongoing charge figure (OCF) and TC.

[358] **most important economist of the late 20th century:** "Paul Samuelson – Wikipedia." toreset.me/358.

[359] **"A Challenge to Judgment":** "The inspiration for John Bogle's great invention – MarketWatch." 5 Mar. 2014, toreset.me/359.

[360] **$403bn:** "VFINX - Vanguard 500 Index Fund Investor Shares | Vanguard." toreset.me/360.

[361] **29% of the entire US market:** "Index funds to surpass active fund assets in U.S. by 2024: Moody's." 2 Feb. 2017, toreset.me/361.

[362] **"Something new under the sun":** "The inspiration for John Bogle's great invention – MarketWatch." 5 Mar. 2014, toreset.me/362.

[363] **but it's a lot more rational than us:** "Is the Market Rational? – Kiplinger." toreset.me/363.

[364] **"who employ high-fee managers":** "Warren Buffett to heirs: Put my estate in index funds – MarketWatch." 13 Mar. 2014, toreset.me/364.

[365] **Peter Lynch:** "Peter Lynch – Wikipedia." toreset.me/365a. Lynch is an amazing investor, a once-in-a-lifetime who, statistical analysis shows, consistently beat the market in the long-term. But when it came to picking his successor at the Magellan fund, Lynch couldn't pick someone who could beat the market. toreset.me/365b.

[366] **"in an index mutual fund":** "Investing's Great Minds Think Alike – Forbes." 3 Jun. 2010, toreset.me/366.

[367] **"they should go to the racetrack or play the lottery":** "Quotations on index investing: 'Refusing to believe in magic'." 23 Jun. 2014, toreset.me/367.

32. Section 3: Investing (RESET's 10-Point Investing Plan)

[368] **"Stick with a broad mix of low-cost index funds":** "US Weekly responds to Sean Spicer insult with solid investment advice." 13 Feb. 2017, toreset.me/368.

[369] **it's 3% and 5% respectively:** "Workplace pensions: What you, your employer and the… – GOV.UK." toreset.me/369.

370 **Trustnet:** "FE Trustnet." toreset.me/370.

371 **Morningstar:** "Morningstar: Share Prices | Fund Prices and Data." toreset.me/371.

372 **capital gains tax:** "Capital Gains Tax: Capital Gains Tax rates..." toreset.me/372.

373 **in an Isa:** "Full ISA Guide – Money Saving Expert." toreset.me/373. The maximum one person can invest in an Isa in any one year (as of 2018/19) is £20k.

374 **One is a co-operative:** "Why ownership matters at Vanguard – About Vanguard." toreset.me/374. The six funds that comprise the *RESET* portfolio cost 0.12% with Vanguard and 0.08% with Fidelity. Fidelity charges 0.35% on funds under manage-ment (Sipps and Isas combined) lower than £250,000 and 0.2% if your portfolio is worth between £250,000 and £1m. Vanguard charges corresponding fees of 0.15% and 0%. There are no charges for buying and selling funds with either, apart from the odd ETF. But watch out for transaction costs (see Glossary of Terms).

375 **one family firm that has embraced passive investing:** "Fidelity's lessons for the asset-management business – The Economist." 22 Jun. 2017, toreset.me/375.

376 ***RESET*portfolio:** "Vanguard." toreset.me/376.

377 **Sipps up and running in the UK:** Ibid. By end 2018, according to Vanguard, in January 2018. In Sep. 2018: "ASAP, but no fixed or proposed launch date as yet."

378 ***pick Fidelity*:** "Fidelity International | SIPPs, ISAs & Investment Funds." toreset.me/378. N.B. At time of going to press (late August 2018), Fidelity now offers a share dealing service to direct customers without an adviser whereas Vanguard has no plans to offer this service, albeit Vanguard is guided by its members.

379 **"put a kilt on":** Meaning, as used in this sentence, translate US advice to a Scottish/UK context, particularly regarding the tax system and fund selection.

380 **(...rules are slightly different in Scotland):** "Tax relief on pension contributions explained – Which.co.uk." 24 May. 2018, toreset.me/380.

381 **a note on asset allocation:** "Asset Allocation – Investopedia." toreset.me/381. Asset allocation is an investment strategy that aims to balance risk and reward by apportioning a portfolio's assets according to an individual's goals, risk tolerance and investment horizon.

382 **according to the Office for National Statistics:** "Most common age at death, by socio-economic position in England..." 21 Feb. 2017, toreset.me/382.

383 **Here's how the overall charges stack up. The calculations:** "How to work out your portfolio's actual cost – Monevator." 16 Jul. 2013, toreset.me/383. The calculations for combined OCF and combined TC charges are made using the formula in this post.

384 **in line with Vanguard's approach:** "Vanguard: 'We're nudging investors away from their UK bias'." 14 Oct. 2016, toreset.me/384. The UK makes up 6% of the world market. Vanguard's LifeStrategy funds favour a 25% UK weighting, as does the suggested *RESET* portfolio. For instance, Vanguard's LifeStrategy 100 fund (in August 2018) has a 25% weighting to the UK, comprising one index fund and two ETFs.

385 **maximise returns and minimize risk:** "Does International Diversification Improve Safe Withdrawal Rates..." 4 Mar. 2014, toreset.me/385a. The article also finds that for UK investors between 1900 and 2012 a globally diversified portfolio performed better in 78.6% of the cases versus 21.4% for domestic portfolios. Nobel prize-winning economist Harry Markowitz's modern portfolio theory was the first

to show that a diversified portfolio can improve performance and decrease risk over long periods: "Modern Portfolio Theory (MPT) – Investopedia." toreset.me/385b.

[386] **one-stop options:** figures correct as of end August 2018.

[387] **helps with currency risk:** "Currency risk – Monevator." 4 Jul. 2013, toreset.me/387.

[388] **23-country MSCI World Index:** "Featured index – World – MSCI." toreset.me/388.

[389] **"Betterment...in preference to Vanguard":** Betterment Cranks up Features and Costs – is it Still Worthwhile?." 1 Feb. 2017, toreset.me/389.

[390] **"includes both value and small-cap tilts":** "The Nobel Prize-Winning Investing Research Behind Betterment." 7 Nov. 2013, toreset.me/390.

[391] **outperform their growth and large-cap counterparts:** "Fama And French Three Factor Model – Investopedia." toreset.me/391.

[392] **23-country MSCI World Small-Cap Index:** "MSCI World Small-Cap Index." 31 Jan. 2018, toreset.me/392.

[393] **"FTSE Developed All Cap Index and Russell 3000 Index":** "Global Value Factor UCITS ETF – Vanguard." toreset.me/393.

[394] **your own low-cost globally diversified set-and-forget eight-fund portfolio for the UK investor:** "An International Portfolio from The Escape Artist – jlcollinsnh." 12 Jan. 2018, toreset.me/394. I know how hard it is translating the US advice to the UK, so I can only imagine how difficult it must be if you live in other European countries. A blog to follow on this topic is JL Collins's, 25% of whom's readers are international. This is a guest post for Europeans from The Escape Artist on how to build a Vanguard passive portfolio, using mainly Exchange Traded Funds (ETFs).

[395] **this provides all the global diversification you need:** "The Simple Path to Wealth: Your road map to financial... – Amazon UK." toreset.me/395, p. 110. Collins discusses plenty of other options in this, the best book on index investing I have read. The bond fund he recommends for US investors is the Vanguard Total Bond Market Index Fund (VBTLX). Collins is not averse to investing in an all-world Ex-US, or total international, or total world stock index fund, but favours the one-fund VTSAX approach pre-retirement.

[396] **Writing in 2011, Pete Adeney recommended a similar approach:** "How to make Money in the Stock Market – Mr. Money Mustache." 18 May. 2011, toreset.me/396.

[397] **Goldberg five funds:** "The Only 5 Index Funds You Need to Own – Kiplinger." toreset.me/397.

[398] **This passive portfolio uses threshold rebalancing:** "Use threshold rebalancing to lower your portfolio's risk – Monevator." 22 Jun. 2016, toreset.me/398.

[399] **In April 2018:** "The Slow and Steady passive portfolio update: Q1 2018 | Monevator." 3 Apr. 2018, toreset.me/399.

[400] *Mr. Money Mustache* **forum:** "Advice for a UK mustachian – Mr. Money Mustache Forum." 13 Jun. 2012, toreset.me/400.

[401] **Bogleheads...with 60 chapters worldwide:** "Investing Lessons From Vanguard's Bogleheads – Kiplinger." toreset.me/401.

[402] **The three funds recommended are:** "Three-fund portfolio – Bogleheads." 10 Aug.

2017, toreset.me/402. These are the US ones; UK equivalents are available through Fidelity and Vanguard UK.

[403] **Compare fees and ease-of-use first:** "Compare the UK's cheapest online brokers..." 11 Feb. 2018, toreset.me/403.

[404] **I picked online share portal IG:** "Share Dealing | Buy and Sell shares from as little as £5... – IG." toreset.me/404.

[405] **the chances of the market going up are 77%; down 23%:** "The Simple Path to Wealth: Your road map to financial... – Amazon UK." toreset.me/405, p. 194.

33. Section 3: Investing (Final Salary and State Pensions)

[406] **only 1,650,491 UK residents are members of defined benefit/final salary schemes:** "The pensions landscape – Defined benefit pensions 2016." 1 Nov. 2016, toreset.me/406.

[407] **up from 80,000 in 2016/17:** "The great British pensions cash-in – Financial Times." toreset.me/407.

[408] **He's received a fair valuation of £142,571:** "Final Salary Pension Transfer Calculator – Drewberry Insurance." toreset.me/408.

[409] **Online calculators:** Ibid.

[410] **Did you know that the full new state pension stands at £8,546.20 a year or £17,092.40 a couple?:** "How much will the State Pension pay in 2018/19? – Lovemoney." 9 Feb. 2018, toreset.me/410.

[411] **draw the state pension when we're 67/68:** "Proposed new timetable for State Pension..." 19 Jul. 2017, toreset.me/411.

[412] **never mind a triple-lock:** "State pension set to rise by 3% thanks to triple lock – This is Money (UK)." 17 Oct. 2017, toreset.me/412.

[413] *google "Check Your State Pension":* "Check your State Pension – GOV.UK." toreset.me/413.

[414] *It's complicated:* "The new State Pension: How it's calculated – GOV.UK." toreset.me/414.

34. Section 3: Investing (Legacy: After You've Gone)

[415] **Beagle Street:** "Beagle Street." toreset.me/415.

[416] **two-thirds of UK citizens aged 35 to 54:** "Nearly 60% of Britons have not written a will – This is Money UK." 26 Sep. 2016, toreset.me/416.

[417] **free solicitor-drafted wills in March and October if you live in Scotland, England or Wales (if you're 55 or over):** "Free Wills Month." toreset.me/417.

[418] **(there is more protection for those who die without a will in Scotland):** "What are my legal rights in Scotland? – Redstone Wills." 9 Sep. 2016, toreset.me/418.

[419] **Vanguard LifeStrategy 80:** "LifeStrategy® 80% Equity Fund – Accumulation – Vanguard." toreset.me/419.

[420] **A steal at 0.22%:** "VANGUARD REDUCES ONGOING CHARGES ON LIFESTRATEGY..." 18 Jan. 2017, toreset.me/420. (Watch out for the 0.1% TC though.)

[421] **Consider setting up a Lasting Power of Attorney:** "I have a will, so why do I need a Lasting Power of Attorney? – Care to..." 26 Mar. 2015, toreset.me/421.

[422] **you can leave up to £1m to your now 61-year-old kids:** "Discussing inheritance is too important to be left until someone has died." 13 Jan. 2018, toreset.me/422. According to British think tank the Resolution Foundation, the average age someone will benefit from an inheritance is now 61.

[423] **(assuming part of that inheritance is your one main home):** "Inheritance tax – how much will I pay? – Which.co.uk." toreset.me/423a and "Inheritance tax planning: Rates and advice – Money Saving Expert." toreset.me/423b. The £1m figure assumes you, the last woman or man standing, die in the tax year 2020/21 onwards, not before.

[424] **listen to podcasts:** "The Tim Ferriss Show | Listen via Stitcher Radio On Demand." toreset.me/424. I recommend *The Tim Ferriss Show* and *Freakonomics* (not by any means restricted to FIRE, but they've both had plenty of FIRE-related guests on their shows, eg, Jack Bogle on *Freakonomics* and Mr. Money Mustache on *The Tim Ferriss Show*).

[425] **Read the best FIRE books:** "Best Books – Rockstar Finance Directory." toreset.me/425.

[426] *Budgets are Sexy*: "Budgets Are Sexy." toreset.me/426.

[427] *Millennial Revolution*: "Millennial Revolution." toreset.me/427.

[428] *Physician on FIRE*: "Physician on FIRE." toreset.me/428.

35. Part IV Index Card

[429] **Walter Isaacson:** "Walter Isaacson – Wikipedia." toreset.me/429.

[430] **all "searching" for meaning in life and our place in it:** "Lessons from Steve Jobs, Leonardo da Vinci, and Ben... – Tim Ferriss." 14 Oct. 2017, toreset.me/430.

Part V: Core Principles to Guide You in Work and Life

[431] *"And that has made all the difference"*: "The Road Not Taken – Poetry Foundation." toreset.me/431.

36. RESET's 11 Core Principles

[432] *"Conformity is the jailer of freedom and the enemy of growth"*: "35 Inspiring Quotes for Kids About Being Different... – Inspire My Kids." 30 Jul. 2015, toreset.me/432.

[433] **"Because to stand out you must become the exception, not the rule":** "Different: Escaping the Competitive Herd: Amazon.co.uk: Youngme..." toreset.me/433, back cover blurb.

[434] **To think outside the box it helps if you've been in the box first:** "Lessons from Steve Jobs, Leonardo da Vinci, and Ben... – Tim Ferriss." 14 Oct. 2017, toreset.me/434. A point made by Walter Isaacson on Tim Ferriss's podcast.

[435] **"watches four hours-plus of TV every day":** "One in four people in Scotland ditch their device to digitally... – Ofcom." 4 Aug. 2016, toreset.me/435.

NOTES

436 **"without being a joke and embarrassment to others"**: "The Subtle Art of Not Giving a F*ck: A Counterintuitive... – Amazon UK." toreset.me/436, p. 17.

437 ***"I run because it always takes me where I want to go"***: "Ultramarathon Man: Confessions of an All-Night Runner: Amazon.co..." toreset.me/437.

438 **like Oprah:** "Running Quotes About Life – ThoughtCo." 12 May. 2017, toreset.me/438.

439 **Ask 1980s basketball legend Larry Bird:** "Basketball Player Larry Bird Grit And Discipline Helped Him Lead..." 31 Jan. 2001, toreset.me/439.

440 **"Then another step"**: "Quote by Antoine de Saint-Exupéry: "What saves a man is to take a..." toreset.me/440.

441 ***"Excellence, then, is not an act, but a habit"***: "Habit Quotes – BrainyQuote." toreset.me/441.

442 **"They never lose a minute. It is very depressing"**: "Daily Rituals: How Great Minds Make Time, Find Inspiration, and Get..." toreset.me/442, p. xviii.

443 **fluctuating fortunes of the Roman Empire:** "The History of the Decline and Fall of the Roman Empire – Wikipedia." toreset.me/443. Gibbon wrote this book.

444 **Exist.io:** "Exist.io." toreset.me/444.

445 **track and tweak their habits:** "Spotlight Your Potential with Keystone Habits – Minafi." 11 Dec. 2017, toreset.me/445.

446 **"Someday/Maybe list"**: "Getting Things Done: The Art of Stress-free Productivity: Amazon.co.uk..." toreset.me/446, p. 177.

447 ***"Stickability is 95 per cent of ability"***: "Magic of Thinking Big: Amazon.co.uk: David Schwartz Dr..." toreset.me/447., p. 31.

448 **"But great power lies in the other ninety-nine percent"**: "Quiet: The Power of Introverts in a World That Can't Stop... – Amazon UK." toreset.me/448, p. 169.

449 **Life isn't *The X Factor:*** "The X Factor – Wikipedia." toreset.me/449.

450 ***"throw stones at every dog that barks"***: "13 Things You Should Give Up If You Want To Be Successful – Medium." 26 Dec. 2016, toreset.me/450.

451 **"Deep work is like a super power in our increasingly competitive twenty-first century economy"**: "Deep Work: Rules for Focused Success in a Distracted... – Cal Newport." 5 Jan. 2016, toreset.me/451.

452 **David Allen's GTD system:** "Getting Things Done – Wikipedia." toreset.me/452.

453 **If you're one of the 70%:** "Quiet: The Power of Introverts in a World That Can't Stop... – Amazon UK." toreset.me/453, p. 76.

454 **"They make people sick, hostile, unmotivated and insecure"**: Ibid., p. 84.

455 **"freedom from interruption"**: "Why You Can Focus in a Coffee Shop but Not in Your Open Office." 18 Oct. 2017, toreset.me/455.

456 **Hofstadter's Law:** "Hofstadter's law – Wikipedia." toreset.me/456.

457 **Bill Clinton said every big mistake he had made in life was due to lack of sleep:** "Bill Clinton: The Importance of Sleep | Sleep Education Blog." 20 Feb. 2010, toreset.me/457.

458 **"Because people don't want to get rich slowly"**: "Don't Start a Company — Be Obsessed With Something... – Medium." 21 Sep. 2015, toreset.me/458.

[459] *"Procrastination is opportunity's natural assassin"*: "Procrastination is opportunity's natural assassin." ~ Victor Kiam | The..." 9 Sep. 2015, toreset.me/459.

[460] **"feel tomorrow, or the next day"**: "Procrastination | Psychology Today." toreset.me/460.

[461] **Imposter syndrome**: "Impostor syndrome – Wikipedia." toreset.me/461.

[462] *Art of Charm*: "Tim Urban | Wait But Why (Episode 522) · The Art of Charm." toreset.me/462.

[463] **"Inspiration is perishable...do it now"**: "ReWork: Change the Way You Work Forever: Amazon.co.uk: David..." toreset.me/463, p. 271.

[464] **"take the current when it serves, or lose our ventures"**: "Julius Caesar (play) – Wikipedia." toreset.me/464.

[465] *"Heav'n of Hell, a Hell of Heav'n"*: "Paradise Lost, Book I, Lines 221–270 by John Milton – Poems | poets.org." toreset.me/465.

[466] *"Nothing gets me more worked up than someone who doesn't believe in me"*: "AskGaryVee: One Entrepreneur's Take on Leadership... – Amazon UK." toreset.me/466, p. 22.

[467] **Michael Caine's headteacher told him he'd be a labourer**: "They Did Not Give Up." toreset.me/467.

[468] **"we can use them to fuel positive, constructive change"**: "The Compound Effect: Amazon.co.uk: Perseus: 9781593157241: Books." toreset.me/468, p. 68.

[469] *The Subtle Art of Not Giving a F*ck*: "The Subtle Art of Not Giving a F*ck: A Counterintuitive... – Amazon UK." toreset.me/469.

[470] **story (widely known...**: "Dave Mustaine: Early Megadeth Vision Was 'Destroy Metallica'." 14 Jan. 2018, toreset.me/470.

[471] **"A Renaissance man"**: "Renaissance Man – Wikipedia." toreset.me/471.

[472] *"use the income from that to pay for everything else"*: "Early Retirement Extreme: A Philosophical and Practical... – Amazon UK." toreset.me/472, (Kindle version) Location 1,151.

[473] **"Character is destiny"**: "Character is Destiny – Thoughts And Ideas – Medium." 31 Jan. 2017, toreset.me/473.

[474] **Charlie Munger...gave a talk to USC Business School in 1994**: "Y Combinator: Elementary Worldly Wisdom." toreset.me/474.

[475] **"The future belongs to those who learn more skills and combine them in creative ways"**: "Quote by Robert Greene: "The future belongs to those who learn more..."" toreset.me/475.

[476] **"It is this stamp of personality, of individual view, which is known as individuality"**: "Jack London's Wisdom on Living a Life of Thumos – The Art of Manliness." 11 Dec. 2017, toreset.me/476. Jack London, "The Writer's Philosophy of Life," *The Editor*, October 1899.

[477] **parrot owner and qualified bricklayer**: "The other lives of Sir Winston Churchill | Express Yourself | Comment..." 14 Mar. 2011, toreset.me/477.

[478] **and whisky, by all accounts – knew no bounds**: "Famous Whisky Drinkers: Sir Winston Churchill | Scotch Whisky." 11 Jul. 2016, toreset.me/478.

[479] *"the resulting emotions and thought patterns are our data"*: "The Subtle Art of Not Giving a F*ck: A Counterintuitive... – Amazon UK." toreset.me/479, p. 117.

[480] **Like an estimated two million people across the UK:** "Are we becoming a nation of runners? – BBC News." 30 Nov. 2014, toreset.me/480.

[481] **you'll add three years on to that early retirement:** "How to Add Three Years On to Your Life | Blog – Zude PR." 28 Dec. 2017, toreset.me/481.

[482] **"physical activity provides a rare opportunity to practice suffering":** "How Exercise Shapes You, Far Beyond the Gym – Science... – The Cut." 29 Jun. 2016, toreset.me/482.

[483] **"You've always got to think that you're young":** "The Wolf Man of Harrisburg | Running blog – Zude PR." 16 Nov. 2014, toreset.me/483.

[484] **2012 best-seller** *The Power of Habit*: "The Power of Habit: Why We Do What We Do, and How to Change..." toreset.me/484.

[485] **"They change our sense of self and our sense of what is possible":** "How Exercise Shapes You, Far Beyond the Gym – Science... – The Cut." 29 Jun. 2016, toreset.me/485.

38. 12 Do's

[486] **interactions with loved ones that contribute to their (and your) happiness:** "Want a Happier, More Fulfilling Life? 75-Year Harvard Study... – Medium." 25 Jan. 2018, toreset.me/486.

[487] **force a smile, it works:** "Study: Forcing a Smile Genuinely Decreases Stress – The Atlantic." 31 Jul. 2012, toreset.me/487.

[488] **"London...that you still have to learn":** "How to be a Graphic Designer, Without Losing Your Soul: Amazon.co..." toreset.me/488, p. 138.

[489] **"sometimes risky, undertaking":** "Adventure – Wikipedia." toreset.me/489.

[490] **1 Second Everyday app:** "1SE." toreset.me/490.

[491] **"ghosts haunting the lost landscapes of our childhood":** "THE WRITING LIFE: TALES OUT OF SCHOOL – The Washington Post." 18 Mar. 1997, toreset.me/491.

[492] **The Pomodoro [productivity] Technique:** "Pomodoro Technique – Wikipedia." toreset.me/492.

[493] **In a meta-analysis of 300,000-plus people:** "Social Ties Boost Survival by 50 Per Cent – Scientific American." 28 Jul. 2010, toreset.me/493.

[494] **Watch Susan Pinker's TED talk:** "The secret to living longer may be your social life – TED.com." 18 Aug. 2017, toreset.me/494.

[495] **businesses fail within the first 18 months, according to** *Bloomberg*: "Five Reasons 8 Out Of 10 Businesses Fail – Forbes." 12 Sep. 2013, toreset.me/495.

[496] **joining the ranks of the one in 25 UK workers who work for themselves**: "Rise in self-employment transforms UK – Financial Times." 15 Oct. 2017, toreset.me/496.

[497] **"Anyone who runs a business...should be proud":** "ReWork: Change the Way You Work Forever: Amazon.co.uk: David..." toreset.me/497, p. 23.

[498] **"You're likely to become wealthy":** "The Millionaire Next Door: Amazon.co.uk: Thomas J. Stanley, William..." toreset.me/498, pp. 227 and 228.

39. 12 Don'ts

[499] **"assign too much or too little importance to others"**: "HELP!: How to Become Slightly Happier and Get a Bit More Done..." toreset.me/499, p. 151.

[500] **"Perfectionism...will keep you cramped and insane your whole life..."**: Bird by Bird: Some Instructions on Writing and Life: Amazon.co.uk: Anne..." toreset.me/500, p. 28.

[501] **"Everyone else cares only what they can get out of you, how you can benefit them"**: "6 Harsh Truths That Will Make You a Better Person – Cracked.com." 17 Dec. 2012, toreset.me/501.

[502] **google "Alec Baldwin Speech *Glengarry Glen Ross*"**: "Leadership – Glengarry Glen Ross – YouTube." 18 Jun. 2009, toreset.me/502.

Nirvana

[503] **"There is no escape from anxiety and struggle"**: "Quote by Christopher Hitchens: "The search for Nirvana, like the..." toreset.me/503.

[504] **"A transcendent state...neither suffering, desire, nor sense of self..."**: Nirvana | Definition of Nirvana in English by Oxford Dictionaries." toreset.me/504.

Conclusion

[505] **But listen – for your own sake and your family's – to Bronnie Ware:** "Regrets of the Dying – Bronnie Ware." toreset.me/505.

[506] **In the opening sequence:** "The greatest thing you'll ever learn is just to love and be... – YouTube." 8 Aug. 2011, toreset.me/506.

[507] **"The greatest thing you'll ever learn is just to love and be loved in return"**: "Nature Boy – Wikipedia." toreset.me/507.

Afterword

[508] **one Renaissance man**: "Renaissance Man – International Churchill Society Canada." toreset.me/508.

[509] **"'We are still masters of our fate. We are still captain of our souls'"**: "The Churchill Society London. Churchill's Speeches..." toreset.me/509.

Acknowledgements

[510] **doubloons:** "How much was the treasure of Sparta in The Count of Monte Cristo..." toreset.me/510.

[511] **Jools Holland-esque:** "Videos – Jools Holland & His Rhythm & Blues Orchestra ... – BBC." toreset.me/511.

INDEX

INDEX

INDEX

Exchange-Traded Funds (ETFs), 195, 211, 213
    definition of, 314n357
Exist.io, 242

Fama, Eugene, 194, 197, 214
Fama, Eugene, Jr., 194
Farah, Mo, 8
Fatal Attraction (film), 71
Fazackerley, Brendan (Bren) and Mary, xxv–xxix
fears, 2, **7–10**, 11, 18, 39, 49, 273
    colleagues, xxxiv
    conquering myth, 8
    list of, 7
    public speaking, 9
    thoughts, 8, 12
Feedly, 58
Fernandez, Doug, 256
Ferriss, Tim, 112
    5–Bullet Friday (newsletter), 112
    Tim Ferriss Show (podcast), 62
Feynman [Richard] Technique, 60
Fidelity, 188, 192, 210, 211, 225, 233
    ethos, 204
    Index World Fund P Accumulation, 213
    investing through, in the UK, **204–206**
    RESET portfolio funds/charges, 209, 212, 311–312n320
    share-dealing service, 218, 219
Financial Conduct Authority, The, 122, 222
financial independence (FI)/financial independence retire early (FIRE)
    benefits of, 129
    brief history of, 127–128, 307n242
    definition of, 127, 285, 286
    FIRE Triumvirate, 151–233
    general, xv, 234
    recognition of term, 128
    savings rate, 167–168
    12 essential disciplines of, 129–130
    US community, xviii, 65, 113, 170–171, 206
Financial Times (newspaper), 76, 101
FIRECalc, 142
Fisker, Jacob Lund, xxxiv, 105, 252
five-year plan, 28
Flynn, Yvonne (89 books), 249
Forbes (magazine), 62
Ford, Henry, 251

Fortnite, xxxii
four-day weeks, xxxiv
401(k), 118
403(b), 118
France, 162
    Provence, 309n282
Franklin, Benjamin, 234
Frankl, Victor, **12**, 14, 21, 24
    meaning of life, 20
    on purpose, 18
Freakonomics (podcast), 62, 101, 194
French, Bob, 194
French, Ken, 214
Freud, Sigmund, 15
Frey, Bruno, 168
Fried, Jason and Hansson, David Heinemeier
    on inspiration, 249
    on obscurity, 62
    see also *ReWork.*
From Last to First (Spedding), xii, 26
Frost, Randy O., 100
Frost, Robert, 235
FTSE 100, 187, 195, 197, 286
FTSE All Share, 216
    performance of, 191
F.U. Money, 81, 123, 142
    definition of, expanded, **127**, 286
    definition of, initial, 25
    Kiyosaki, Robert, 30
    Loadsamoney, confusion with, 25

Gandhi, Mahatma, 9
Gates, Bill, 27, 87
GDPR, 70
Georgetown University, 243
Gibbon, Edward, 241
Gibson, Neal, 282
Giffnock North A.C., 257
Gladwell, Malcolm (ten-thousand hour rule), xxii
Glasgow, xxxiii, 14, 19, 48, 66, 282, 293
    City Council, 54, 301n106
    communities, 75, 83
    recognition of FI or MMM in, 128
    size of, 51
    time lag for ideas to reach, xxi
Glengarry Glen Ross (film), 272
glide path, 201
Godin, Seth, 62

INDEX

329

INDEX

INDEX

Did you enjoy *RESET*? What did you learn? Use these blank pages to jot down what resonated while it's fresh in your mind. What small actions will *you* start taking after reading this book?

(And good luck; you won't need it. Follow the practical steps in *RESET* and you'll make your own.)

Printed in Great Britain
by Amazon